Breathing New Life into Faith

Ancient Spiritual Practices for the 21st Century

by Richard Dahlstrom

Breathing New Life into Faith

Ancient Spiritual Practices for the 21st Century

Tea & Bacon Productions
PO Box 222, Snoqualmie Pass, WA

www.stepbystepjourney.com

ISBN-13: 978-1983719653

CONTENTS:

5

Preface to 2nd Edition

I wrote *"O2: Breathing New Life into Faith"* ten years ago, because I could see a vital need, both in my own life and in the life of faith seekers everywhere, for a move away from expressions of spiritual life that left people hollow, burnt-out, bored, and cynical. The church I led then was in the midst of rapid expansion, and I was in the thick of all the headaches and opportunities that come with that. The national economy was expanding too, even while trust in leaders of all sorts was eroding. We didn't know it then, but the expansion was a mirage, a bubble created by easy credit, inflated housing prices, and the belief that tomorrow would always be better than today.

Shortly after the book came out two things happened to our social landscape. **First, our capacity to trust was severely damaged.** As the lies and corruption that left countless families facing foreclosure were uncovered, it became clear that the perpetrators of these crimes would largely escape unpunished, some even receiving large financial bonuses for their actions. This would lead to further erosion of trust in our country. The problems weren't limited to financial institutions, though.

Catholic churches with pedophilia scandals, new mega-churches with isolated leaders at the helm and commensurate downfalls, government "truth" claims, officials in high places using power to get sex, increasing media bias, companies demanding employee loyalty and then outsourcing work to cheaper places - no institution, it seemed, was immune from our increasing awareness that honor and integrity were evaporating like water on hot pavement. Anxiety and cynicism were on the rise, as was the destructive tendency to withdraw from those with whom we disagree, isolating ourselves in small, self-referential communities which fragment and alienate. As a result, we're much more cynical and polarized than we were ten years ago.

Second, social media displaced reality. Facebook moved from a university phenomenon to a mainstream means of communication. Since Facebook's inception, thousands of other social media platforms have also launched. While examining the cultural consequences arising from this are far beyond the scope of this book, one thing is certain. We now have a new way of squandering our time, and we're squandering it in a big way. Two hours a day translates to over 700 hours a year, and that becomes about one month of our precious 12, each year, spent passively digesting what others are doing, living vicariously, and missing reality. Our bodies like it, apparently, as a little feel-good hormone dopamine spike rewards our brain while we're there, making us glad we clicked and more likely to click again. Most of this time, though, is stolen from our potential to bless, serve, give, create, and celebrate in the real world.

Tragically, many of us may never feel the loss, because we haven't thought about what our life should be or could be. Instead, allowing our lives to be shaped by the overwhelming forces of culture, we've increasingly surrendered to all that surrounds us, leaving us alternately bored, anxious, afraid, and often lonely. None, it seems, are immune from this hijacking of the life for which we're created - including people of faith.

The cumulative effects of these and other cultural upheavals have left us more isolated, afraid, and addicted than ever. My response to this has been a rediscovery of God's invitation for times such as these: *This is what the LORD says: "Stand at the crossroads and look; ask for the ancient paths, ask where the good way is, and walk in it, and you will find rest for your souls.¹"*

We don't need a new experience, new place to go, new methodology. We need to rediscover an old thing, recover its primacy, and learn, by practice, how to live in accordance with it. The old thing we need is a path, one that's always been there, but has become overgrown due to neglect because newer, shinier, "more relevant" routes have arisen. The well-lit, heavily travelled super-highways are leaving us polluted, alone, sick, anxious, overmedicated, in debt, angry, and afraid. Maybe it's time to clean up the old path that's been there all along and give it a try.

The ancient paths are needed now, perhaps more desperately than when they were first created. In a world of isolation and fragmentation, the ancient paths lead to community and coming together. In a world of fear, the ancient paths lead to a peace beyond earthly comprehension. In a world of consumerism and greed, the ancient paths open a way for contentment and generosity.

We don't know much about any paths these days, let alone ancient ones. Freeways? Highways? Toll roads? Information highways? These are all familiar to us. They're well-lit and travelled by the masses, smacking of commerce, power, and pleasure. We're either passing or being passed, and the environment is incidental, a space through which we must pass in order to get "there," wherever that is.

The superhighways are shouting "buy me," "wear me," "taste me," "sleep with me," "vote for me," and "protest with me," each one over-promising but under-delivering. Those voices are more, and louder, than ever. Just listening to them has robbed us of riches, leaving our souls wallowing in an impoverishment we sometimes don't even recognize, let alone understand.

The ancient paths don't shout. They're humble and unassuming, requiring a bit of intentionality to find, and a bit of discipline to travel. In a loud world, we're invited to walk the path of silence; in a greedy world, the path of generosity; in a world of insulated living, the path of encounter with creation. You get the picture. These paths are *contra mundum*, in defiance of general opinion. As such they require more investment.

The well-lit highways of culture, enticing us away from the ancient paths, are increasing in both number and force with each passing day. And that's why, when it comes to rediscovery and traveling of the ancient paths, I believe that these practices are needed.

Now more than ever! The material has been updated, with sections on Confession, Meditation, Gathered worship,

So welcome to a consideration of the ancient paths. May you not only learn of them, but walk on them, and in the process find not only peace, but the good life for which you were created.

How to Use this Book

This book is more like a guide to running a marathon than a book of history, science, or philosophy. Based on the belief that each of us is a vast storehouse of potential, by virtue of the reality that nothing less than the resurrected Jesus desires to express His life through us, this book was written to help the reader develop a cadre of practices which will release this potential. Here are some suggestions that will help you maximize the use of this book:

Best digested with others. As I'll share in a later chapter, the journey of spiritual transformation is best undertaken with others, for a host of reasons. You can surely read the book alone and seek to apply its principles, but for the most part, we're made to walk together on our journeys of transformation. If possible, find a few friends interested in developing habits that will strengthen your journey of transformation in Christ, and work through the material with them. If you want to supplement the reading material with teaching, you can find an entire series of studies on the subject under on the podcast app from iTunes.[2]

Best applied with by declaration. Nobody climbs Mount Everest accidentally. It requires preparation, aerobic conditioning, mountaineering skills, and a deep commitment to achieving the summit because the reality is that parts of the journey will be uncomfortable. The same thing is true with your spiritual formation. Nobody ever woke up one day and accidentally began thinking and behaving more like Jesus. Such change is always a conscious choice. The spiritual disciplines articulated are of no value unless they translate into practices in your life. It's right here that many faith journeys are ultimately shipwrecked. We don't take God's time-honored practices seriously enough to incorporate them into our lives, and then we wonder why they don't work. On the other hand, those who do the work of creating their own rule of life will discover that, in spite of the sputters, failures, and frustrations common to all who undertake such a bold pursuit, the end result will be profoundly life-giving!

A tool to help you build your rule of life can be found here: churchbcc.org/ruleoflife   As with anything else worth doing in life, start small, be patient with setbacks, and enjoy the "little by little" adventure of lifelong transformation!

I've been living by a rule of life with greater and lesser success and consistency for nearly twenty years now, and can tell you that it's worth the effort. There's been plenty of neglect, hitting the reset button, and adaptation along the way, and that's OK. For those who think that "effort" is incompatible with following Jesus, later chapters will remind you that your effort, without the indwelling Christ, won't produce any more transformation than a farmer's effort would produce a crop if he or she lacked seed.

On the contrary, on this path of transformation all of us will come to discover the glorious truth that the seed of Christ has been sown in our hearts, but that God dignifies us with all the responsibilities of the farmer. Care for the soil. Provide the water and sunlight. Be patient. Deal with the weeds.

Do these things and a crop of "abundant life," the life for which you were created, awaits you. I'm thrilled that you're interested in the journey and pray God will use these chapters to help equip you for the adventure of lifelong transformation.

In His Service,

Richard Dahlstrom

stepbystepjourney.com

Chapter 1

Breathless

It happens every weekend. This Sunday hundreds, even thousands, of people will leave their place of worship after the final benediction or "Amen," and never return to that dying thing we call "church." This is because every week, many of the faithful who gather are secretly harboring doubts as to whether any of it is true or, if it's true, whether it makes any vital difference in daily living. Once those seeds of doubt have germinated—once it becomes evident, by personal experience, that the church is, indeed, irrelevant to the realities of daily living—it's only a matter of time before the departure is finalized. Their disillusionment likely won't be with Jesus. Rather, it will be with the institution of Christianity, which, for all goodness that has poured through it down through the centuries, is increasingly weighed down with various sorts of sickness, rendering it impossible to be the healing community of hope for many. That's why you'll hear, "I've nothing against Jesus. In fact I follow him. It's the church that I can't endure."

Of course, they're often right to harbor doubts about the church, because for too many, being religious or spiritual makes no vital difference. We who gather for worship on Sundays are increasingly becoming a statistical parallel to the rest of the culture in some unflattering categories. Does our culture have a hard time with marriage? The church does too. Does our culture encourage consumerism and reckless spending as a means of keeping the economic fires burning? The church is following suit. As the culture has increasingly moved to a recreational sexual ethic, has the church maintained a distinctive? I could go on, continuing to ask questions about the health of the church and making comparisons between it and the culture at large, but statistics indicating a general decline in church participation offer chilling evidence that the most honest answer to the question, "How is the church in North America doing?" is to say that it is dying[3].

All of our meetings and activities apparently haven't led to an explosion of love, grace, hospitality, celebration, humility, purity, and passion for the kingdom of God. If this is the case—if we see little difference between the church "joiners" and those who stay on the sidelines—we may legitimately ask why anyone would want to participate. After all, if the only differences between being people of faith and people of "the world" is that people of faith lose their free Sunday mornings, and that a good chunk of their income goes to the offering, what's the point? I'll keep my Sunday mornings, with good coffee and more sleep, and keep my money too. As a result, many have stopped gathering. Others continue to gather while still harboring these doubts and wondering if what they've stumbled into, or been born into, is real after all.

If people don't experience an increase in joy or peace or meaning, maybe they are right to leave. If the Jesus that is embodied by our gathering together in community looks like the self-centered, arrogant, stressed-out, upwardly mobile North American whose only distinction from culture is the size of his Bible or the fish on her car, certainly the whole matter needs to be revisited. In order to do that together, and to help us recover a vibrant, life-giving, and life-imparting faith, I hope you'll join me in a little exercise. Please make yourself comfortable, sitting in a chair if possible, with no distractions. Are you ready? Good.

Breathe. You're already doing it, or you wouldn't have this book in your hand right now, but for the next moment or two, pay close attention to what's going on as you breathe. Inhale slowly, allowing your lungs to fill from bottom to top as you feel your diaphragm and chest expand. Let your lungs fill until you're convinced they can't hold any more. How does that feel?

Now exhale, slowly letting the air leave your lungs until, toward the end of your exhale, you're forcing air out of your lungs until there's nothing left to release. Now notice how much you long to inhale again and how much joy you feel as you draw in that next breath.

But notice too how quickly the initial joy of inhaling becomes satisfaction. And just as quickly, satisfaction becomes fullness. Fullness becomes satiation. In a matter of just a few seconds, you've moved from a longing to inhale to a serious need to exhale.

Do this as slowly as possible, counting ten complete breaths.

Are you finished? You've just participated in one of the great miracles of nature: the respiratory system. Here's what has happened.

The muscles of your diaphragm have combined with the action of your ribs to create an open space with lower air pressure than the outside air. This has the effect of drawing air into the lungs where blood, rich in carbon dioxide but lacking oxygen, passes through, and an exchange nothing short of miraculous occurs. Through a complex action, oxygen diffuses into the blood and the carbon dioxide is moved out of the blood into the lungs. This will then be expelled as the muscles of the diaphragm relax, sending out a carbon dioxide blessing to other life-forms that need it, while the oxygen-enriched blood is now equipped to provide the fuel necessary for virtually every bodily activity. Thinking, loving, running, creating, cooking, eating, sleeping, dreaming—all require the oxygen that we can receive only through the rhythm of inhaling and exhaling.

Of the two, which is more important, inhaling or exhaling? For the human body, the question is ridiculous, because of course you can't have one without the other. But the body of Christ misses this balanced perspective. The church body, fractured and divided as it is, has the unhappy reputation of fighting against itself, like a human body with some sort of autoimmune disease, attacking itself with sickening regularity because it mistakes its own saints for the devil. History has often shown the church body to be at civil war over the merits of inhaling and exhaling.

Champions of inhaling, who represent our need to receive life-giving strength from Christ through things like study, prayer, and silence, treat the exhalers, who represent our need to serve and be involved in the issues of this world, with varying degrees of disdain, often portraying them as proponents of a different gospel and a different Jesus. Meanwhile, the exhalers have turned a suspicious eye toward the inhalers, who are so heavenly minded with their praying, reading, fasting, and solitude that they are no earthly good. The exhalers say the inhalers would rather give a starving child a Bible than food because the "food which perishes" (John 6:27) will only cause the poor children to hunger again, but the "food which endures to eternal life" will satisfy forever. And the tragedy is that some inhalers really think this way.

The champions of each camp raise their voices, shouting across the chasm that divides them. "Exhale!" cry those who are committed to the kingdom ethic of Jesus: service to the poor, hospitality, and generosity. "Fail to do these things and you fail completely!" they shout as they quote Jesus' words:

> I was hungry, and you gave Me something to eat; I was thirsty, and you gave Me something to drink; I was a stranger, and you invited Me in; naked, and you clothed Me; I was sick, and you visited Me; I was in prison, and you came to Me (Matthew 25:35-36).

"This," they shout, "is the Christian life."

The cries come back from the far side of the chasm: "Inhale!" The inhalers quote Jesus' own words from the very same Gospel:

> Many will say to Me on that day, "Lord, Lord, did we not prophesy in Your name, and in Your name cast out demons, and in Your name perform many miracles?" And then I will declare to them, "I never knew you; depart from Me, you who practice lawlessness" (Matthew 7:22-23).

They shout this in order to prove that knowing Jesus is the true essence of a faithful life, chastening and warning the exhalers that their misplaced zeal could land them in the fires of hell. They have many more verses to offer, immersed as they are in Bible study. But their zeal sounds like arrogance to the people on the other side of the canyon, who often hear the loud Bible-quoting with such disdain that it only confirms their own entrenched ways of living. "If I ever become like that, just shoot me," one of them says to a like-minded friend.

The very existence of the dichotomy reveals our pathologies of fragmentation and division. Each of us is bent—by family upbringing, emotional constitution, church background, and other influences—toward either engagement or withdrawal, body or spirit, doing or being. Each position has deeply entrenched camps eager to reinforce their predispositions. When we join such movements, we become so focused on ourselves that our imbalances become not just a way of life, but *the* way of life.

Sadly, these imbalances have the effect of distorting Christ. The activist creates Exhaling Jesus (EJ, I like to call him). His version of Jesus is endlessly involved in service to others at the cost of his own well-being. He is the Jesus who is always on mission trips, always serving in the soup kitchen, always throwing a party, always involved in issues of justice and mercy. He's diligent at home too, often scrubbing the grout in the bathroom tile with a toothbrush. He's on a thousand mailing lists and is working hard to change the world. But all this activity is wearing him thin, and he's showing some signs of cracking. Rage is often lurking underneath his smooth and helpful exterior, and it's only a matter of time before it escapes. He starts to look like Billy Joel's "Angry Young Man"—active, passionate, and committed to changing the world, but angry at everyone who doesn't agree with his assessment of things, at everyone not as committed as he is to changing the world, and at the structures and systems of the world that create pain for so many.

Of course, the rage will only leak out if he lasts that long. EJ sometimes just melts into a pile of uselessness, because he's absolutely run out of breath. My wife, Donna, and I were reminded of this some years ago, when we were running a retreat center and wilderness Bible school in the Cascade Mountains of Washington State. It was a few weeks before our summer programs were to begin, and I was in Europe doing one thing: teaching. My wife was at home doing many things: preparing the grounds for summer, homeschooling the children, cleaning up after vacationers who rented our cabins, mowing lawns, shopping, cooking, making final contacts with incoming students, and arranging the details for our cook, who was arriving from Canada. Oh, we also had a house church that met in our living room on Sundays.

When one particular Sunday came around, Donna had been exhaling for far too long. She hadn't had enough rest or enough margin in her life, so when our anticipated cook for the summer called from Canada to let us know she wouldn't be coming down after all, Donna didn't take the news very well. She learned this on a Sunday morning, just moments before people started coming for worship, which didn't make it any easier. But come they did, with their happy faces on, ready to sing praise songs. With me in Europe teaching, the piano player was missing, and so the small crowd called for my wife to play her guitar. "Not this morning," she said, fighting hard to hold back tears of frustration (over the cook) and exhaustion (because she'd been carrying the entire parenting, schooling, working, cabin, property, ministry, home-church load for two weeks while I was doing one thing—alone—in Europe) and anger. How dare these people be here! How dare they smile! How dare the cook change her mind! How dare my husband do one thing in Europe while I do ten here! How dare it rain!

But the guests were persuasive, so soon she was standing in front of 30 people, playing her guitar and singing about entering God's gates with thanksgiving, about rejoicing and being glad. Picture this happening with tears of frustration and weariness streaming down the guitar player's delicate features, and a voice that is sobbing out the "glad" lyrics, and you get a picture of Exhaling Jesus: too tired for her own good or for anybody else's good. Slowly, people stopped singing, realizing that their musician was not glad in spite of the fact that her song said she was. When the music stopped, she poured out the litany of problems, obligations, and activities that had emptied her. There's little room for gladness when one is completely spent. For the exhausted, always-exhaling Jesus, words of gladness, peace, and rest seem incongruent to reality. It feels like a sham.

18

"Poor woman," said I, as I heard of what came to be known among our friends as "Black Sunday." I quickly returned to prayer and study in preparation for teaching, after which I would face a rough afternoon of journaling and reading C.S. Lewis. We teachers always need to be growing in knowledge and thinking about ideas that might be of value someday, in some lecture in the future, somewhere in the world. Having read myself nearly to sleep, I went for a short walk and came back to brew a cup of tea before attending a meal that I'd neither prepare, nor clean up after, because the only thing in the world I had to do was say words in front of students and answer their questions. The difference between our lives couldn't have been greater.

I'm more balanced now, but you can see how easily I have sometimes embraced the distortions of Inhaling Jesus (IJ to me, as we're definitely close friends). For us IJs, it is enough to know Jesus, sit in silence, read the Bible, pray, meditate, walk through the woods in solitude, listen to creation speak of God's glory, and then tell others what we've learned. At my most imbalanced, I'm perfectly content to sit in the morning with my coffee and Bible, and "watch the trees grow," not caring a bit if I make any difference in the world. Inhalers are at risk of spiritual narcissism.

Some of us inhale so well that our lungs are about to burst. But since the prospect of actually getting out into the world and doing anything of real tangible value for or with other people is so terrifying to us, we content ourselves with a definition of spiritual health that is purely interior. The IJs lead many people to believe that Jesus' concerns have nothing to do with politics, economics, the environment, the IMF, G8, HIV, ISIS, healthcare, racism, "just war," homelessness, or any other matter of critical importance to the well-being of the planet. Though the IJ's misrepresentation of Jesus is more complex than simply inhaling without exhaling, it is undoubtedly a key factor in the church being pushed to the margins of irrelevance by the vast majority of twenty-first-century people. It may be "good for feeling good." It might be an "opiate for the masses," the many who can be distracted from the tragedies of our indulgent, unjust, isolated, often boring lives by a dose of quiet hymns and a few psalms, or maybe some candles, fair trade coffee, and Hillsong worship music, if you're young enough. But life-changing? Relevant? Get real.

So which is better, inhaling or exhaling? Of course we know the answer. Breathing is better than either on its own, because it requires both. We're born to breathe, not inhale or exhale. When we learn habits of spiritual breathing, we will recover some measure of holistic health and balance, both in our individual selves and our faith community. This book is about learning to breathe by stepping into the rhythm of inhaling and exhaling that permeates all creation.

Part One

The Case for Breathing

Chapter 2

Waiting to Exhale

Try it. Put the exhale first, and then follow your
breathing in this manner for a few minutes.
Deliberately breathe several complete cycles by
emptying yourself first then inhaling. Empty
yourself, squeeze more breath out, then inhale.
Start the cycle again by exhaling and finish the
cycle with an inhale.

Dan Brule

Better Breathing

"I see more passion for trees in the Sierra Club than I do for Jesus in the church." Her youth pastor was relating these words to me in the midst of a conversation about why Christianity is often so boring for young people. This particular young woman went on to study environmental science, but was never able to see any connection between her love for the environment and the Christian life. She never saw that her passion for trees and her desire to address the corrupting effects of global pollution, and the consumerism that caused it, could in fact be an expression of love for Jesus, so she left.

Why did she miss the connection? My own assessment is that the few teachings about simple living, creation care, and economic justice issues that she might have heard in church couldn't possibly counteract the avalanche of destructive lifestyle choices she saw all around her in the faith community as a whole. Perhaps she saw wealth and consumption without active engagement in solving the pressing issues of poverty, racism, and environmental destruction. Maybe she heard that young people shouldn't sleep together before marriage, but heard nothing about the desperation that drives many to prostitution in many parts of the world, including America. She might have heard people talking about the end of the world and living environmentally reckless lives in the present because "the end is near—why save a sinking ship?"[4] After a while, the disconnect between her passions and her faith became too large a canyon to cross. Forced to decide, she stayed on the side of passion, abandoning her faith in favor of environmental activism. That she felt compelled to choose is an indictment on our faulty breathing habits as people of faith.

In our own recent history as a nation, most people who have joined up with Christ have done so because they've become convinced of a sense of personal sin, failure, guilt, or alienation from God. They've come to understand that God made a way for reconciliation with God and healing of our brokenness through Christ. The only condition for enjoying this transformative healing is that a person must believe it is for them, and thankfully receive it from God. It's all good news, true and beautiful.

The difficulty often comes right on the heels of that glorious moment of new life and conversion. Rather than telling the story of God's plan to do away with all greed, injustice, pollution, destruction, hate, oppression, lust, and those other elements that have rooted themselves in us and among us because of sin, we talk about how great it is that we get to go to heaven someday. Rather than inviting people to actively participate in the hope-filled story God is writing in the world, we invite people to come and sit, to listen and learn: learn doctrine, learn to pray, learn to be silent and not ask questions, learn the Bible, learn to sing songs never heard anywhere ever before. The exceptionally zealous also help people learn what to wear to church, what music to listen to while at home, and what to drink (or more importantly, what *not* to drink). This entire system has the unfortunate effect of taking Jesus' explosive and revolutionary movement of hope that Christ began and shrinking it, reducing it to something largely interior, with a few added cultural initiations thrown in to help people get along with other Christians.

We proclaim this largely interior faith when we care more about our church sanctuary's well-being than the well-being of the homeless people in our city, or when we worry about the style of music in our churches more than the fact that 30,000 children die every day of treatable diseases, or when we dismiss calls to care for the earth as a political issue. We imply that if the only things that really matter are the soul and spirit of a man, the cars we drive and the stuff we consume have nothing to do with the faith we profess.

The new convert, initiated into this privatized way of thinking and living, is now at a dangerous junction, and the two most commonly traveled paths at this crossroads are both destructive. On the one hand, she may resonate completely with this interior, privatized version of the faith, and become one of a large crowd whose theology and lifestyles are mostly concerned with the invisible, "spiritual," and future aspects of faith. Once reconciled to this paradigm, she will feel safe, comforted by assurance that the practices she's developing here will give her peace in her heart now and the assurance of eternal life after she dies. She'll define her faith as a few private devotional practices and the careful avoidance of a few select sins, especially sexual ones.

On the other hand, she may become one of the millions of faith casualties who start down the road of following Jesus, but eventually become disillusioned with the whole thing. Her passions for living in a more just, clean, and hopeful world will find little room for expression among those faith communities concerned predominantly with the development of the interior life, certain lifestyle constrictions, and habits of the heart.

There's a "yes, but…" thing that happens to these people as they stand at that crossroads. It's not that they don't believe that Jesus died for their sins, or that heaven is real, or that reading the Bible is vital to one's spiritual health. To all of that most of them would say, "Yes. Of course I believe." "But," they would add, "I'm dismayed about the rain forest disappearing and species becoming extinct, because this is far from the kind of 'caring for the earth' that I think God has in mind for us. I'm concerned about the increasing gap between the rich and the poor, homelessness, human trafficking, terror, and our bent toward violence as a first solution when threatened. It bothers me that abortion is so easily available as a form of birth control, and that many who abort do so because of poverty. I'm concerned about police shootings of unarmed black men, and the shooting of police officers, too. I'm worried that our lifestyles as Christians look too much like those of the surrounding culture as we buy, sell, consume, recreate, elevate individualism, and worry just as much as our neighbors without faith."

When the church is silent in the face of these social and cultural questions, or when the church's only answers have to do with a larger dose of Bible reading, or a promise of personal prosperity if you have the faith to give more and take a class, the tension in the hearts and minds of these friends becomes too great. They need to leave the church or they'll snap. The disconnect between their heart and the gospel they're hearing is just too much to endure. I don't blame them for leaving.

A Different View of Salvation

The tragedy is that they've rejected a caricature of the faith life rather than the real thing, and this caricature is, for many, the only experience they ever have of the gospel. This caricature focuses on the glories of the afterlife, the work of preparing to get there, and the work of getting others there. Its emphasis is on what is coming rather than what is already, and on the state of your heart rather than the state of the world. Such a view of the Christian life quickly becomes tedious and boring for people who can't seem to extinguish their flame of hope for a world of justice, mercy, peace, hope, and so much more right now, in this present age.

The gospel Jesus articulated is quite different from this popular view. In His opening day of ministry, He stood up in the temple, unfurled the Old Testament scroll, and read from Isaiah:

> The Spirit of the Lord is upon Me, because He anointed Me to preach the gospel to the poor. He has sent Me to proclaim release to the captives, and recovery of sight to the blind, to

set free those who are oppressed, to proclaim the favorable year of the Lord (Luke 4:18-19).

So Jesus' first articulation of His message was the promise that He would be moving into people's lives with the express purpose of blessing them in very tangible, visible ways. Good news for the poor. Release for captives. Recovery of sight for the blind. It would be fine to spiritualize these things if Jesus did, but He proclaimed good news to the literal poor when He multiplied loaves so that hungry people could eat. He dignified a poor woman by calling her offering the greatest given among the temple donors. He actually freed people who were captive, physically, emotionally, and spiritually. By healing the lepers, He freed them from their life of isolation. By turning the tables on her accusers, He spared the woman caught in adultery from the death penalty. He healed people who couldn't see the light of day or who had withered hands, unstoppable bleeding, or paralysis. These events are not merely metaphors for inward transformation. On the contrary, Jesus' starting point for salvation was usually in the exterior world: sparing a newly married couple the humiliation of running out of wine at their reception, feeding hungry people, enabling a handicapped person to walk, or sharing a meal or a drink of water with someone who'd been socially marginalized.

And though these were typically the beginnings of His interactions, His ministry never remained purely external. He engaged a woman in conversation because He was thirsty, and the conversation ended up being about personal sin and questions of worship. He saved someone from the death penalty and then challenged her to clean up her sexual life. He fed 5,000 and then chastened them for following Him only because He was a source of good food. Though He began with external issues, He was relentless in turning the discussion back to interior matters of the heart.

We see an ongoing dance between internal and external manifestations of the gospel. This makes sense, because salvation is holistic, transforming spirit, mind, will, emotions, body, family, ethic, politic, culture, environment, and eventually the whole cosmos. In fact, the apostle Paul speaks of "...a long-range plan in which everything would be brought together and summed up in him, everything in deepest heaven, everything on planet earth" (Ephesians 1:10, The Message).

Essentially, that powerful word tells us that history is moving toward a climax, a new cosmological order of sorts, in which every molecule in the universe is transformed, by virtue of being shot through with the glory of Christ. Christ is whole, so all things will be whole. Christ is just, so all things will be just. The beauty, peace, glory, and vibrancy of such a cosmos is beyond our imagining capacities. I get chills even thinking about it.

A Different View of Ethics

But of course, Isaiah, Jesus, and Paul don't talk about such things so we can get chills. They cast this vision because we're called to embody it in some small measure right now in this present time and place. This is what Jesus meant when He called His followers to a different way of living in His Sermon on the Mount. Stanley Hauerwas and William Willimon explain the implications of this for us:

> Imagine a sermon that begins: "Blessed are you poor. Blessed are those of you who are hungry. Blessed are those of you who are unemployed. Blessed are those going through marital separation. Blessed are those who are terminally ill."

> The congregation does a double take. What is this? In the kingdom of this world, if you are unemployed, people treat you as if you have some sort of social disease. In the world's kingdom, terminally ill people become an embarrassment to our health-care system, people to be put away, out of sight. How can they be blessed?

> The preacher responds, "I'm sorry. I should have been more clear. I am not talking about the way of the world's kingdom.

I am talking about God's kingdom. In God's kingdom the poor are royalty, the sick are blessed. I was trying to get you to see something other than that to which you have become accustomed.[5]

Followers of Jesus are invited to live in ways that run completely counter to the prevailing winds of culture, taking their cue from the One who, Himself, lived a contrarian life at every level. All of us who follow Christ nod our heads in agreement over that last sentence. But the devil, as they say, is in the details. Though we know that we are to live differently, all of us remain blind to certain areas where we are not embodying the hopeful and spacious ethic of Christ. All of us are guilty, in those blind spots, of practicing "business as usual," the conventional wisdom of the prevailing culture. Our passivity leads to an unconscious adaptation to whatever winds of culture happen to be shaping the world. As a result, we end up, as we've seen, looking remarkably similar to the surrounding culture. Make no mistake about it; all of us have such blind spots. All. Of. Us.

A Different View of Inviting

If you had only four sentences in which to articulate the gospel, what would you say? Would you begin with the bad news that humanity has failed and is cut off from God, but that Christ's death paid the penalty for our failure? Maybe you'd start with an explanation of how all people have sinned, and then press people to acknowledge their failure to perfectly fulfill the moral demands of the Ten Commandments. Perhaps you could move from there to the good news that though you failed, Jesus didn't. But you'd better hurry—you're going to run out of sentences soon.

My intrigue regarding how best to invite people to meet Jesus was sparked by looking at Jesus Himself. We don't find Him inviting people to Himself by beginning with three or four propositions about how messed up they are and how He's their solution. Here's what I found instead.

Jesus invited two fishermen to follow Him with the promise that if they do, they'll start catching men instead of fish (Matthew 4:18-20).

He followed this invitation with a similar one among the net menders. He invited a despised tax collector to follow Him (Matthew 9:9-11), which led to a complaint on the part of the religious elite that Jesus was spending far too much time with the wrong people (the "unchurched" as some would call them today). He called Philip the same way, and Nathanael, too. Even in the "you must be born again" passage of John 3, Jesus hinted that what Nicodemus really needed to do was to simply trust Jesus and start *following* Him out into the literal highways and byways of life, where he would be led by the Spirit of God into new challenges, new relationships, new adventures, and new ways of thinking.

In every case, Jesus was inviting those who would eventually become His disciples to simply follow Him. It was very practical, decidedly non-theological. He'd been speaking of a new reign, a new King and kingdom. He already had begun His ministry of showing people hints of the new kingdom by healing, by casting out demons, by challenging the religious orders of the day to rethink and reprioritize, and by turning the social order upside down through His contacts with the poor, sick, demon-possessed, and otherwise marginalized sections of the society.

Then, having exemplified these different ways of living, He invited others to simply follow Him, to step into the work that He was doing of being a blessing and embodying some sort of hopeful new world order.

What if we were to do the same? What if the starting point of our message was simply an invitation to step into the work God is doing, to follow Jesus by embodying a hopeful new world order? What would this mean?

It would mean that we might invite our environmentally aware neighbor to help rebuild a salmon stream, because our church is working on that project right alongside a local preservation group. Or it might mean inviting a friend who is a boat builder to go with our mission team to Asia after a tsunami. Perhaps we'd invite a businesswoman to join us in Rwanda as we help teach ethics and economic development in that part of the world. It could be as simple as inviting a friend to distribute blankets and hot chocolate to street people on a rainy night in Seattle or spend the night in the homeless shelter our church sponsors.

This seems to be how Jesus did it. He'd start by inviting people to exhale because when we do, we discover our need to inhale. I know someone who is about to go spend some time in Central America, and when she told one of her friends about the work she'd be doing building an orphanage, her friend decided to go too. This is how many people are discovering Christ. They're learning that Jesus cares about the world in which we live, and that He's inviting us to be bearers of good news and hope in the midst of it. It's an invitation that I'm convinced many people are longing to hear[6].

Waiting to Exhale

Lots of people are waiting to exhale. They've travelled the path of upward mobility and harvested more than enough of everything except meaning. So now they're looking for ways give expression to their longings. They want to serve a continent ravaged by famine and disease, or to preserve the environment by challenging people to live more simply, or to care for the elderly, the poor, the homeless. Some of the people who are waiting to exhale walk right past the church (or they drop in and quickly drop out) because they haven't seen the church as a place where one learns to breathe, but as a place where one only inhales and then waits for the spectacular removal of the faithful from this earth in the rapture. Such a vision is neither inviting nor accurate. We're not made to inhale endlessly. What's more, we can't hold our breath forever.

That's why the *first* invitation for so many needs to be an invitation to exhale. Once this happens, lots of good things are sure to follow.

Exhaling Our Way Back to Health

The untimely death of my dad during my senior year in high school plunged me into a crisis of faith, during which I doubted the goodness, trustworthiness, and love of God. Why does a man who never let tobacco touch his lips die at the age of 53 of lung disease? When people found out the cause of death they usually said something like "Cigarettes kill," and I wanted to hit them. We're always looking for a formula, an explanation. But the reality is that good people die too soon all the time, and there's no explanation, no formula.

This very lack of formula, this sense of God as the capricious, random being who either actively instituted or passively allowed immense suffering, caused me to withdraw from my faith. I decided to pursue a career in architecture so I could leave my mark on this earth and build some creations of my own before I too died, God only knows when.

I'd still sit in church, but nothing angered me more than hollow platitudes about how "all things work together for good" quoted from the Bible by well-meaning friends, along with mild exhortations to make sure I kept reading the Bible and praying.

No thanks. I'd lost my dad. I was depressed, and I was losing my health, too. Words about everything working out for the best felt like a hollow mockery, and I didn't know the Bible well enough to find the parts where people who loved God expressed their rage and lament.[7] Those sections weren't covered in church, or I missed that Sunday. I thought the faithful were the ones who kept smiling, no matter what, and I realized I couldn't keep my plastic smile pasted on anymore. I kept my Bible on my shelf and pursued architecture with a vengeance, hoping to find comfort in the fact that, though the grim reaper would win someday, I'd leave my mark in the form of buildings scattered across California.

I'd been on the coast at my new college for only a week before meeting Cindy in the dining hall. "You're a Christian?" I asked, as I'd seen her praying over her food. She smiled and nodded, her eyes bright with hope. "And you?" she asked. The story was too long, and she was too attractive. To keep it simple, and in the hopes of keeping it going, I said yes.

We ate together, and as soon we returned to the dorm, she introduced me to Jim, a big hulk of an architecture student. Some moments abide in our lives long after most memories have faded.

One of them is what happened next. This big, hairy guy with a red, bushy beard looked at me, his eyes filled with as much hope and twinkle as hers, and he said, "God is going to do some amazing things this year in our dorm. And you're going to be a part of it." And then he wrapped his arms around me in a great big bear hug. I had disengaged from hope a few counties back on the road of life, and now a guy was hugging me and assuring me that I was about to be part of something big. I didn't know what to think of it.

He went on to ask me how I wanted to help. Could I sing, play guitar, lead games, play piano? I could bang on the piano, so I showed up for the Sunday evening Bible studies he led. Seven people become ten. Ten became twenty. Twenty become forty. Then sixty. The Spirit of God was sweeping through our dorm, people were going to the beach to get baptized, and I was somehow involved in seeing people trust the same God whom I doubted I could ever trust again.

Had the hairy guy just invited me to a Bible study, I'd likely have said no. Had he challenged me to pray more or begin a regime of witnessing, I'd certainly have said no. I'd inhaled enough platitudes and frustrations recently, and felt as if I was choking. But I wasn't invited to sit or study or pray. I was invited to participate, and that made all the difference. I was doubting, failing. I was in a frustrated space where I had more questions than answers, and the answers I did have were ringing hollow. But I could play piano. Being asked to play rather than sit was just the wooing I needed.

The rediscovery of Christ as a source of hope and healing began with exhaling for me. It doesn't work that way for everyone. But based on the way Jesus invited His followers, the weight of evidence is that exhaling comes first.

Jesus meets a couple guys who are wondering if their lives are amounting to anything and He says, "Come with me. We'll catch men instead of fish!"

Sounds pretty inviting to me.

Chapter 3

Spiritual Asthma

Whenever I feel blue, I start breathing again.

L. Frank Baum

You never really think about inhaling until you can't. But if you're tempted by the slide at the swimming pool, even though it's in the deep end and you're only in second grade and can't swim, your glee as you descend is quickly replaced by a panic that you're sinking to the bottom and can't come up for air. Suddenly, inhaling is the only thing that matters. Afterward, when the lifeguard plucks you out of the pool, sets you on the warm cement, and lectures you about staying in the shallow end, you won't remember much of the speech. But you'll remember those first few inhalations of oxygen as if they were nectar from heaven, which, in a way, they were.

I remember travel games of childhood, when my sister and I would try to hold our breath as we went through a tunnel. It was tough work because it was so counterintuitive. Everything in us was crying *Inhale!* and it took, we thought, great courage and stamina to resist. This is because the body knows the dangers of hypoxia. It knows that only a few minutes of oxygen deprivation results in the death of millions of brain cells, and that these deaths carry with them loss of functionality. The miracle of inhaling occurs 20 to 25 thousand times each day without us even thinking about it. But when we're deprived of even one breath, our body screams its demands, and this becomes the only thing we think about, desperately.

The process of taking in the oxygen that feeds our spirits, however, is much less intuitive, requiring discipline and intentionality if we're to attain the peace, joy, hope, mercy, and wisdom that God wants to impart to us. The fact that we can easily bypass the regular habits of inhaling has led many to believe that no oxygen for the spirit exists, that such habits are a mirage, a waste of time. Having dabbled in these habits at different times and having seen no results, we discard them. Making matters more difficult, we can quickly point to people who lack any silence, solitude, Sabbath, or prayer in their lives, and who appear to be getting on with life just fine.

It's as if we're looking at fish swimming in the sea of a materialistic worldview. Ancient saints are standing on the shore, heralding the need for spiritual inhaling as a means of sustaining life. Meanwhile, an ocean of creatures seem to be doing just fine without these practices. Instead of solitude, their schedules are booked solid with social events, business engagements, and parties where deals are closed and connections made. One study in 2011 discovered the average father spent seven minutes a day with his teenage daughter because there are so many more important people to see. Of course, all the obligations on the schedule crowd out the habit of slowly and prayerfully reading through the ancient wisdom found in Scripture. Besides, the words are dense and hard to absorb, and our minds wander off into thinking about the "real" things we should be about. Soon we drop the habit as our desire to produce visible results trumps all others. We see people swimming in the sea of commerce, growing fat. They apparently don't need to inhale, so why should we?

This was the assessment of Asaph when he pondered these matters millennia ago. You can read about it in Psalm 73. I paraphrase him this way:

> *There's a problem, God. As I'm looking around at those who have no habits of the heart, no apparent intimacy with You, they not only appear to survive but actually seem to have an advantage! They're healthy. I see them in the window of the Cross-fit gym as I drive by, working out and checking their phones. Their bodies are trim, tan, and sexy. They're wealthy. Using their energies to better themselves and acquire more, and*

they seem to float through life with the greatest of ease. They don't worry much about the untidy consequences of their prosperity. "Life has winners and losers," they say. "Do you know what being a good loser makes you? A loser!" they say. They turn their philosophy into a seminar, peddle it in the corporate world, and retire rich. And each night they toast themselves as they fall into a contented sleep on their custom-made beds.

So tell me, God, what advantages come to those who do it Your way? Because frankly, I'm just not seeing it. Instead I behold loss, deprivation, and suffering among those of us trying to serve You and others, while the rest of the world swims along merrily in a sea of self-interest and consumption. This really isn't working for me.

And the reality is that it *won't* work for you or for me, if we believe that the goal in life is to have more, do more, see more, taste more, earn more, save more, know more, travel more, and buy more. The problem is with that little word *more*. More is always just beyond our reach. This is one of the realities that Asaph doesn't yet see. He sees the "wicked" as content. But John Rockefeller, with all his immense wealth, was the one who, when asked how much money he needed in order to be content, answered, "Always one dollar more." The contentment of driven consumers is, of course, a mirage. It appears as contentment only from a distance, as in TV commercials or a casual glance at the well-dressed people attending the symphony or professional basketball game. These are people with intelligence— erudite, sophisticated, and urbane. Surely they have all they want, because I want all they have.

Stop right here and ponder with me. I've been on this path too many times to recount. If I go just a few steps further, the slope will get quite steep, and sliding further down will be much easier than returning. I'll find myself, almost against my will, plunged into a dangerous sea of discontent and seeking. In my pursuit of becoming the consummate human, I'll make a plan and fill my days with education, work, networking, social webs, club memberships, and self-improvement. Perhaps I'm not so crassly materialistic as my friend in Psalm 73, so I add to this list a few good deeds as well:

golfing for the cancer fundraiser, Lions Club, booster club for my child's volleyball team. It's a good life, but full. Very full.

This paradigm leaves no time for reflection, but then why should it? In this worldview, we don't *need* reflection. We already know what we want. We know what we need to do to get there. Let's get on with it. Silence? Solitude? Prayer? These are for those who are still uncertain about meaning, vocation, or direction, or for the wounded and weak. But for those who know, who've seen the promised land and are going after it, nothing remains but to do it.

Our mistake happened in our paraphrase of Psalm 73. We stopped at verse 14, and that was a big mistake. What we needed most were verses 16 and 17: "When I pondered to understand this, it was troublesome in my sight until I came into the sanctuary of God." If only I'd stopped to enter the sanctuary *before* stepping into the whirlwind, if there in the sanctuary I'd entered the silence and solitude that attune my heart to the voice of God, I would have seen things differently. Then, having seen differently, I would have chosen differently, and lived differently.

Therein is the value of inhaling. The nourishment we need in order to choose wisely is only offered to us when we pause, ponder, wait, listen. My daughter and I were climbing in the Cascades once, a route I'd previously done with friends. Unfortunately, on my previous trip I'd not paid attention to the final details of our destination. After a two-hour hike, I said to my daughter, "This is it: The Tooth. Are you ready to climb?" She nodded and we set up our gear—harnesses, ropes, carabiners, and protection. I began to climb as she belayed. *Why is this popular climbing route filled with brush? Ouch! Stinging nettles too? What a dirty climb. I hope the second pitch is better. Why am I not seeing farther up the route? Where are the anchors for the belay?* Then, before I could ask another stupid question, I ascended high enough to see, across a short gully, the real object of our destination. We were climbing the wrong mountain. I'd stopped one gully short of the true objective. Something didn't feel right at the time, looking back, but you know how it is. I was so excited to get going that I didn't stop to make certain we were on the right mountain.

This is, of course, one of the reasons we desperately need to inhale. The oxygen of the Spirit offers us a reference point, so we can discern whether the step we're taking, the mountain we're climbing, is the right one or the wrong one.

Choosing Our Author

The teachings of B.F. Skinner have played a major role in the field of psychology. His teachings are often summarized (and oversimplified) by the concept that man is a blank slate, and the forces of society hold the pen. These forces include the media, our family, educational systems, and prevailing social mores and taboos. Christians often reject the teachings of Skinner, because they seem to lead to some sort of fatalism, a sense that we are merely a passive parchment, waiting to be written upon by forces beyond our control. We recoil at the loss of autonomy and individuality implied in the model, preferring to think of ourselves, as our poets have said, as masters of our own fates, captains of our own ships, determiners of our own destiny. We like to picture ourselves as "out there," apart from the crowd, paving a new way, making our own path.

Of course that's why we seek the latest phone and wear denim, or a suit and tie, or whatever the crowd we run with happens to wear. We're all out there seeking to be individuals together. Clever, isn't it? We think we're pioneers, but powerful forces actually are at work, intentionally attempting to shape our lives so that even if we listen to indie bands or shop at Goodwill, we're part of a subculture that does the same. It's rare to find people truly shaped by their own internal values, for such thinking would presuppose that our values are already in place at birth, waiting to express themselves as we grow older.

Call me a heretic, but I think the Scriptures largely tend to agree with part of Skinner's theories. The Bible indicates that our lives, indeed, are a sort of slate that will be written upon. People of faith do part ways with Skinner, however, in believing that the individual can choose to change which author will do the writing on the blank slate that is our lives. And by changing the author, we change the story, change the script.[8]

But this change of author requires disciplined intentionality. Every day, powerful forces seem to be at work in us, seeking to write scripts on our souls that would pull us toward fear, greed, lust, self-centeredness, mistrust, violence, pride, and so much more. We turn on the TV to watch news, and we learn to fear terrorists, Islam, immigrants. We learn that a drug is available for erectile dysfunction or heartburn or anxiety, and so we learn that we can buy a life free of suffering. The pen is writing, changing the way we think about people, time, money, and more. And so we subtly step into the script, playing out the part that our environment is writing on our hearts. Eventually, it takes its toll. Some honest reflection finds us admitting that we're weary, anxious, afraid. Perhaps there's a better way.

It would be nice if there were only one alternative to this destructive storyline. But often, having become weary of the story this world is inviting us into, we try to leave it behind by joining a church, hoping that perhaps this is the place where we will finally find peace and rest. But church life and the commensurate indoctrination into the life of faith lead many people to simply replace one set of ambitions and obligations for another. They begin to feel as if Christ's invitation was not to come and find rest, but rather to continue the sweat and toil with a new set of goals. There's a whole menu of activities to choose from, all of them seemingly important.

This new life in Christ, it turns out, is often busier and more tiring than the previous life. There are mission trips to take, classes to attend, children to care for, meals to cook, buildings to clean, committees on which to serve, men's groups, big groups, small groups, retreats, conferences, and prayer meetings. And of course, though we may have invited a new author to write our story, the old story isn't exactly finished. We're still working. We still have rent or mortgage payments, relationship problems, credit card debt, and hobbies. Six months to a year after coming to Christ, many who are new to the faith must face the dawning realization that the story of peace they were hoping to enter is more elusive now than it was before. Adding a layer of Christian activities to our already full lives is certain recipe for some form of exhaustion. What we needed was certainly not recruitment to the organizational goals of yet another institution.

A second problem arises for many who join up with the church. Having been attracted initially by Jesus' ethic of peace, simplicity, generosity, and His amazing capacity to build bridges across social and cultural divides, we find ourselves part of a movement that seems in contradiction to these very pursuits. Consider the bridge-building example.

Sociologist Sam Reimer conducted a study to determine whether people of faith were more tolerant of people who were different from themselves. They determined people of faith both by their beliefs and by their level of church attendance. Their findings? Interestingly, they found that orthodox beliefs neither increase nor decrease tolerance of those who are different. However, if one regularly attends church, tolerance of differences actually decreases![9] In other words, if you want to learn how to be less tolerant of others, go to church!

The thoughtful person finds herself asking important questions. If Jesus' ethic speaks of loving one's enemies, why are we praying for American soldiers, but not their enemies? Why are we passionate to protect life in the womb, but often apathetic about the plight of single moms trying to raise their infants without health insurance or access to living-wage employment? Why are we working just as hard as everyone else to perpetuate an American dream that results in our 5 percent of the world's population consuming 26 percent of the world's resources? When thoughtful Christians articulate these questions, they are too often told to stop thinking so much and get with the program.

There, I believe, is the crux of the problem. Evangelical Christians have a rich history of activism over the past half-century. We've been busy adding radio and TV stations, magazines, camps, retreats, political committees, fundraisers, lobbies, therapy centers, Bible schools, mission agencies, and more. And the second- and third-generation workers have been taught to perpetuate the activist story. We have learned how to work smarter and faster, how to bring technological advances to the aid of our cause, and how to align ourselves politically. Yet I fear that we've lost our capacity for thoughtful reflection about whether this is really God's story. Or, to switch analogies, I wonder if we're taking the time to be certain our train is actually on the right track.

Going Faster in the Wrong Direction

We'd landed in Milan, found the train station, and tasted our first Italian food. I made my way to a counter to buy train tickets to the Italian coast for a hiking vacation. My wife, Donna, and I were headed to the Cinque Terre, Italy's now-famous quintet of fishing villages that can be visited by hiking from one to another, through glorious, ancient olive groves and fertile vineyards. We needed to pass through Genoa on our way, so as the time for boarding the train arrived, I showed my wife how to read the departure schedule and find the right platform. I was excited to show Donna my skills as a world traveler, as I taught regularly in Europe and was quite comfortable navigating the trains.

We settled into our seats and began to enjoy our first experience together on the continent. About an hour into the trip, the ticket taker came by, and I showed him my ticket. He glanced at it, and his brow furrowed as he looked up at us.

"These are tickets to Genoa," he said in a strangely punishing voice. I couldn't understand why he'd be angry.

"Yes," I said confidently.

He pointed to the mountains that were increasing in size out the window as our train sped forward. "This train is going to *Geneva!*" Oops! I'd misread the sign on the platform by glancing too quickly at it. The mistake cost us. We had to disembark, buy a ticket back to Milan, return to the train station, and start over. This delayed our arrival at our destination by nearly half a day. Were it not for the food and wine from heaven itself that awaited us that night, I'm not certain my wife would ever have forgiven my careless mistake. We drank a toast to the ticket taker, for without his rebuke, we might have been eating fondue in the Alps and wondering what happened to our plans for Italy.

This is why inhaling is of great value. We need someone to look at our ticket and say, "You're supposed to be heading for generosity, but look! Your consuming habits are leading you to the land of greed. You need to get off this train immediately." If our lives are ordered in such a way that we have no time to encounter the conductor, we're likely to become lost. If we're hiding from the One who knows the schedules and destinations because we're afraid to hear what He'll say, we'll run into trouble. We'll find ourselves in the wrong place, and addictions, phobias, frustrations, and fears will fill our landscape, because we didn't make time for listening and carefully reading the signs.

The church has historically offered several practical means for meeting Christ. These allow Him to assess our lives and redirect, encourage, nurture, heal, and refresh us. This is precisely why the habits of inhaling discussed in this book are vital.

So why are these practices conspicuously absent from most of our lives? Different people have different reasons, many of us more than one. But these are some common responses to the inhaling disciplines:

> I'm not made that way. I'm into doing rather than being. This stuff is for poets and philosophy majors. Let them sit and think while the rest of us make the world work.

> I don't have time.

> I've tried these things before, and they haven't worked for me.

> These things sound too Catholic.

> I don't know how to practice these disciplines.

Let's consider each objection briefly, in hopes of providing the motivation and framework needed for developing these vital practices.

I'm Not Made That Way

Dietrich Bonhoeffer was a German pastor who lived during the rise of the Third Reich. His open resistance to Hitler's vision forced him out of the public arena. While he was training young pastors in his underground seminary, he wrote a book about learning to live in community and titled it *Life Together*. He pointed out that people who are in love with solitude need to be more with people, and those who most enjoy being with people need to intentionally focus on developing habits of solitude. His point is that we can easily hide behind our temperaments, saying, "This is the way God made me," and avoiding those things most necessary for our transformation[10].

We do well to remember that God is seeking to *change* each of us so that our daily lives, our agendas, our social interactions, and our personalities become more Christlike. The one given over to solitude must be driven into the arena of relationships, and vice versa. We all need to move out from behind the comfort zone of our strengths and into precisely those areas where we feel most challenged. Thus the practical person needs to set her heart intentionally toward the disciplines of inhaling. To be visiting senior citizens all the time or to be involved in justice projects may appear spiritual, but the reality is that a fixation on doing can easily be a way of hiding, a way of avoiding listening to God.

We all have ways of avoiding naked intimacy in relationships when such intimacy is too threatening to us. One of those ways is to simply get busy. Do you see that couple over there in the corner of the restaurant? She's trying to share something deep and intimate with her lover, and her exposure is having the effect of exposing him as well. You can tell that he is beginning to feel uncomfortable as his own pain, his own longings, and his own anger are all quickly surfacing. He doesn't like facing them, and he has worked hard to build a life where he doesn't need to face them. But now, here she is talking like this, and all the things he's worked so hard to suppress are bubbling up like some Yellowstone cauldron, exposing the activity of the soul he has so deeply buried.

He can tell that this conversation will lead to confession, truth telling, and vulnerability. He can feel tears welling up in his eyes. And then—THANK GOD!—his cell phone rings. He picks up. It's a business matter. Very quickly his armor is back on, and the eruption of the soul is brought under control. "Now," he says after he ends his call, "where were we?" He is relieved because he knows that wherever "we were," it will be a long time before we go there again.

Unfortunately, our culture encourages such disruptions, and they become rabbit trails that lead us far from those deep places in the soul, places we can reach only through time spent together, whether with those we love or with God. The phone rings, and we pick up, often allowing the demands or needs of the caller to mask what God is trying to reveal in our own souls. We do this not only with the phone but with all our compulsive doing, running from task to task until we drop into bed, exhausted. We can go on like this quite happily for days if we're wired this way. But we don't realize that the soul healing that can only take place through silence and solitude will forever elude us, and we'll never live fully human lives. *All* of us need to inhale.

I Don't Have Time

Does the marathon runner have time to ingest water along the route? Does the hiker have time to check the map and compass? Does the woodcutter have time to sharpen the saw? Does the Iditarod musher have time to care for his doggy's feet?

In every case, although progress appears to have temporarily stopped, these respites are necessary for strength and rejuvenation, assurance of direction, nurture and healing. If I don't have time for these elements in my life, I'm doing too much. The antidote to my apparent frenzied life and shortage of time is incredibly counterintuitive. It requires that I stop, inhale, listen for God's voice, and embrace God's agenda. Jesus invites us into this very posture when He says, "Get away with me...and work with me—watch how

45

I do it. Learn the unforced rhythms of grace. I won't lay anything heavy or ill-fitting on you. Keep company with me and you'll learn to live freely and lightly" (Matthew 11:28-30, The Message).

When we take the leap of faith and carve time for inhaling into our daily and weekly routines, the promise of Jesus comes true. We slowly, over days, months, and years, learn to live more freely and lightly.

It Doesn't Work for Me

I have a wacky hip that makes jogging difficult. No doctor has been able to help. Physical therapy offers relief, but not real healing. It appears the problem is structural. I tend to obsess about these kinds of things and so, after a great deal of research, I purchased a book that seemed to promise relief. It prescribes a series of exercises for just my malady. And yet, after owning the book for nearly two years, I still have a hip issue. "Stupid exercises," I say, sounding like Homer Simpson as I prepare to toss the book aside.

I can't, though. The author has brilliantly included a little section called "Don't Blame the Exercises." His summary point is that this little series of exercises must be done daily and in the right order, with the proper motion and number of sets and reps, if they are to work. When people claim his program doesn't work, he always asks if they're doing the routine daily and in proper sequence. When the answer is no, as it invariably is, then he says, "Then don't blame the exercises." Of course, that's been my problem: sporadic attempts, selective application, cheating on reps. And then I say it doesn't work.

The reality is that it's never been tried. This is most often the case with the disciplines of inhaling. Maybe you attended a silent retreat, and after five minutes of silence, you found your mind racing from your to-do list, to your relationships, to *Why am I wasting this time here?* to *I hate my job.* Or maybe you fell asleep. Either way, you've tried it, and it's not for you.

Don't blame the exercises. Maybe you went from sitting on the couch to running a marathon without taking the proper steps for training and progressively increasing challenges. Such behavior will cure you of jogging forever. You need to start slowly, reasonably, and with some help. And you need to set some achievable goals for these disciplines and stick with them for six months. If you slip into old patterns, pick yourself up and continue. These disciplines have been around for centuries and have been the mainstay of vibrant lives around the world. Please, don't blame the exercises.

This Is Too Catholic

This objection is born from the misguided evangelical notion that the church was invented by Martin Luther. This one sweeping misunderstanding conveniently negates 1400 years of church history, relegating all of it to the dustbin labeled *heresy*, where it can be dismissed. After all, the Catholics were guilty of the Crusades, indulgences, and the abuse of papal authority. How can they be trusted?

Yes, and Luther was guilty of anti-Semitism and persecution of his dissenters, and the church that has grown off his branch of church history's tree is rife with dissent, war, sexual misconduct, colonialism, and the sanctioning of slavery. If we're to be consistent when we negate branches of the church because of impurity, we need to burn the whole tree.

Maybe I would, except for the reality that throughout both the Catholic and Protestant branches, countless people have displayed Christ's redemptive, healing life in powerfully undeniable, life-changing, culture-blessing ways. So even though the whole tree is tainted with dysfunction, throughout the tree we can still find examples of fruitfulness hanging delicately and often inconspicuously from the branches, right there in the midst of the less healthy fruit.

My own journey into these disciplines came about because I, a Baptist since the cradle, was drawn to the life of Henri Nouwen, a Catholic theologian and academic who left his teaching position in order to serve in a small community for the developmentally disabled. The spacious spirit of Christ was so evident in his writing that I was drawn to read more in hopes of learning from this one who was such a genuine expression of Christ's life. I found his little book called *The Way of the Heart,* and it infected me with experiences of silence, solitude, and prayer from which I've never recovered[11].

Perhaps we need to drop the labels and look for the spirit of Christ wherever He can be found. In our finding, let's absorb, learn, and feast on Jesus' life. We'll not only learn more; we'll also contribute to breaking down the walls that have for too long fractured Christ's church and set people against each other.

I Don't Know How

When my oldest daughter began violin lessons, she didn't know how to play. Those first months were, to be polite, not the most pleasant experiences for the ears. I'd try to time my running routine with her practicing routine so I'd miss the endless renditions and variations of "Twinkle Twinkle, Little Star" executed so painfully. And yet the girl played on. Days turned into weeks and months and years. She still plays, now beautifully.

Why are children so willing to learn new things with such abandon? Why are they so uninhibited by their initial rough steps in mastering a new skill? When they fail, why do they pick up and try again so easily?

Children evidently suffer from an appalling lack of pride (or perhaps an abundance of humility). They seem to be able to celebrate small steps without worrying about whether or not they're the greatest of all. The joy is in the doing for them, not the triumph. Jesus indicates that this posture is precisely what we need if we're to develop the practices that will enable us to express Christ's life more fully. We need to become like little children: uninhibited, willing to try new things, willing to fall down and pick ourselves up.

Are you unsure about how to practice silence, solitude, spiritual reading, prayer, Sabbath rest? Don't worry. At one time, you didn't know how to use a fork either, but you learned. You dropped your fork a few dozen times. The first attempts at stabbing your food were probably comical, but you kept at it. And perhaps now is the time to become a child again and learn to breathe. You will experience frustrating moments, just as you did when you were mastering the use of your fork. Keep learning and growing. Spacious new arenas of grace await those who stay on the path.

Part Two

Inhaling and Exhaling Breathing Practices

Chapter 4

Word Problems: Assessing Our Problems with the Bible

Sink the Bible to the bottom of the ocean, and still man's obligations to God would be unchanged. He would have the same path to tread, only his lamp and guide would be gone; the same voyage to make, but his chart and compass would be overboard!

Henry Ward Beecher

The Bible has been the Magna Carta of the poor and oppressed. The human race is not in a position to dispense with it.

Thomas Huxley

What We Know

Have you ever heard of a Gideon Bible? A group called the Gideons is on a mission to distribute Bibles, and each year they hand out millions of copies of the Scripture in thousands of locations around the globe. Our church receives an annual offering for them to help in the fulfillment of their mission. Each year, we hear stories of people who found a Bible in a motel room, a hospital, a halfway house, or somewhere else, and upon reading it, came to the conclusion that Christ is the source of all that is good and beautiful and true, the only real source of life. A recent baptism at our church included the testimony of a young man whose first contact with the Bible was in a hotel in Las Vegas. His initial reading started him on a path that eventually led to his standing in the waters of a lake in Seattle, awaiting baptism as a way of declaring to the whole world that he was putting his hope in Christ.

Stories of people reading a Bible and responding to its revelation in ways that changed them forever are scattered throughout the pages of church history. Some people know intuitively that this Word we call the Bible is powerful. Others know because of the stories they've heard or because of what they've experienced in their own lives. But however we know it, the Bible itself reinforces this position many times:

> All Scripture is inspired by God and profitable for teaching, for reproof, for correction, for training in righteousness; so that the man of God may be adequate, equipped for every good work (2 Timothy 3:16-17).

> With all my heart I have sought You; do not let me wander from Your commandments. Your word I have treasured in my heart, that I may not sin against You (Psalm 119:10-11).

> How blessed is the man who does not walk in the counsel of the wicked, nor stand in the path of sinners, nor sit in the seat of scoffers! But his delight is in the law of the Lord, and in His law he meditates day and night. He will be like a tree firmly planted by streams of water, which yields its fruit in its season and its leaf does not wither; and in whatever he does, he prospers (Psalm 1:1-3).

The testimony of changed lives and the testimony of Scripture itself combine to declare that when we're holding the Bible, we're holding in our hands an inspired collection of words that have the power to reveal the source of truth and life. We should take it seriously.

At one level, the Bible *is* taken seriously. It's a perpetual bestseller. Every Sunday around the world, people gather together in order to listen to the words of the Bible, whether they are sung, read, taught, discussed, prayed over, or all of these things together. In many churches, the sermon is the centerpiece of the worship service because of the life-changing power available to those who will hear and respond to the Word of God.

Christians are encouraged to learn their Bibles, and so reading programs, weekly Bible studies, and countless devotional options are made available, all in the hopes that those who follow Christ will follow His example by gaining a solid grounding in Bible knowledge[12]. In short, the Bible is honored as God's written revelation to humanity, and those who follow Christ are encouraged to become "people of the book."

What We Do

So it might come as a surprise to discover that both the Bible reading habits and Bible knowledge of those who claim to know Christ are appallingly low. Stephen Prothero, in *Religious Literacy: What Every American Needs to Know—and Doesn't,* says that Americans know little to nothing about religion, and though an overwhelming majority of the nation's population claim they are Christian, only half of the adults can name one of the four Gospels (Matthew, Mark, Luke, and John). Most Americans do not know the first book in the Bible (Genesis). Twelve percent think that Joan of Arc was the wife of Noah.

Thus we are faced with the very strange situation, in which a book that is perpetually the global bestseller, a book that has a reputation for saving people from the depths of despair and pointing them toward a new, hopeful, joy-filled, meaningful life, is also a book that is, frankly, rarely read, even among some of Jesus' most devoted followers.

We've spoken elsewhere of the sad statistical similarities between people who claim to be Christians and the culture at large. The Bible itself expresses that the way to be equipped to live differently is to become saturated in the Scriptures. Romans 12:2 explains that our lives will move toward renewal and transformation to the extent that we are responding to God's revelation found in His Word. Thus, if the Bible remains largely unread, we should not be surprised that the church looks so similar to the surrounding culture. Call me old-fashioned, but our journey of transformation will be severely hampered if we don't develop habits of hearing from God on a regular basis, and hearing from God surely includes encountering truth through the text God gave us.

Unfortunately, not all who believe in Christ believe the last sentence of the previous paragraph. Christian colleges everywhere are struggling as the combination of Internet access, gender role confusion, heightened individuality, and postmodern angst are conspiring to thwart some young people from rising up and embracing their callings to be people of purity, hope, and blessing. A leader from one of these campuses and I were discussing how the Internet's easy access to pornography is changing the hearts of so many students, leading to layers of addiction, shame, and disengagement from relationships and service to this broken world. When I asked whether students were encouraged to read their Bibles and pray every day as part of a strategy to address this, the leader looked at me somewhat condescendingly and said, "I don't think that's the real issue here, do you?"

In part, yes I do. The most important thing isn't that we learn how to be relevant, or emergent, or that we understand the inherent weaknesses in the modernist and postmodernist hermeneutics. The most important thing is that we are being shaped and empowered by Christ, so we can live the lives of blessing for which we were created. But that shaping is a response to revelation, and I can't respond to what I don't show up to see.

That seems clear enough. So why don't more people show up? Understanding the reasons will be helpful as we seek to develop our own unique patterns of inhaling the Word. The following parable will lay the foundation to help you better understand the barriers.

The Reasons for the Disconnect

Once upon a time, some people were devoted to the study of maps. The maps were intended to guide people on a journey to a magical land of justice, hope, celebration, peace, enough food and clean water for all, and stunning beauty everywhere. It was an enchanting land, and people who'd had their fill of their own dark land would come together and consider the journey to this new land. They would gather together each week in a big room, and everyone would bring their various maps, all of the same terrain. Studies in orienteering, navigation, and other general skills associated with map reading were a regular part of the gatherings, along with a weekly focus on a particular section of the map. The master cartographer used the map and other sources to describe the magical land. He explained to all the eager listeners what the map was indicating that each one needed to do in order to arrive safely, where to turn and where to go straight. He pointed out the wide roads leading to destruction and the narrow road leading to the magical land. Often the students gathered at a local restaurant after the map-reading session and discussed whether the teacher was wise enough and entertaining enough to keep them coming back for another map session next week.

Sometimes arguments would arise about whose map was closest to the original, but the original maps to this magical place had been lost long ago, so this argument seemed pointless to most. By the end of most map meetings, the group left feeling good about the fact that they'd learned still more about the magical land by studying the map. They felt better prepared than ever for the journey. At the end of one session they were told that the next week, they'd learn about the mysteries of true north and magnetic north, which filled them with a heightened sense of expectation.

Meanwhile, down the road, another group of people also gathered weekly, not to look at maps but to read travelogues and look at picture books of that same magical land. Many of them had once devoted themselves to the study of maps, but they found that the almost obsessive preoccupation with the map had a way of stripping the wonder and beauty from the magical land. This group was far more interested in the nuances of the journey. What was the food like? Were the people friendly? And what about the climate, and the smells, and animals? "You don't get any of that from a map!" one of them shouted one day as he angrily left the map group in order to join the travelogue club.

Every week these two groups gathered. Every week they felt good about the knowledge they gained. And every week, almost none of them actually moved one step closer to the new land. Both groups were convinced that they were closer to the land than their antagonists, and they spent so much time reacting to their enemies that they forgot that the real point of their gatherings was to equip them to move forward on their journey and to celebrate the steps people were taking in that direction.

The ones who met to discuss travelogues would shout across the fence to the other group, "All you care about are lines and dots on a piece of paper."

The map lovers would respond, "You're so enamored with the atmosphere and human-interest stories that you're not paying attention to the route. You're going to end up somewhere bad, somewhere hellish!"

The volume grew progressively louder every week. New people always seemed to be joining the meetings, enchanted by the prospect of a magical land better than the one they presently inhabited. But other people were leaving the meetings and never returning. The ones who departed were tired of the arguments, tired of one group's fixation on map minutiae and the other group's utter disregard of much-needed truths to lead them to their destination. Most of all, they were tired of the fact that for all the studying, all the careful considerations of the magical land, they rarely found a person who was actually traveling toward it.

Always though, a few were on the journey. They were scattered in both camps. Some travelers didn't even go to any of the formal meetings, choosing instead to simply gather around a meal and share stories from the journey. These people used travelogues *and* maps as well as their own stories of steps they'd taken toward the magical land, all as a means of encouraging one another to continue. "Press on through dark forests! Ford raging rivers! Don't turn back. The land they call 'life' is up ahead." These people had little time for the arguments about whether maps were better than travelogues; they were willing to use anything at their disposal in order to keep moving. And their faces looked different, more hopeful than the others'.

Unwilling to Journey

It's not a very subtle parable. In fact, it's not a parable at all. Here's what Jesus said regarding those who thought that all they needed was a map: "You search the Scriptures because you think that in them you have eternal life; it is these that testify about Me; and you are unwilling to come to Me so that you may have life" (John 5:39-40). His complaint regarding the textual experts was that they were unwilling to make the journey, unwilling to come to Him. They studied the text, preserved it, interpreted it, argued over their respective interpretations of it, divided their communities over their interpretations of it, shunned those who disagreed with their views, memorized it, read it aloud, and taught it regularly to the people under their care. And yet for all that, they were unwilling to make the journey that would have led them to the land of life.

What's even more tragic is that they seemed to think that preserving their tiny view of truth was, above all other things, what their lives were to be about. Thus when the One came who was, Himself, the human embodiment of truth—and when that embodiment contradicted their presuppositions—these leaders who knew their Bibles so well presumed that Jesus was in error. Unwilling to move: that was their problem.

This resistance showed up when the religious leaders were continually offended by Jesus. "Why does this man speak that way? He is blaspheming; who can forgive sins but God alone?" "Why is He eating and drinking with tax collectors and sinners?" "Why do John's disciples and the disciples of the Pharisees fast, but Your disciples do not fast?" "Why are they doing what is not lawful on the Sabbath[13]?" Later, when Jesus cast a demon out of a man, the textual experts finally had Him figured out: He was possessed by a demon and could therefore cast out demons! Such astute minds and hearts! So thoroughly did they know their Bibles that they came to the conclusion that God in human form was inhabited and empowered by demons!

For this group, the Old Testament Scriptures had become nothing more than a map, or perhaps more accurately, a legal code to be studied. They dissected and debated the particulars of the text with literary and philosophical tools in order to arrive at the perfect meaning. We'll see later what this did to the Sabbath. But for now, simply note that all this dissecting and obsession with minutiae had the effect of missing the forest for the trees. When the Messiah, about whom the whole thing was written, came and lived among them, they not only didn't recognize Him, they killed Him. Perhaps if they'd seen the bigger picture—the sights, sounds, and smells of redemption, mercy, and God's kingdom—they'd have gotten it right. And they not only missed Jesus, but also profoundly misinterpreted the law because they needed the larger framework in order to understand the particulars.

We can be harsh with these folks, and of course, this is a caricature intended to make a point. But the point is an important one: *The Scriptures themselves can become a hindrance to our living the life of faith!* We too can fixate on minutiae to such an extent that we fail to see the larger work to which we're called, fail to see the story that God is writing in history. When this happens, we reduce salvation to a tiny little transaction, executable with the simplicity of paying bills online[14]. We reduce discipleship and ethics by restricting movement to only certain areas on the map (don't have sex before marriage, don't get an abortion, stay sober, read your Bible, tell others about your faith) and conveniently ignoring others (justice for the poor, care for the environment, following Jesus' example of nonviolent resistance and loving enemies). Our obsession with the text might just make us equally as equipped to miss the point as the first-century Pharisees were.

We stand at a grave crossroads, where we're in danger of so fixating on the minutiae that these elements end up shaping our personalities, our churches, our investments of time and energy. That's why so many think of people of faith only in terms of what they're *against*, which is so strange because Jesus' life was characterized much more by what He was for. His life and words indicated He was *for* breaking down social barriers, giving a voice to the marginalized, caring for the poor, healing the sick, inviting people to know true life, loving enemies, practicing hospitality, and learning to speak truth and forgive those who've wronged us. That's just a short list. And yet my friend who is a musician working in New York says that he tells his coworkers he's a follower of Jesus rather than using the word *Christian*. He avoids the label, because it's come to mean "people who persecute gays and bomb abortion clinics." Sure, it's fair to say that such generalizations misrepresent. But these perceptions weren't fabricated out of thin air. They were forged through encounters with legalistic obsession with minutiae. Is standing in front of a gay rights rally with a sign that says, "You'll burn in hell forever" really our calling? Does it truly embody the Spirit of Christ? All such gestures do is give rise to negative generalizations about people of faith, creating ill-will and building walls that shut out all healthy dialogue.

Not everyone stays on that path. There are more than a few who, when they step away from the minutiae and seek to get the global view, realize that they've missed the point. They step back and see that Jesus probably wouldn't have spent an afternoon painting a colorful fire on a protest sign, making the Ls in "hell" look like pitchforks, or shaking the sign at gay people while shouting slogans. When they really think about it, they suddenly see that their faith expressions have misrepresented Christ.

Danger exists at the other end of the pendulum, too. The church eventually discovered that the Bible was never written as a law brief (for wrangling over words) or science textbook (for debating or defending the age of the earth). This shift began with a clash between scientific inquiry and the textual expert's interpretive methods.

"From the rising of the sun to its setting the name of the Lord is to be praised" (Psalm 113:3). Thus did the textual experts declare that the Bible clearly teaches that the earth is the fixed center of the solar system, and the sun is the moving object. Any other view is heresy! This is why Galileo found himself in trouble when he came to the conclusion that the reverse was true, but his discovery was just one of many during that period in history that contributed to a reconsideration of how the Bible is to be read. The emphasis on discovering some of the contextual nuances and allowing those to govern interpretation became more popular.

But nuances and context are also a slippery slope, as the postmodernist has come to discover. Nobody comes to the text with perfect objectivity, dispassionately sorting words and context in order to arrive at "the" interpretation. When we of the North American middle class, who send our children to college, read "blessed are the poor," we like to come to the conclusion that Jesus is speaking of the "poor in spirit." Perhaps that's one of the reasons Matthew's version of the Sermon on the Mount is more popular than Luke's version in our part of the world. But in Central America, some families work for 60 cents a day or less, without health care, education, or the possibility of ever escaping the scourge of poverty that causes so many children to die before the age of ten. For these people, Luke's version, carrying the unmistakable reference that people who are living in true financial poverty are blessed, carries the day[15].

Liberation theology was shaped in the fires of poverty and oppression. Prosperity theology was forged in the heart of the richest nation on earth. The notion of approaching any text in a purely objective vacuum no longer appears realistic to readers. But this opens the doors to a different kind of danger, the danger that the meaning of a particular text is either completely unknowable or so flexible as to mean virtually anything.

At this point it's tempting to throw up our hands in frustration, set our Bibles on our shelves, and just walk away. Many have. And when asked why they don't read their Bibles, many people, even though they've never been to Bible college or seminary, offer answers that seem to come from the front lines of these interpretive battles we've been considering.

"The Bible Is Misused"

The Bible was quoted by both sides in the slavery debate. Genocide has been justified by quoting it, and it has been used to support both capitalist and socialist ideals. The marginalization of women has been based on certain interpretations of biblical text, with the result that spouse abuse is statistically higher among Christians than among the culture at large. The Bible has been used to endorse the pillaging of the earth, as I once heard a preacher on the radio explain that

God killed the dinosaurs to give us oil. People have sustained oppressive regimes, mocked worldviews before they fully understood them, and justified consumerist lifestyles—all by simply quoting chapter and verse.

One author makes a pointed charge against the conservative churches of the West in this regard:

> We wanted a simple, clear, efficient, and convenient plan for getting to heaven after death. Between now and then, we wanted clear assurance that God didn't like the people we didn't like, and for the same reasons we didn't like them. Finally, we wanted a rule book that made it objectively clear, with no subjective ambiguity, what behaviors were right and wrong for all time, in all places, and among all cultures, especially if those rules confirmed our views and not those of people we considered "liberal[16]."

"The Bible Is Hard to Understand"

Pick any social or ethical issue: War? Divorce? Homosexuality? Gender roles in marriage and society? Is Jesus the only way to heaven? Does man choose God or does God choose man? Once someone has gained salvation, can it be lost? For every question, people who are completely committed to the authority of the Bible will have different, even conflicting, answers. And precisely because it's not rocket science, these varied contradictory interpretations can't be tested in a lab to see whether they fly. I've had countless discussions regarding these kinds of issues with people who love God and are committed to the authority of the Bible, just as I am. So why don't we agree? People who need things to be rock solid, linear, and verifiable through the scientific method get frustrated with all this gray, all this seeing "through a glass, darkly," and so their Bible, shrouded in mystery and revealing more questions than answers, remains unread[17].

"The Bible Is Boring"

You learned somewhere along the way that reading the Bible is important, and so you dig in. No matter where you begin, you quickly come to some parts that seem quite remote to your daily living or hard to understand. This distance from reality, and the disconnect that these little (or big) sections of the Bible seem to have with any sense of a larger story, have the effect of lulling you to sleep. "Please, I don't need to hear any more about a woman's issue of blood[18]. It's too much information!" "Does it really matter if silk touches wool[19]?" We tend to wear fleece in the Pacific Northwest, so what relevance does this have for my daily living? Perhaps the front page of the *Times* would be a better use of my time (or maybe I'll skip the front page and dive into the comics).

"I Read It When I Was Young"

Some people went to Sunday school and know the famous stories about Noah's ark, Moses and the tablets, and David killing a giant. Others went to a weekly Bible study at their high school youth group or were in a Christian group in college that stressed daily Bible reading, so they've memorized lots of verses and know the stories really well. Both groups feel that even though they don't fully understand the Bible, they understand it enough for life in this present moment.

Familiarity breeds disengagement. For some, the Bible has become a little bit like those movies we buy because we loved them so much. We buy them and watch them once, twice, maybe even a third time. But after that, we have a sense that we've seen it all before. The jokes aren't funny anymore. The parts that made us cry don't make us cry anymore. And Meg Ryan and Tom Hanks are still covered in sap the third time you watch them e-mailing each other while you run on your treadmill. Pretty soon the movies just sit there, next to our Bibles. I don't worry much about Tom and Meg just sitting there on the shelf, but the Bible? That's a different story.

These are some of the major reasons that this powerful text sits unread in so many homes. But as we've seen, when we stop showing up to receive revelation through the Scriptures, we stop moving on our journey because our movement and growth come as responses to revelation. We simply can't go forward without meeting Christ, and we can't meet Christ if we're neglecting the primary source through which God has chosen to reveal Him.

In the midst of all these issues, how can we recover a healthy view of the Bible? How can we develop regular habits of encountering it in a healthy way, so that we're shaped by the heart of Christ as we continue on our journey? The answer is in the next chapter.

Chapter 5

Inhaling the Bible Without Choking On It

I heard, and I forgot.
I saw, and I remembered.
I did, and I understood.

Chinese Proverb

I was in Germany shortly after the Iron Curtain had rusted through, allowing democracy and capitalism to pour into what was once East Germany. My friend Michael had invited me to spend time with him, and so we spent a day driving through what was, just a short time earlier, forbidden territory. We talked of the Marshall Plan and communism, of Christianity in East Germany and the remarkable tenacity of the German people in their rebuilding work.

The day ended back at Michael's home, where his parents were hosting an amazing supper party. Michael's sister, brother-in-law, parents, and grandmother were all there. The grandmother spoke not a word of English. Please understand that, for a guy who'd grown up Baptist, what unfolded in the next several hours was an assault to my sensibilities. Michael worked for a ministry in Germany, and his parents were devout Christians as well. In spite of this, these people were washing down their bratwurst, sauerkraut, and the best bread in the world with draft after draft of beer! You wouldn't find Christians in my part of the world drinking beer. No sir. Never mind that Jesus turned water into wine at a party. I'd heard a sermon or two on how it was impossible that the wine Jesus had created was strong enough to create any problems. I don't remember the reasoning, only the conclusion: Alcohol and the life of faith don't mix.

I'd lived a culturally sheltered life, so I was really having a hard time making sense of the way these hospitable people, whose faith was so vibrant, were drinking beer like this. Worst of all was the grandmother. I didn't know anything of her faith story because of the language barrier, but even though she was small in stature, she seemed to me to be the biggest drinker at the table. I wasn't watching carefully, but she always seemed to be filling her glass.

The food and conversation were incredible, and the evening was already indelibly marked in my mind as the new gold standard for hospitality. But the most earth-shattering part was yet to come. After hours of conversation, the grandmother, through the translating abilities of her grandson, invited me to her home, a few hundred meters down the road. Once there, she showed me a scrapbook of pictures and headlines from World War II, including the bombing of Dresden. She told me what my country did, and the horrific losses her people suffered. Then she asked me why we felt the need to kill so many.

I was speechless, but she didn't really want an answer. I think she just wanted me to see an event through a different lens. She then recounted much of her story. Her father died early, in combat in World War I. Right after her marriage, her husband was conscripted into Hitler's army and hauled eventually to the Russian front, where he found himself when the war ended. He was told the war was over and that he was free to go home, but he had no means to get there. So he began to walk. More than a year later, he arrived home. Meanwhile, the dividing line created in Germany split her family and resulted in profound losses. She didn't know whether her husband was dead or alive. Finally the day came when he walked through the door, so many months after the war had ended. I listened, and the room became silent.

"Life has been hard," she said. I nodded, speechless. "Do you know what kept me going and gave me hope?" I waited for her answer. She pointed to a large Bible on the coffee table and said, "Every morning, on my knees, I meet with Jesus in His Word. He's always given me what I needed for the day: joy, wisdom, strength." This from the one who seemed to enjoy her beer more than anyone at the party. In one evening, my whole tiny world had been shattered, and the faith that would grow out of the ashes of that night would be much different. It would be more spacious, forgiving, and kingdom oriented than the faith of my childhood.

Please don't miss the point. The story has nothing to do with beer, and everything to do with how our cultural conditioning shapes our understanding of the Bible—why we read it, when we read it, and what we understand as we receive it. In other words, we never approach the Bible in a vacuum. Consider, for example, the "Why should I read the Bible?" question. I have serious doubts that this woman woke up in the morning during those dark days of the war and said to herself, "Hmm. I know that I'm supposed to have a quiet time, so I'd better get up and read my Bible." No. When your entire world collapses, you are drawn to the Bible as a source of sustenance. You needn't have your city bombed, though, in order to sense your profound need for what God has to offer through the Bible. You simply need to be about what God is about, committed to being a light of hope in a hopeless world. That—along with dating, marrying, parenting, dealing with financial and sexual choices and employment issues, facing the challenges of aging parents and your own aging—ought to be enough to keep you coming back for more, day after day.

We began the previous chapter with a consideration of 2 Timothy 3:16, which reminds us that the Scriptures are "inspired by God and profitable for teaching, for reproof, for correction, for training in righteousness." This brings us to the first principle regarding Bible reading.

I Must Be Committed to the Journey

We're invited to participate in making the character of the invisible God visible through our lives, our homes, and our faith communities. This is no small task, and it entails both personal transformation and practical commitment to be a blessing to the world through acts of service. But when we've been captured by this vision and are committed to making forward progress, the Bible once again becomes the source of fortification and equipping that God intends it to be.

All of these breathing practices are interrelated. I'm not motivated to inhale the Word if I'm not exhaling acts of service, hospitality, and generosity. All through the history of the church, people have accepted the Bible as the source as long as they were coming to it to be equipped for the journey. Like thirsty travelers, they drink deeply and get back on the trail.

This cycle of revelation and response becomes self-sustaining. When revelation leads to obedience, the obedience creates a context in which we long for more revelation, which leads to more obedience, which creates longing for more. You get the picture. Conversely, revelation that's ignored creates a backwater in which truth putrefies, which makes further drinking unpleasant, which weakens us so that we're no longer motivated for the journey, which further poisons our perceptions of the Word. Again, you get the picture. This is why James tells us to make certain that we respond to what God is revealing[20].

I Must Look Through the Interpretive Prism

If we approach the Bible as nothing more than a book filled with moral precepts, we will ultimately misuse the Scriptures and misrepresent the heart of God. If we look at it only as a nice book of stories from which we draw warm feelings and inspiration, we end up with the same problem. We saw the dangers of both of those tendencies in the last chapter. In order to avoid these minefields, we need to continually hold the Scriptures up to what I call an interpretive prism, reading them through different lights.

The Narrative Light

The Bible is, above all else, the story of God's activity in history, beginning with creation in the distant past and stretching forward to the culmination of history in the distant future. The plot of this grand story could be summarized this way:

Act I: Man's movement from glory to rebellion

Act II: The judgment that arises out of the rebellion

Act III: The restoration that arises out of the judgment

This is the grand "meta-narrative," or large story, running through the Bible. This same plot is also played out in smaller stories within the larger story: another rebellion, another judgment, another restoration.

Because we're reading a story (please don't misunderstand: not fiction, but *story*), we must realize that God and the authors inspired by God are often simply describing what happened. This is quite different from sanctioning what happened, forming it into precedent and setting law for all time. Thus the genocidal practices of Israel in their early days of settling their land are seen as aberrations rather than the way God always does things. The same thing is true with respect to how we treat fortune-tellers and how we no longer forbid menstruating women to gather for worship.

We need to see the big picture, the upward trajectory of God's movement in history. It's a movement away from slavery, violence, isolation, and economic oppression. In short, it's a movement toward the restoration of all things[21]. This larger view of narrative will help inform our interpretation of the particulars.

The Encounter Light

The book of Hebrews tells us that the Word of God is living and active, sharper than any two-edged sword. That little truth is tucked into a passage where the author is admonishing people who are tempted to give up on the journey[22]. He reminds them that an entire generation of Israel in the Old Testament spent years wandering around in frustration, because they refused to keep moving forward toward their God-appointed destiny. In order to avoid having the same fate fall to us, we're admonished to continue encountering the Word of God, which is somehow living.

Listening for God's voice through the Scriptures, then, is one of the primary ways I'm able to sustain a genuine relationship with the Creator of the universe. Because my times in the Word are "relationship times," I need to treat them as such. Unfortunately, we often view time spent in the Bible through a decidedly non-relational lens. We view this time as more of a transaction, whereby we give God time, with the tacit expectation that God gives us something tangible in return. If you view the other relationships in life through that same conditional lens, there is a word that describes you: *lonely*. "I met with Sally for coffee, but she really didn't have much to offer me today. And yesterday when I met with her, she wasn't encouraging at all. In fact she told me some things about myself that I didn't really want to hear. So I'm rethinking our friendship."

It's not a very healthy way to relate to people. Or God. Rather, we show up because we're in relationship, and because showing up sustains relationship. Somehow, in the process of showing up, we trust that we'll be transformed. Sometimes we'll come away from "coffee with God" with very practical steps we know we must take in our lives. Other times we'll come away encouraged by having heard something true about ourselves, about God, or about the future. Other times we'll be deeply convicted. And other times, just like in other friendships, we'll be bored. But we keep showing up because there is no transformation without encounter, and no encounter without presence.

The Precept Light

The light of the precept is as important as the light of encounter and narrative. It simply means that out of this story and the encounters we have with God through the living Word, we will learn precepts: principles, ethics, and convictions by which to order our lives. Because our calling is to make the invisible God visible through the way we live, God has a great deal to say about that subject. God cares about what we do with our bodies, who we sleep with, how we treat our enemies, what we do with our money, and much more.

Convictions must be forged through a continual process of approaching the Scriptures and allowing them to speak to us. Often, this approach will bring confirmation to convictions we already hold, but sometimes our convictions will be shaken as we receive new understanding. That happened to Peter in Acts 10, when God told him to eat meat that he had always viewed as unclean and therefore forbidden. Later, the church shifted in its position on eating meat sacrificed to idols. It had been forbidden, but Paul acknowledged that the act is, in itself, harmless[23].

Likewise, the church has shifted its views on slavery, racism, colonialism, and other issues. I'm glad the shifts occurred. Without them, the world wouldn't see Christ's character as clearly. Still, we have a long way to go. Will our convictions shift regarding our responsibilities to the environment or regarding the economic inequities brought about by our current structures?

We must watch out for two dangers when looking through the precept lens. Some people seem afraid to land and declare what they believe to be the truth. Their fears of being wrong, being unpopular, or being like the textual experts of Jesus' day have paralyzed them. As a result, they are always discussing, always considering, and always debating, but never coming to any convictions. It's vital that we see the deception in this. We're called to live our lives in obedience to what God is revealing, and though we don't understand it perfectly, we must nevertheless commit to living out our convictions with courage and humility.

The humility part of living out our convictions is critical, and speaks to the second danger as we look through the precept lens. That danger is to hold our convictions with such stubbornness that we become immovable even when the Holy Spirit is seeking to bring about a shift in our thinking. Without such movement, African Americans would still be sitting at the back of the bus. There would still be inquisitions and witch burnings. I'd still be presuming that everyone who enjoys beer doesn't know God. The movement from darkness to light is thwarted as much by people holding convictions too tightly as it is by people not holding any convictions at all.

I'm very concerned for people who respond to any challenge to their understanding of the Scriptures as a threat. We need never be afraid of a challenge to our convictions if, in the core of our being, our desire is to know the truth. If we're already walking in the truth in some area of our lives, it will withstand challenge. If we're wrong, it won't, and we should thank God because our transformation will be progressive, "from glory to glory[24]." I can't keep growing if I continue staying the same!

I Must Practice

Scripture is given to us, we're told, for "training in righteousness." Paul was well-versed in the culture of the Olympic games, and he often offered word pictures of an athlete in training. The most pointed references are found in his first letter to the Corinthians, in which he notes that everybody runs in a race, but only one wins the prize. He goes on to encourage us to "run in such a way that you may win[25]." Nobody who does anything worthwhile in life does it without discipline. I don't wake up one morning and play Beethoven piano sonatas. Before the sonata, I learned hand positions, notes, rhythm, and phrasing. I practiced scales and arpeggios. And before Beethoven, I played "Mary Had a Little Lamb." To run a marathon, we must first run a mile. To climb a summit, we start with a StairMaster. And so it goes.

All these endeavors, says Paul, pale in comparison with the greatest undertaking of all: embodying the reign of Christ in our lives and faith communities. Like playing the piano, running, or climbing, we will only go as far as our commitment to the endeavor. If we continually choose to be shaped by forces other than the Bible, our capacity to make Christ visible through our lives will suffer. You can't get around the reality. We need to develop a consistent practice of inhaling the Word that works for us.

It can be short, but it should be consistent. You don't need to read through the whole Bible in a year. If you're not presently being consistent, you need to find a way to read a little section of the Bible every day, prayerfully asking God to show you what He wants to teach you. If you feel nothing, you feel nothing. Don't be discouraged. You have a vision. You're on a journey of transformation. You're learning how to bless and serve others, how to offer light to a darkened world. God will show you what you need to know, when you need to know it, if you'll just keep showing up. Supplement your reading by learning other facets of the Bible, such as historical context and various ethical or interpretive issues. Perhaps you can find classes in your area. If not, you can find good online resources through my Web site[26].

What This Looks Like

Two temptations arise when we try to make this deeply practical. The first temptation is to universalize any person's experience of digesting the Bible, making it *the* way to approach God. No single way is universal. If you're learning to play the piano, you can adopt the Suzuki method, the Canadian graded system, or the infinite variety of methodologies available in our American system. You're free to find what works for you.

Likewise, some people use devotional books with a verse and a little commentary or story. Others simply read the Bible in either short or long sections. Some underline. Some journal. Some simply pray when they're finished. Some practice what's called *Lectio Divina,* an ancient practice that encourages slow, prayerful, meditative reading of the text. Some people get the "verse of the day" by e-mail and read it when they get to work. The important thing isn't what technique you adopt, but that you are consistently inhaling the Word. Your practice is working if you're not just doing a ritual but actually meeting and being shaped more fully by Christ.

However, the very freedom we ought to have, so that we can find what works for us, is also dangerous. We can shop perpetually for the perfect technique, discarding too quickly our approaches to meeting Christ because we get easily bored, with the result that we never establish a practice that we can call our own. If I try to learn piano by the Suzuki method this month, the Canadian method next month, followed by the improv method and scales after that, I will eventually decide that I'm not made to play the piano, which of course may or may not be true. I'll never know until I develop a consistent practice.

For this reason, it's good to talk with people about how they digest the Bible and what God is teaching them as they make themselves available to be taught by the Word. Are people actually meeting

Christ? What does that mean? Do people who have a regular practice see how it is connected with the lives they're living? This kind of sharing proves helpful as we begin to develop our own habits. We needn't copy anyone exactly. But we do need to learn from one another and move toward consistent habits of our own that work for us. We seem to shy away from sharing our stories in this realm for some reason. And precisely because I'm not sure if anyone will share his story with you, I'll share mine.

This habit has waxed and waned in my life for a number of reasons. Sometimes I've been lazy, sometimes so disengaged from God's purposes that I've not felt the need. Sometimes I've been too busy. But "coffee with God" is often critical to the life to which I'm called, and not because I'm a pastor (though that would be reason enough). Rather, the calling to serve and bless my wife and children requires skills, wisdom, and purity of heart that I don't have. Or sometimes I feel awkward when I try to be a good neighbor, fearful that my calling as a pastor is creating a veil between me and others. Perhaps I'm dealing with some interior struggles and need God's wisdom and power. Maybe I desperately want to make the most of each day, being a voice of hope and blessing, enjoying life fully and entering into God's purposes. These are the reasons that, though I fail to show up with perfect consistency, I keep showing up as often as I do.

I've spent many years reading big chunks of the Bible and writing a short response in a journal, but I don't do either of those things presently. Instead, I simply sit, and after a short prayer, I begin to read very slowly. I'll keep reading, chewing a bit on meaning, looking for something that will reach out and grab me, something that will speak to me like a living personal word. Usually, by the time I'm finished with a short section, something has done just that. Not always, though more now than when I first began.

Then I'll ponder that word and pray about it, asking God to cement this truth in my heart. This is, I believe, how our lives are transformed—not through spectacular lightning flashes of revelation but through the tiny little additions that are made day after day, just one more brick on the wall of truth. One brick! It's nothing. You could skip it without feeling much of a loss. But the power is in the addition of a brick a day. Soon you're a foundation. Then a wall. Someday we'll be strong towers, lighthouses, or places of safety for others who are weary, all because we added a brick most days.

Once God has shown me something, I'll run with it. Literally. It will become like a mantra that I'll try to carry through the day, beginning with my morning run. "Let the words of my mouth and the meditation of my heart be acceptable in Your sight, O Lord, my rock and my Redeemer" (Psalm 19:14). I repeat the verse in my mind over and over as I run. I begin to long for the very thing I'm repeating; long for my words and heart to be pure. Later in the day, my mind begins to wander down a dark alley. I'm reminded of what I read. It happens again the next day. Again Psalm 19 is mine, like a voice warning me not to walk down that alley. Over time, many portions of the Bible are hidden in the recesses of the soul and arise, often unbidden, by my conscious heart, to speak to me in a moment.

I read because I need that voice in my life. There are too many alleys that look attractive to me, too many dead-end options, too many ways to be hijacked. This, of course, brings us full circle. If we're not involved in the exhaling habits, we've no need to inhale either. But there's a word for people who aren't inhaling or exhaling: dead.

Chapter 6

Journey

God counseled Abraham to leave his own country and go in pilgrimage into the land which God had shown him, to wit the "Land of Promise"—Now the good counsel which God enjoined here on the father of the faith is incumbent on all the faithful; that is to leave their country and their land, their wealth and their worldly delight for the sake of the Lord of the Elements, and go in perfect pilgrimage in imitation of Him.

St. Columba

God be with thee in every pass,
Jesus be with thee on every hill,
Spirit be with thee on every stream,
Headland and ridge and lawn,
...Each step of the journey thou goest.

Mary MacDonald

"Are you ready to climb this mountain?"

I shout the question to the other eleven of our group who stand, packs on back and trekking poles in hand, at a visitor center parking lot. It's the staging point for climbing Mt. Rainier, one of the tallest peaks in North America. Our excited group shouts back, "We're ready!" as they pose for the departure photo, fresh socks on blisterless feet, hair shining and clean. After the picture, we take our first steps away from the pavement, upward and onward toward the summit.

The difference between the *notion* of ascent and *actual* ascent is enormous. Sitting by the fire and looking at maps with friends, we can easily romanticize the climb. We can picture ourselves tied together with rope, ice axes in hand, negotiating a crevasse field on a glacier under the clear blue sky as the sun rises over the horizon and turns the glaciated ice to ethereal hues of pink and blue. We can feel the crunch of our crampons biting into the ice as we breathe deeply and press forward, higher and higher, until the final obstructions recede behind us and everything is down. We imagine ourselves taking pictures at the top, basking in the warmth of the sunshine and accomplishment and enjoying the vast views and deep fellowship of a job well done. Then, in our minds, we reluctantly begin our descent to our base camp, where we gather our goods and head for the car, arriving there just as the sun is setting.

The actual climb is so *otherwise* as to be almost unrecognizable. As we find ourselves climbing Mt. Rainier, and as reality displaces fantasy, we discover several things that our romantic ascent ignored. We completely forgot about slogging six miles to base camp, enduring relentless sun, and carrying 55 pounds of gear on our backs. Our backs! The weight has compressed our vertebrae together, so that when we arrive at base camp and discharge our load, movement is difficult, and even without the burden, the new spinal ache torments us. The thought of carrying any weight at all to the summit in this condition is repulsive. The altitude has given us headaches, and when the sun drops below the ridge, our burnt skin quickly becomes deeply chilled. We are tired, achy, and grumpy, but we must immediately dig a snow shelter, set up a tent, melt snow for our water, and cook our meal. We want desperately for someone to serve us, for someone to care for us, but no one is here but us. We must care for ourselves. We finally manage to carry out these necessities, void of any joy. Then we drop into our sleeping bags for a few fitful hours of sleep, somewhat alarmed that our pulse is still raging, even though we finished hiking more than three hours ago. The altitude is having its effects.

The next day begins early, as the alarm beeps at 12:30 a.m. to call us from our restless sleep. We fumble in our tents and get dressed for the summit: layer upon layer of clothing, two pairs of socks, cold boots. Next we add all the climbing paraphernalia: harness, rope, crampons, ice axe, carabiners, extra loops of rescue rope, headlamp, helmet, whistle, and climbing protection. If we forget a single element, we put the safety of the whole team at risk. And forgetting is easy to do at this altitude, at this time of night, in this cold, with our aching backs, lack of sleep, and splitting headaches. Nevertheless, we persevere, and soon we are dressed, equipped, and ready to climb.

The ascent itself is arduous. Our hearts are pounding in our heads. Climbing the steep sections in all this clothing makes us hot, but when we stop to catch our breath, the chill is immediate. The route across the first ice is beautiful, but the next section of the ascent is on rock, and our crampons clang against the rocks as we ascend, roped together, breathing the dust we kick up. We feel like a chain gang doing time for some horrific crime. *What terrible deed have I committed that I am forced to endure this punishment?* And then we remember that we *chose* to be here while looking at pictures in a brochure, sitting by a fire, sipping hot drinks.

At twelve thousand feet, two of our party throw up. The altitude is getting to them, and they contemplate turning around but decide to continue. Some of the rest of us *wish* we would throw up so we could return early with dignity, but the "mountain gods" are not so kind to us. We press on. A rock slide sends boulders careening down the side of the mountain, narrowly missing several members of our party. It is still dark, so we cannot see the toaster-oven-sized boulders until they fly past us as fast as cars, missing us by less than 15 feet before they're launched into a free fall to land somewhere far below, in eastern Washington.

Later, we enjoy a few minutes of incredible beauty as the sun rises over the eastern horizon, turning the icy mountain into a riotous array of color. But our joy is short-lived, as the sun soon begins to bake our bodies, which were only moments earlier chilled by the wind whipping against our sunburned faces.

The altitude is taking its toll. Each step is labored. Our legs are made of wet cement. Judging time and distance becomes impossible. The summit looks close, but we carefully negotiate a crevasse field and are disappointed to look up and see that though the goal seems no nearer, another two hours have passed. The morning sun continues to rise.

Finally, we reach that point where there is no farther to go. We are at the crater of Mt. Rainier. We sit for a few minutes. The wind is relentless, chilling us to the core. All of us are nauseated, yet we need to eat for the strength to negotiate our way down the mountain, which will be dangerous slush, riddled with rockfall, in just a few hours. We cannot stay at the top, nor do we want to, but we feel too weak and tired to leave.

Yet leave we do, and the next four hours are spent in descent, regaining air in our lungs but becoming utterly dehydrated and finding new places to get sunburned. We have made it to the summit, and all has gone pretty much as planned, yet the experience was somehow different from what we had envisioned. As I descend, I envision a classified ad: "Mountaineering equipment. Used once. Like new. Sell cheap—or best offer."

Soon we're eating burgers and telling stories back in the valley, and before the meal is over, I've cancelled my classified ad and am planning my next climb. Like a mother who has recently given birth, I forget the pain quickly while the glory and beauty of the experience endures for a lifetime. For those of us hardwired for a love affair with the mountains, the journey never ends.

The Real Journey

Climbing is more than recreation for me, because every time I pursue a summit, I'm struck with the realization that these journeys in the mountains are metaphors for the real journey, the faith journey that is central to our growth, transformation, and fulfillment as humans. Every journey, as the ancient proverb tells us, begins with one step. But every journey requires more than just one step. It requires thousands, tens of thousands, of steps, and any one of those steps can so challenge, frighten, or overwhelm us that we simply stop moving and settle into a lifestyle of preserving the status quo, rather than moving into the future God has for us. The rockfall of economic uncertainty makes us afraid to follow the way of generosity, so we get comfortable with our fear and greed. The endurance required to take another step toward purity or truth telling or forgiveness is simply too much, so we make a pact with lust, duplicity, and bitterness. We park ourselves, making a home in a spot wholly inhospitable to our real calling, our real humanness.

The life for which we're created is available to us only if we come to grips with this fact early on: *We're called to a journey of continual transformation.* And like the journeys I take in the mountains, journeys which are at best weak shadows of the more profound and important journeys of the heart, each step, though challenging, will lead to much-needed transformation. Strength, hope, honesty, humility, and so much more await us if we'll commit to keep moving forward.

An Invitation to Disruption

Every encounter with God in the Bible was an invitation to leave the present behind and move into a different future. Noah would leave desert life for shipbuilding and animal husbandry. David would leave shepherding for the throne. Gideon would move from wheat farmer to warrior prophet, and Jonah, from whale watcher to whale food to preacher in a hostile land. And so it goes. Saul became Paul and moved from persecutor of the church to its most vocal and articulate defender. Cephas became Peter, moving from fearful crowd pleaser to the bold leader of a church that confounded Rome's best attempts to silence it. Later in church history, John Bunyan's *Pilgrim's Progress* became a bestseller, describing the Christian life through the metaphor of journey.

Every case included a transformation, but just as importantly, every journey was disruptive to the sojourner's comfort zone and status quo. And so it must be, for our truest and deepest selves were never made to feel at home in this world, filled as it is with lust, war, disease, hate, jealousy, oppression, and so much more that is contrary to everything we know to be true and good. Though we know that we're not made for these dark elements, something within each of us clings to the present. Why is that?

One reason is that we give lip service to the realities that we live in a broken world and that we ourselves are broken people, but we're also comfortable. Many of us in the developed world are the recipients of great ease and prosperity in a world we know to be filled with suffering. Why would we forsake such ease? A journey from the life we've known, at first glance anyway, appears to offer everything to lose and nothing to gain.

Another reason we cling to the present is that we fear the unknown chasm that any change will bring to our future. We know that God is calling us to a vocational move, or to speak truth or forgiveness into a relationship, or to live more generously, or to get involved in crossing the social and racial barriers that are all around us, but doing any of these things requires letting go of the status quo. The paradigm of the change-resistant personality is, "I may not like the present, but it's all I've got," which is a way of saying that I'll choose a mediocre life that's a known entity over the risk of an unknown future. After all, to let go of the present might lead to a future that is *worse* than my predictable yet seemingly boring present. Or so the thinking goes.

One summer, my daughter and I were climbing a Pacific Northwest volcano, and when the alarm went off at 3:00 a.m., I stuck my head outside the tent long enough to feel a stiff breeze and realize that the glacier had frozen up in the night. In such moments, getting out of one's sleeping bag and getting dressed is completely counterintuitive. That's the moment I love in mountaineering. Will I stay or will I go? It's the crux moment of the whole adventure, really, because we know we can be back in the city inhaling pancakes just as the sun is coming up. Everything depends on which way we turn in that moment. Though we're uncomfortable, we both know that the summit is why we're here and that unmatched beauty and challenge, some fear of the unknown, and great joy lie ahead. And so we get up, confident that we have all we need to keep going.

Crux moments are happening all the time in our journey with God. As I'm hiking in the silence of the morning, I think of Dietrich Bonhoeffer leaving the relative comforts of America in order to return to Germany at the height of Nazi power and expansion.

Germany was where he began an underground seminary, and his return to his homeland led to his eventual arrest and execution. I think of Amy Carmichael, leaving the beloved cool and moisture of her British homeland in order to help young women break free from temple prostitution in the heat of southern India. I think of William Wilberforce, who didn't change geography but embraced his calling to render slavery illegal, a calling that would stretch his limits of endurance and political will to the breaking point. Wherever anything significant has happened in this world, it's happened through the hands, feet, and voices of people who were willing to move into previously uncharted territory, whether geographical, spiritual, emotional, relational, or economic. No growth, no transformation, no fulfillment of the destiny for which we were created is possible without movement.

All we need to do in order to become people of movement is embrace the reality that Jesus calls us sheep and offers Himself to us as the good Shepherd, a word picture that powerfully encapsulates the reality of life as a journey. He tells us that the world is filled with sheep thieves, those whose aim is to steal the lambs or kill them or maim them in order to render them useless to the good Shepherd.[27] Until you've spent a little time with sheep, you might not appreciate what Jesus is saying. An unlikely encounter with sheep a few years ago seared in my mind forever the reality that I'm at my best—ironically, even at my boldest—when I know myself to be a vulnerable, frightened sheep, for that's when I'll cling to the Shepherd.

One glorious autumn, after I'd finished my teaching responsibilities in Austria, I spent an afternoon climbing with a friend who grew up raising sheep in the Alps. We were climbing near the bottom of a ski area where European championships and World Cup events have been held. The final slope down to the parking lot is long, steep, and green in late October. But just this week, the snows began to dust the higher reaches of the Alps, and these snows would soon overtake the lower portions as well.

This steep green slope had been food for a delightful flock of sheep all week, their bells ringing as they grazed and munched the lush

85

Alpine meadow. The school where I had been teaching is located just 50 yards or so from the gondola that ascends through the meadow, so I awakened each morning to the blend of church bells and sheep bells. One morning, I rose early and hiked up the slope. I turned a corner and came out of the trees right into the midst of grazing sheep. Though I tried to speak gently with them, and though this was their slope and not mine, their food and not mine, their country and not mine, my presence was no comfort to them. They had plenty to say to each other about my presence, and instantly fled from me as if I were a wolf.

So later that day I was climbing with my friend Martin, and at one point I was just hanging from the rope, resting my arms, gazing up the hill at the sheep dotting the still-green ski slope, and enjoying the gift of the moment. Then I noticed, far up the slope, a man and his son walking down the mountain, passing through the sheep. Suddenly the man said a few German words. He wasn't shouting or cajoling; he was just speaking. The effect, however, was immediate. All the sheep came running toward him, first the older sheep and then the lambs. When they were all within spitting distance of the shepherd, he walked down to the ski area parking lot, and they all followed. From there, he led the sheep through town, right down the main street, where some people were sitting down to eat ice cream and roasted chestnuts and where other people were buying their clothes and doing their banking. Right in the midst of all these terrifying people—sheep! And on they walked, in the middle of commercial chaos, as fearless as armed soldiers because of the presence of their shepherd.

Martin told me, as we watched this unfold, that any other person could say that same German word to call the sheep, but that those sheep would respond only to the voice of their own shepherd. Suddenly, the Scriptures converged with what I'd just seen! "The sheep hear his voice, and he calls his own sheep by name and leads them out. When he puts forth all his own, he goes ahead of them, and the sheep follow him because they know his voice. A stranger they simply will not follow, but will flee from him, because they do not know the voice of strangers" (John 10:3-5).

I always wondered why Jesus, when empowering His disciples to go, preach, heal, and serve, said to them, "Behold, I send you out as lambs in the midst of wolves" (Luke 10:3). This is not an encouraging simile, at least not until you consider the presence of the shepherd. Wolves are predators, the poster children for Darwinian living—it's kill or be killed—so they must continually assess whether a potential prey is worth the fight.

Sheep, on the other hand, are bold with respect to only one prey: grass. They eat it with reckless courage and abandon, fearless of retaliation. But before most *other* living things, sheep shake with terror. They know themselves to be prey, and live fearfully in the midst of wolves—unless they are with their shepherd. The presence of the shepherd changes everything for them, enabling them to walk with boldness into places where they would otherwise flee. No wonder they know the shepherd's voice. He is their source of security, direction, provision, protection.

Embracing my identity as a sheep is what makes the journey possible, even enjoyable. In fact, the older I get, the more often it becomes true: I *want* to hear the voice of this Shepherd and follow Him, because I'd rather be with Him in the chaos and disruption that is all of our journeys than be anywhere else on my own. But make no mistake, such a commitment to follow in the footsteps of the shepherd will be disruptive. For example…

I'm sitting cross-legged on the deck of our chalet in the mountains. It's sunny, and the first hints of summer are in the air. We've lived here for six years and don't have any plans of leaving. We moved here after some years doing the pastor thing on a small island, after which I'd decided that I was done with that role. Up here in the clean, wet air of the Cascade Mountains, I am my own boss. So I'm cleaning backpacking stoves that afternoon, preparing for our summer ministry season, when the phone rings. It's Dave from Bethany Community Church in Seattle. "Richard, I'm calling on behalf of the search committee. We'd like you to consider filling out an application for the job of senior pastor."

87

Had it been any other church, I'd have started laughing and hung up the phone. But something about *this* church and *this* invitation had the voice of the Shepherd in it.

Two years prior, I'd been in India teaching at a Bible school. A riot in the city forced my early departure, and I soon found myself in New Delhi, staying in the home of a man I'd never met while I waited for my flight out. We were sitting at breakfast one morning, and the man, who spoke English very well, said, "So you're from Washington State?"

I nodded an affirmative.

"I know it's a big place, but perhaps you've heard of Bethany Community Church?"

I told him that, yes, indeed I had, told him that I attended there while in college, told him that it's a very good church.

He continued eating, and when he found room to speak, he told me that he was a missionary supported by that church. Then he said, "Did you know that pastor is retiring?"

I told him I didn't know that, and I asked how long Pastor John had been at that church.

"Thirty-eight years," he said, and I told him, in my best Mr. T imitation, that "I pity the fool" who tried to walk in his footsteps. "PJ," as he was called, was legendary. I told him that the only sermon I remembered from my college days was one PJ preached when he had just returned from India and was reading from his diary. It was one of the most powerful sermons I'd ever heard. The man smiled at me. "PJ stayed with me while he was in India. We ate breakfast together just like you and I are doing right now."

Then something strange happened. This man, who was some sort of charismatic and thus prone to hearing special words from God, told me that he thought God was calling me to become the senior pastor of that church. I laughed. He didn't. He told me that God had just spoken to him. I told him that it would never happen, that I was having too much fun living in the mountains and not going to committee meetings. He told me to remember this day. I told him I would, fully intending to quickly forget.

All of that—the riot, the unlikely stay with the stranger, and his prophetic word on my life—comes rushing back when this man asks me to consider applying for the job of senior pastor. Thus begins a journey of application, interviews, meetings with various people, and more than a few nights of tears and prayers for my wife and me, articulating hopes and fears to God and each other. Eventually, I preach for the congregation, and they call me to become their senior pastor. The voice of the Shepherd is so unmistakable that I can't say no.

So off we went, out of our mountain comfort zone and into the big city, knowing only that such a move would forever change our family. Would we succeed or fail? Would "the world" from which our children had been so easily protected forever pollute them, stealing their hearts, or would their encounters with culture equip them to become capable of greater lives of blessing and service? We didn't know the answers to these or a hundred other questions, but we knew this much: We'd heard the voice of the Shepherd, and so we needed to go. And what an adventure it's been, far more blessed than I could have imagined, thanks to an incredible, patient, loving, and forgiving congregation these past twenty-two years. 300 people have become 3500 people. One location has become six, and I'm now privileged to meet with all my teaching pastors regularly, as we study together weekly in preparation for our teaching and preaching. I get chills just thinking about the loss that it would have been had I said no[28].

Leaving a place and work I loved wasn't easy, but it was necessary. Such is often the case with our journeys. We need to face up to the truth that the journey that is the Christian life will be disruptive, shaking our core and revealing our fears, insecurities, and unhealthy attachments. These revelations are, of course, good for us, but they're good for us like surgery is good for us, or exercise or collard greens: unpleasant in the moment but making us healthier for the long haul, better able to live the life for which we were created.

The Journey to Be a Blessing

And what is the life for which we were created? Let's be clear when thinking about journey. We weren't invited to follow Christ *so* that we could live lives of disruption, as if the whole point of the matter were to keep us forever wondering what's around the next corner. Disruption for disruption's sake has its roots in boredom, not obedience to God.

Neither were we invited to follow Christ for the purpose of adventure or the enjoyment of the many gifts and comforts that might come our way. We're not invited on this journey so that we can gain heaven when we die, as glorious as eternity will be. All of these things unfold in some way in the context of our journey, but they aren't the point of the journey. Unless we get the point seared into every fiber of our being, we're in danger of never embarking on the real journey, or worse, embarking on the wrong journey. So what *is* the reason we are called to embark on a journey?

The answer runs like a thread throughout the whole Bible. God calls us out of our comfort zones in order that we might become a blessing to others: our families, our neighbors, our faith community, and our work environments. God's vision for our lives is for us to shine as light in the midst of this darkened world so we can, as St. Francis prayed, sow love where there is hatred, joy where there is sadness, hope where there is despair, light where there is darkness.

Regardless of whom we're talking about in Bible lore, the theme of calling and journey always carries with it the same principle. God is challenging people to move out of their present situation for one reason: so that they might become a blessing to others. God tells Abraham to leave his country and embark on a journey. The end result will be that whole world will be blessed[29]! Moses? He was called away from his comfortable life in the desert so he could put an end to slavery for his people and lead them to become a free nation[30]. Joseph? A source of deliverance for his family, who would have otherwise perished in a famine[31]. Gideon? A farmer become warrior in order to free people from oppression[32]. Esther? The one who journeyed into the palace "for such a time as this" in order to save Israel from genocide[33]. "Shepherds, leave your flocks and go pay a visit to God. He happens to be sleeping in a feeding trough in a cave outside Bethlehem, but seeing Him will give you capacity to bless the world[34]." The point of every encounter with the holy, of every invitation to journey, is that our movement will create in us an increased capacity to serve and enrich those around us.

God is still writing such stories today through anyone He can find who is willing to leave the present and step into the unknown future of God's journey.

Be Careful How You Walk

I love that moment on the mountain when you get out of your tent and make the decision. Left and down to pancakes and bacon, or right and up to the summit? It feels like the most important step of the whole trip. But the reality is that every step along the way is equally significant. At any point we can stop and turn around. The seemingly big decisions we make in life aren't really any more important than the countless little ones.

A step on the journey might be admitting that I'm addicted to shopping or food or sex, and taking steps to be liberated, embracing the honesty and suffering that true wholeness, freedom, and intimacy demand. Perhaps a relationship has been damaged, and I've simply discarded it rather than working to fix it. Now God is calling me to move toward reconciliation. Maybe I've always taken indulgent vacations, and now God is calling me to use that precious time to serve others in some practical way. The next step may be as simple as meeting my neighbors. Perhaps learning some of the breathing habits you'll be reading about is where God is calling you to move. Whatever the step, it's important to remember that God isn't moving us onward and upward just for our own well-being, though better we will be. God is increasing our capacity to bless this broken world in fuller measures.

"Journeyisms"—The Things You Need to Know

The Bible is filled with stories of those who settled down somewhere along the road and made a home out of what was supposed to be only a stop along the way. This happens for many reasons, but perhaps the most common reason people end their journey too soon and settle before arriving is that they had wrong expectations. Thinking that the journey would play out in a certain way, their disillusionment with reality was too great for them. They stopped trusting and believing the Shepherd, choosing instead to cut their losses and hold on to what they had left in life. They fired Jesus and became their own CEOs[35].

In order to avoid this common fate, it's vital that we see the journey for what it really is. This is not a vacation, not a therapy session, and not a movement toward self-actualization. This journey will challenge us to the core, and the sooner we accept that, the better we'll be able to accept the reality of how things unfold as we seek to live out our lives in the midst of this fallen world. The realities are encapsulated in several "journeyisms"—truths for each of us as we embark on the adventure of following Christ.

A Step at a Time

We're given next steps, not final destinations. Can you believe what God said to Abraham? "Go forth...to the land which I will show you" (Genesis 12:1). That's all God offers. No GPS coordinates, no map, no itinerary, no agenda, no timetable. Simply this: Follow Me! Jesus' calling of the disciples was pretty much the same way. He encounters some fishermen and says, "Follow Me, and I'll make you fishers of men" (Matthew 4:19). What in God's heaven is that supposed to mean? A desk job? A raise? Little did Peter know that it meant he would become the spokesperson for a new movement called the church, and that this role would place him in the public eye, leading eventually to his imprisonment and untimely death by crucifixion. He didn't know any of that when he followed, didn't know that "fishers of men" would include all this.

In a consumerist culture such as our own, we are likely to do a cost-benefit analysis before embarking on any endeavor. The problem, though, is that Jesus doesn't play His hand, doesn't let us in on what the cost will be. In fact, the letter to the Hebrews tells us that those who've taken the journey have had all kinds of experiences: some seemingly easy, some immensely difficult[36]. This leads us to the next important journeyism.

Obedience Includes Struggle

God doesn't offer us a formula that links our obedience to our comfort and ease of journey. Our modernist construct leads us to think of faith matters in the same mechanistic way we think of the rest of life. If our car or computer or smartphone or even our body is broken, we know what to do. We run diagnostics until we find out what isn't right, and then we fix it. We take out the broken part and insert the proper one. Then everything is supposed to work.

We face a real danger when we approach our calling to journey that way. I'm struggling with self-doubt, so I run a diagnostic and find out that God is inviting me to go on a short-term mission trip. I do, but I'm sad to discover that the machinery that is my life is still broken, that I'm still plagued with self-doubt, perhaps now more than ever. Obviously, I misdiagnosed. So I run off to a conference and discover that what I was really lacking was a commitment to prayer. Presto! I begin a practice of daily prayer, but I'm sad to discover that I'm *still* plagued with that same problem I had before I took the mission trip, before I started praying more. Why aren't my steps fixing things? Shall I try another diagnostic, or do I just decide that this whole faith thing is bogus and set the journey aside, settling down in the pursuit of the American dream?

The problem lies in the original formulaic assumption. Abraham set out on a journey, and instead of making him a model citizen, the journey revealed his feet of clay. His journey revealed his propensity to lie and doubt and be afraid and sleep with the maid. With character qualities like that, he wouldn't be able to serve on the board of your local church, yet the book of Hebrews lists him as a faith hero. Why? Because though he fails often, he sticks with the journey, so that by the end of the story, his faith is gutsy, solid stuff. It's the kind of faith that's forged less by singing hymns and going to potlucks than by taking faltering steps of obedience on the journey, listening for the voice of the shepherd, and following. Such following doesn't promise ease—only transformation. And when does the transformation end? This leads to the final important journeyism.

A Rhythm of Moving and Stopping

Israel's journey in the Old Testament was out from the confines of slavery in Egypt, with the goal of entering into the freedom and abundance of a new land God was giving them. Though it was only an eleven-day journey "as the crow flies," God had plans for the "space between" Egypt and the promised land, lessons for Israel to learn that could best be learned in that space and time. God's intent was that the journey take two years instead of eleven days.

As a result, God guided Israel through the wilderness with a miraculous cloud during the day, and a fire during the night. Numbers 9:15-23 is where God goes to great lengths to explain to the nation of Israel that when the cloud moves they're to move. When the cloud stays, they're also to stay, right where they are, and wait.

> "...Whether it was two days, or a month, or a year that the cloud lingered over the tabernacle, staying above it, the sons of Israel remained camped and did not set out; but when it was lifted, they did set out." (Number 9:22)

God is telling us that being people of the journey doesn't mean being a people who are always on the move. Rather, it means that we've learned when to stay, and when to go. That, it seems, is a difficult lesson to learn, because all of us, by nature, are at risk of either moving too soon, or staying too long. Some of us get comfortable and stay, long after God has called us to move on. Others move too quickly, often because they're running from lessons that can only be learned by cultivating the much needed discipline of endurance. They resist showing up at the same job, faith community, or marriage, precisely because of an addiction to "the new", an addiction which is nearly pandemic in our culture of easy disposability.

Which kind are you? If you move too soon, God will likely plant you for a long time in places and relationships. If you are afraid of change, expect your world to be rocked on a regular basis. The important thing isn't staying or going; it's learning to hear the voice of the shepherd whenever He says its time to break camp and go, and then to go wherever He leads, and not a single step further.

The Journey Is the Destination

The ultimate destination is nothing less than a perfect display of the character of Jesus, revealed through us in totality because we're totally available, accurately hearing His voice, and perfectly following it. Yes, that should work out for me—in two or three hundred years. I'll never get there in this life, so for now the journey *is* the destination. Perhaps I'll enjoy life more if I let go of the shame and condemnation that I heap on myself, that I heap on others, and that others sometimes toss my way for not being perfect. The truth is, God may be leading me toward the summit, but getting there is less important than getting up every morning and being willing to break camp and move on to new heights. That mindset of never settling down is what is most significant, because it enables me to live with humility, knowing that I don't yet have the whole Christlike thing wrapped up. The day I stop learning, stop accepting new challenges, stop allowing the safe places in my world to be deconstructed—that is the day I stop journeying and so stop growing in my capacity to bless others.

This commitment to journey will enable me to process the oxygen I need to live. Are you ready to climb this mountain? It begins by committing to citizenship in God's kingdom.

Chapter 7

Sabbath Rest

Are you tired? Worn out? Burned out on religion?
Come to me. Get away with me and you'll
recover your life. I'll show you how to take a real
rest. Walk with me and work with me—watch
how I do it. Learn the unforced rhythms of grace.
I won't lay anything heavy or ill-fitting on you.
Keep company with me and you'll learn to live
freely and lightly.

Matthew 11:28-30, The Message

Oh, and one last question. When did you
become the Messiah?

From a college minister's performance review

We listen to lots of words over the course of a lifetime. Many of them
pass through our minds and exit as just so much waste, in much the
same way excess food passes through our bodies. But some words
penetrate and transform if we let them, if we listen. They find their
way past our minds, and settle in the recesses of our hearts, there
becoming the soil from which fuller life, blessing, and fruitfulness
germinate. I call them "sticky words," because of their tendency to
remain deeply embedded in our souls. Whole lives have been
altered, for better or worse, by sticky words.

Some sticky words came my way while I was attending a conference
overseas years ago. The event had come three years after my wife
and I had started our work in the mountains. The ministry of
teaching and hospitality we began had no major donors, no assured
funding, no visible means of support. In fact, more than a few people
told us we were crazy to quit our stable work and venture out as we

did. And indeed, it was either reckless insanity or an act of faith for us to join with another family and buy the run-down mountain property. The income to keep the whole thing going came from a variety of places: teaching honorariums, small donations, renting the cabins to vacation travelers, a bookkeeping job for my wife, hundreds of basketball games officiated by me, and a small amount of program income from retreats.

The combination of all these efforts paid off. The plan was working. That was the good news. The bad news was that we were working too much: 14-hour days on many days, often seven days a week. I'd be off speaking somewhere, and then someone would call and ask if we could host a retreat for their group. They'd be coming in Friday night (and so would I, on a plane, at the end of five days of teaching and counseling students) and staying through Sunday supper. Without hesitation I'd say, "Sure! See you Friday," fearful that if we said no, we'd lose much-needed income and would somehow perish.

People would come to the mountains for a weekend and be sitting at our table for breakfast. They'd look out at the sun lighting up the fir-covered butte across the street, while deer meandered through the yard, and they'd say, "It must be nice to live up here, where you can sit and enjoy creation all day!" My wife would catch my eye, and we'd smile because we were both thinking, *Yes! After homeschooling, changing sheets in the cabins, buying food for guests that are coming, writing newsletters, studying, teaching, refereeing basketball games in town, running a home church in our living room, paying bills, and fixing clogged septic systems, we love sitting around watching the deer!* But we never said that, because in spite of the busyness, we genuinely loved where we lived and felt called to what we were doing.

Still, it wasn't quite healthy. During those years, the word *no* disappeared from our vocabulary almost entirely, with one glaring exception. We nearly always said no to rest. I felt invincible; my calling was important enough that God was granting me an infinite supply of energy. I never really stopped long enough to realize how full my life had become, how I'd given away all the margins in my life and had no time for restoration.

Three years into this habit of saying yes to everything except rest, I attended a conference in England. I was to speak for one session, but I was there mostly to listen and enjoy catching up with old friends and meeting new ones. The first night our speaker, whose name I can't remember, began: "Some of you are thrilled with the work you're doing. Some of you are frustrated. Some of you are confident regarding the future. Some of you are perhaps frightened. Some of you are arriving here well-rested. *And some of you are tired—very, very tired.*"

Suddenly I felt as if the room were empty, and this man seemed to be speaking a word from the mouth of God directly to me. I could feel hot tears welling up in the corners of my eyes, and I fought to hold them back, all the while wondering why that little phrase, "some of you are tired," was having such a profound effect on me. Surely the first reason was that it was true, and for the first time in many months I could acknowledge reality: I was exhausted.

But as his words sank in, something else happened inside me, a seismic moment that shook my thinking. Prior to hearing those words, I had somehow assumed that a full calendar was a sign of importance, that busyness was a sign of spiritual maturity. Self-esteem isn't handed out in exchange for sitting around and watching deer in the front yard. It comes at the price of producing, or so I thought. But as this man spoke, I suddenly knew that my weariness was not a sign of importance or spiritual strength. It was a result of disobedience to God and revealed a deep personal insecurity. This, more than my actual weariness, was the source of my tears. I would spend a great deal of time over the next months pondering why that word was so powerful, why I was so tired, and what steps I needed to take to live differently. The pondering would include conversations with friends and study of the Scriptures. Those ponderings led me to rediscover a practice that has long been forgotten in our culture at large and in most of our communities of faith. We're tired because we've lost the Sabbath.

Two Schools of Sabbath

This matter of the Sabbath is subject to two large schools of interpretation. Both seem to contain vital truth, and neither seems complete without the other. The first school interprets Sabbath literally, as a day for rest. This, of course, is rooted in the Ten Commandments.

> Remember the sabbath day, to keep it holy. Six days you shall labor and do all your work, but the seventh day is a sabbath of the Lord your God; in it you shall not do any work, you or your son or your daughter, your male or your female servant or your cattle or your sojourner who stays with you. For in six days the Lord made the heavens and the earth, the sea and all that is in them, and rested on the seventh day; therefore the Lord blessed the sabbath day and made it holy (Exodus 20:8-11).

This is quite simple, really. Take one day a week to stop, rest, and inhale. It makes sense for a whole host of reasons, some of which we'll consider in a moment. But this simple command, intended by God to be a source of healing, joy, and liberation, has often been a source of great grief for many believers. It becomes a huge burden when we begin to define *rest.* Definition becomes law, law leads to nuanced interpretation of law, and nuanced interpretation of law leads to a sense of fear and fighting over tiny words. *Perhaps I will unintentionally violate the Sabbath,* we think, wondering whether we can light a fire, play soccer, watch a movie, or go for a long hike. Why would anyone have such fear?

Jewish law prohibits 39 specific acts as violations of Sabbath-keeping, that's why. And the interpretation of those prohibitions can get tricky. Here's an example of the extreme ways religious experts interpreted the law. God's people were not to bear a burden on the Sabbath. Simple enough. But the scholars went to work immediately, describing two ways of bearing a burden: either by picking something up or by putting it down. In addition, someone might move the burden from either a public place to a private place or vice versa, creating eight possible ways to violate the single commandment about bearing a burden.

Of course, the weight of the burden comes into play (a burden equals the weight of a dried fig), along with highly detailed definitions of what constitutes a public or private place. And what constitutes carrying? If you were to throw something with your right hand and catch it with your left, it might not be considered sin, but it was obviously sin if the same hand that threw something also caught it (presuming the object thrown weighed more than a dried fig). And let's not forget about the question of what happens when something you're wearing shifts on your body. If it shifts from front to back, you have not sinned, but if from back to front, you've violated the Sabbath. And of course, you'd better not wear your false teeth on the Sabbath, because if they fall out and you put them back in, you're in violation of God's liberating Sabbath gift of rest. Aren't lawyers grand?

As the Christian church adopted Jewish Sabbath-keeping and applied it to the first day of the week rather than the seventh, things lightened up a bit, but there was still a great deal of debate regarding what constitutes work. As a result, for a lot of people, keeping the Sabbath was nothing more than a depressing prohibition: "It was the one day a week we couldn't go outside and play. Cards were forbidden. TV was forbidden. We just sat around. I hated Sundays."

One could easily see how this commitment to Sabbath rest would lead children to see God as the One Who Negates rather than the source of all that is joyful, spacious, and life-giving. This oppressive view of the God of the Bible is still quite popular, in part because of the ridiculous burdens Judaism and Christianity gave people in their interpretations of Sabbath. These perversions tempt people to walk away from the whole thing, or at the very least to walk away from any attempt at keeping a Sabbath.

But rather than discarding the Sabbath, we can move past these caricatured extremes. In fact, they can motivate us to discover what God is really after in giving this gift to us. And make no mistake:

Many rabbinical teachers saw Sabbath as a gift to be celebrated, rather than a precept to be feared. Feasting, making love with one's spouse, enjoying the gifts of friendship and creation, giving thanks to God, and celebration are all part of healthy Sabbath-keeping traditions, and they come much closer to God's original intent. One author who has written extensively about rest writes:

> Sabbath time is time off the wheel, time when we take our hand from the plow and let God and the earth care for things, while we drink, if only for a few moments, from the fountain of rest and delight. Sabbath is more than the absence of work; it is not just a day off, when we catch up on television or errands. It is the presence of something that arises when we consecrate a period of time to listen to what is most deeply beautiful, nourishing, or true[37].

This is closer to God's heart for the Sabbath, and dissolves the legalist's wrangling over whether mowing the lawn on Sunday is acceptable. Instead, the Sabbath becomes an invitation to step out of the daily responsibilities of work. It shows us that God will continue to provide for us, giving us seven days of provision in exchange for six days of work. And it allows us to rest, worship, celebrate, and restore.

In contrast to this literal "day of rest" interpretation is the "Sabbath as a lifestyle" interpretation. This too is rooted in the Scriptures, but in the New Testament rather than the Old. Its roots are in the book of Hebrews, especially in the third and fourth chapters. In these chapters, we learn that Israel's trek toward the promised land under the leadership of Moses is a picture of the journey all of us are invited to make toward a life of rest. Perhaps you know the story. The people who were delivered out of Egypt through the miraculous parting of the Red Sea found themselves, two years later, set to enter the land God had promised to give them. They sent spies into the new land to assess it, and most of them came back determined that any attempt to conquer the new land would be suicidal. Their bad reports doomed the venture, and Israel spent the next 40 years wandering in the wilderness.

We read about God's judgment on Israel: "They shall not enter My rest" (Hebrews 3:11). It's very telling that the judgment isn't that they'll fail to enter *land* (though they will also fail to do that), but that they will not enter God's *rest*. Can you see how the journey to the land becomes a picture of our journey toward a life of rest? You might think this is carrying things a bit too far, taking a verse that hints at a metaphor and building a whole doctrine of rest out of it. I'd agree if only one verse spoke that way. But here it is again: "And to whom did He swear that they would not enter His rest, but to those who were disobedient? So we see that they were not able to enter because of unbelief" (3:18). "Therefore, let us fear if, while a promise remains of entering His rest, any one of you may seem to have come short of it...for we who have believed enter that rest" (4:1,3). The author sums up this picture once more for us very nicely: "So there remains a Sabbath rest for the people of God. For the one who has entered His rest has himself also rested from his works, as God did from His. Therefore let us be diligent to enter that rest" (4:9-11).

Rest as a Lifestyle

This view of Sabbath replaces the duty of a *day* of rest with an invitation to a *lifestyle* of rest, whereby we live in a posture of continual dependency on Christ. The goal is for each of us to rest from *our own works*, as Hebrews 4:10 says. Then we can say with Paul, "I have been crucified with Christ; and it is no longer I who live, but Christ lives in me" (Galatians 2:20). When I've let go of my plans, ambitions, goals for upward mobility, preconceived definitions of success, fears of rejection, lust for approval, and the false sense that I am the only one who will provide for me, I'm beginning to experience being crucified with Christ.

Being crucified, even metaphorically, has a way of clearing your calendar. But being crucified without being resurrected leads only to emptiness, depression, and despair. To simply say "I quit" leads to nothing but futility and boredom, which become the soil for new pursuits, relationships, hobbies, and desires. Soon after quitting, we're up and running again with new ideas and plans. But these too will eventually wear us out, causing us to quit yet again. This is the journey of the perpetually dissatisfied and weary, and it isn't remotely similar to the invitation of rest offered to the Hebrews.

The critical element that makes this new form of rest successful is this paradox: I've been crucified, yet Christ lives in me. I am dead, but I am alive. Dead to my own agenda, alive to God's. I need not only to let go of my autonomous plans and identity, but also to embrace Christ's life as a gift that will liberate, energize, and empower me. Those who are living with the conscious sense that they are in the stream of God's activity are at rest. Christ expresses life through them in a grander way than any of their attempts to live could ever realize. This is true rest. It has nothing to do with taking a day off and everything to do with being energized by this great exchange: God's will instead of my own, Christ's strength instead of my weakness, the Holy Spirit's guidance instead of my feeble attempts to orchestrate life[38].

I know that my own movement toward rest has required learning these vital lessons. Because I didn't believe that God would provide adequately for me, I said yes to every work opportunity for three straight years. Yes to every basketball game, yes to every teaching opportunity, yes to every group coming in to use our facilities. Because I believed that the salvation of the world depended on me, I said yes to every speaking engagement, too. And three years later, when the speaker at the conference told me I was tired, I began to see why, began to see I'd been running my life according to my ambitions, my fears, my insecurities, my greed, and my love of activity. Such a workload can look impressive to those on the outside, but on the inside the physical and emotional weariness and the tension created in relationships were combining to create a person who, beneath the surface of spiritual strength, was becoming strained to the breaking point. Thankfully, I was starting to feel the effects of living out of my own strength when that word came to me and exposed the whole house of cards. I didn't just need a day off; I needed to enter Christ's rest, needed to find rest as a lifestyle.

I spent several weeks that next winter considering what the Bible had to say about rest and weariness. This study exposed the many ways I didn't trust God to take care of me, and I slowly began to let go of those phobias that had been steering the ship, resting instead in God's active care and sufficiency. I began believing that if I needed direction, God would provide it; if I needed provision, He'd provide that, too. He'd provide everything I needed to carry out that which He called me to do. And so I could rest—not a passive withdrawal, but an active trust that as we live in relationship with Jesus, He really does take care of us, just as a shepherd takes care of sheep. This wasn't a promise of wealth or even health. It was an encouragement to stop fretting and sweating and manipulating and living in the continual fear that if I didn't work constantly I would perish. Slowly, I began to stop worrying and start trusting, and the fruits were almost immediately evident[39].

The Path: Rest as a Practice

Advocates of rest as a lifestyle sometimes say we don't need to worry anymore about a specific day of rest, because every day is to be lived resting in the sufficiency of Christ. To focus on a single day, they argue, would be a step back into legalism and away from the full life that Christ came to offer us. "Every day is a day of rest," they say, as they jet off to another activity.

Who could argue with the concept of living our lives out of a heart full of rest? On the other hand, of the Ten Commandments Moses received from God, this seems to be the only one we spiritualize in a way that bypasses any concern for a literal application. Can you imagine trying to spiritualize the command to honor your parents? "Of course, this is speaking of our *spiritual* parents, which means our rabbis (or pastors or universities), which means that we don't need to worry about our literal parents. Instead, we should divert money that would have helped them and give it to the synagogue (or church or college)." Jesus didn't like this kind of twisting, arguing instead that honoring parents meant honoring parents[40]. He is concerned that we not be too quick to spiritualize our application of Scripture at the expense of the plain literal reading. Such twisting leads to loads of pain and sorrow.

I'm concerned with my tendency to theorize and internalize truths, because this can have the effect of neutralizing the life-changing power of Jesus' teachings in real time, in the real world. If things are really to change, they will need to change not only the way I think or the way I pray, but also the way I live. Henri Nouwen writes about this when he says, "We often say, 'all of life should be lived in gratitude,' but this is possible only if at certain times we give thanks in a very concrete and visible way…We often say, 'We should love one another always,' but this is possible only if we regularly perform concrete and unambiguous acts of love[41]." Likewise we can be tempted to say, "All of life should be a life of rest," but this becomes meaningless unless we concretely express our trust, dependency, and ceasing through literal rest.

So in spite of the invitation to enter rest as a lifestyle, we still need to develop a practice of rest that entails ceasing from our normal obligations and devoting time to literal rest. Here's why.

The Testimony of Creation

Everything that lives goes through seasons: sunrise and sunset, resting and waking, working and playing, winter and summer, wet and dry, light and dark, high tide and low, full moon and new moon, birth and death. These seasons come to us with remarkable regularity. Carolus Linnaeus was an eighteenth-century Swedish man who studied plants and knew them well enough to plant a garden that could tell time. He filled it with flowers that opened and closed their blossoms in such precise intervals that he could look at his garden instead of his watch. *Photoperiodism* is a word describing an organism's ability to respond to the rhythms of light and dark. This is why trees know when to shed their leaves and when to invoke new growth. It has to do not only with temperature, but also with length of days.

Look around. What part of the created order doesn't have a pattern provided for it to rest, a time for restoration, renewal, consolidation, gestation? Are we above that created order, outside it somehow?

God's provision for mankind in this created order was simple. We function best when we're awake during the day and sleep through the night. Our internal clock and hormonal balances are geared to enter this rhythm of work and rest. And yet we stomp on this natural order, lighting up the night and pushing ourselves to produce more, do more, consume more, know more, and experience more. This leads to sleep deprivation, which carries with it a host of other pathologies that rob us of our capacity to both enjoy life and serve our world.

We do the same thing when we ignore the time God has provided in our week for restoration of soul and body, a time provided in what He called Sabbath. It's the rhythm He made for us, and physiological evidence shows that we ignore it at our peril.

The Reality of Adaptation

Last weekend, as spring was just beginning, I decided it was time to exercise. So I jumped on my bicycle and rode 20 miles. The next day, I rode 30 more, as fast as I could. The day after that I hiked up a steep hill carrying a heavy load. *After all,* I reasoned, *I need to get in shape for next month's climb.* The day after the hill climb I could barely move. My muscles were sore, but more importantly, I'd lost all motivation to do anything. Getting out of bed seemed a massive chore, requiring all my will. I slogged through the day, oozing ill-will on everyone in my path, went home and sat in front of the TV for a couple of hours, and then fell into a fitful sleep. Isn't exercise grand?

The problem, of course, wasn't the exercise. It was that I forgot about adaptation. That's a principle in exercise physiology that says that the value in exercise comes not only from the stress but from the rest. Without the rest, the body has no time to repair the tiny injuries created each time we exercise, and those little repairs are what strengthen our body. Take rest out of the equation, and our body has no way of strengthening.

The same thing is true of our emotions and spirits. That's why, after intense times of ministry, Jesus took His disciples away for a little while to rest. But if we're convinced that there's far too much to do and that rest is luxury we just can't afford, we'll press through without any time for adaptation. When that's our posture, we never really internalize the lessons we learn through our activities.

One pastor used his Sabbath day to hike with his wife. The two of them packed lunches in the morning and hiked together in silence throughout the morning hours. When they stopped for lunch, they shared with each other their thoughts, prayers, and concerns. Another couple walks to the market and buys fresh food to prepare a meal together. I try to go skiing or hiking on my Sabbath morning and spend the afternoon reading. However it works, the important thing is to provide space for transformation, healing, rest, hearing from God, and learning from the events of previous days. Without this space for adaptation, our spirits and emotions, just like our bodies, don't have adequate time for strengthening.

Trust

The final principle is perhaps the most important. To understand it, we'll go back in time and consider Israel wandering through the wilderness again. Of course, one of the great challenges they faced was the matter of provision. Where were two million people to find sustenance in the arid desert? When you read about God's answer, you think, *Nobody else would even think to do it that way. That's so like God!* God provided in a way that nobody could have anticipated. Bread just showing up on the ground each morning? Who does that? How does that happen? Further, this amazing provision unfolded in a way that would help Israel learn important lessons about God's character and their capacity to trust.

The story is in Exodus 16. One of the major things to see is that God provided exactly what everyone needed, because people gathered based on the size of their families. "He who had gathered much had no excess, and he who had gathered little had no lack" (Exodus 16:18). If only we'd begin with the supposition that there's enough for everyone, our world would be a dramatically different place[42].

The Sabbath principle enters the story because God tells people to gather twice as much on the sixth day, cook what they don't use at the end of the day, and store it to be eaten on the seventh day. No manna would appear on the seventh day: "Tomorrow is a sabbath observance, a holy sabbath to the Lord" (Exodus 16:23).

The plot thickens when some of the people wake up on the morning of the seventh day and, in direct opposition to what they've been taught, go outside to gather manna. They fail to find any, and even worse, God gets angry at them. Here's what God says: "How long do you refuse to keep My commandments and My instructions? See, *the Lord has given you the Sabbath;* therefore He gives you bread for two days on the sixth day. Remain every man in his place; let no man go out of his place on the seventh day" (Exodus 16:28-29).

God was simply teaching Israel that He—not their hard work or cleverness or zeal—was the source of provision for their lives. Thus they could confidently align their lives with His principles, knowing that as they did so, God would provide enough for them. The resting is vital, in part because it's our way of saying that God, not our brilliance, is the source of provision. We can cherish the way He has structured our lives not only for work but also for rest, not only for service but also for celebration, not only for inhaling but also for exhaling. We can enjoy all of it! In fact, the rest principle really is a trust principle. *Do you believe that I'm the One providing for you? You do? Then why do you continue to work seven days a week? Why are you so worried about the future? Why do you continue to hoard the manna I give you, rather than giving it away? Why do you remain stuck on that miserable, driven, self-destructive path? It's because you don't trust Me enough to rest.*

After hearing the word about weariness at that conference in England, after studying the Scriptures and talking with friends about the meaning of Sabbath rest, I realized that my problem was trust. And in response to that conviction, I began to say no. I'd pray about opportunities, rather than just embracing them. Soon I was no longer officiating basketball games at all. This was a big financial step of faith. We also began providing space between my travels and our hospitality ministry. Just saying the word *no* opened up space in my life.

With this newfound space I went for a hike one Monday morning. We'd hosted some guests over the weekend, and they had left, so I was taking a Sabbath hike. (Yes, Monday works as well as Sunday or Saturday. It's the spirit of the thing we're after, not a wooden legalism. This is the case with all the breathing principles.) I hiked to the top of a local peak and then scrambled the rock to the summit.

At the top, I stopped completely and just sat, looking around at the incredible majesty of creation, watching the sun paint the peaks and fill the valley. A verse from the Bible came to my mind in the form of a little chorus I'd sung years ago: "Ascribe greatness to our God— the Rock. His work is perfect and all His ways are just." Indeed, God was the Rock, the One who'd be here long after I'm gone, the One who is solid, stable, trustworthy.

Suddenly I saw the ministry I was leading and the family I was raising in a whole new light. This isn't *my* ministry; it's God's. It's not *my* family; it's God's. I'm just the one chosen to care for these things for a season, and so I'd do well to order my own life according to principles of the One who is really in charge. Then I can relax and begin to enjoy this calling, this place, these mountains. Coming to the realization that I'm not the Messiah was pretty freeing, a liberating turning point that helped me become like a little child again, living out of a posture of joyful dependence. The good news is that you aren't the Messiah either. Relax. Rest. And let the healing begin.

Chapter 8

The Intimacy Invitation: Prayer

To pray is to descend with the mind into the heart, and there to stand before the face of the Lord, ever-present, all-seeing, within you.[43]

Timothy Ware

When my wife and I ran our wilderness retreat center, our affiliation with a camping consortium brought us into contact with a phrase we'd never heard before: *camper days*. Say you have ten beds. That would mean you have a potential of 70 camper days per week. What you are supposed to do, of course, is determine how much revenue a camper day (one camper filling one bed for one night) produces and how much the camp costs to run. Then you can discover how many camper days you need in order to stay in business. Camping is, after all, just like any other enterprise in this world. You need a business model, and you need to stay profitable, or you can't fulfill your mission.

That's all legitimate, to a point. But when doing ministry, or when doing *life* for that matter, such efficiency models can actually become inefficient. In the economy of the Creator, we learn new ways to allocate resources. A model based purely on resource allocation and return would have no room whatsoever for long walks in the park, sunsets, tickle fights with the children, or significantly, prayer.

If we begin with the assumption that we know our goals and have the resources to fulfill them, prayer can seem like a colossal waste of time. Once we've received our marching orders, why not simply get on with it? We are, after all, called to steward the resources of our lives wisely, and one of the most precious commodities of all is our time. Wouldn't it make sense, regardless of how we're spilling the colors of the kingdom into this gray world, to spend more time spilling and less time sitting? I can hear the efficiency experts now. Twenty hours of work on food distribution equals 200 mouths fed for a week. (This is purely hypothetical, but the same line of thought as camper days.) Thus, only 18 hours of work equals 180 mouths fed.

"What happened to the other two hours?" the efficiency expert asks. Twenty people are still hungry because you slacked for two hours. What were you doing?"

"Praying."

"Excuse me? Did you say 'paying'? That's accounting's job."

"No, I said, 'praying.'"

Efficiency guy begins to laugh before he gets mightily angry. And then begins the discourse about efficiency. I'm sad to say, it could have been written by many North American pastors (but not a single Korean pastor, because the latter understands the role of prayer in God's breathing plan far better than the former).

The efficiency model makes sense, but only if its assumptions are true. And Jesus dismantles several of the key assumptions through His teaching and ministry. "Which ones?" you ask. I'm glad you did.

Assumption: We Know What to Do

Earlier, we noticed Jesus' commitment to prayer. Throughout the Gospels, the Father's plans for Jesus often contradicted conventional wisdom. Whether Jesus was leaving a town where all the needs hadn't yet been met (as He often did), crossing social barriers to speak with the marginalized, or refusing to fight back when His life was threatened, His agenda wasn't obvious. He needed to hear from the Father.

And so do I. The church I lead was in the midst of a facilities expansion program, born out of growth in our community and a conviction that God wanted us to be a base camp of sorts, from which a new generation of leaders would be raised up and sent out to spill the colors of hope across the globe in places where they are so desperately needed. But such dramatic and costly changes weren't easy to carry out, especially in an era and place that was suspicious of growing churches, so we needed to be quite convinced that this was God's will. Such conviction isn't born out of common sense. In fact, common sense is worthless. The only sense that mattered when facing decisions of such magnitude was whether or not this was something God wanted. In our particular case, we faced so many obstacles to even obtaining a building permit that in our continued prayers during the planning process we gave thanks that God had so many chances to stop the plan: Parking issues. Buying an alley from the City of Seattle. Funding issues. All were overcome.

Assumption: We've Got What It Takes

The chapter on solitude demonstrates that Jesus Himself didn't sense that He had what it would take to fulfill the destiny the Father gave Him. Everything He did was born out of a conscious sense of dependence on God the Father. Jesus needed not only direction, but also the very power to get the job done.

Praying is, in a strange way, actually easier when we are convinced that we *don't* have what it takes to get the job done. When we are consciously aware of some big lack, be it wisdom, energy, money, connections, authority, or whatever else it is that we might be aware that we need, we seem to fall to our knees (at least metaphorically) and pray.

This has been demonstrated in my life countless times. In one instance, we were out of money, and a road through our retreat property was so damaged by storms that it was impassable, not a very encouraging condition when that road is the means for vacationers with money to come rent your cabins. Out of options, we prayed for gravel. Within 48 hours, the owner of a gravel pit offered us about a dozen truckloads of gravel for free, with the caveat that we find our own dump truck. We prayed for a dump truck, and not too long after we said amen, the phone rang. Leonard was a friend with whom I'd not spoken for some months, and coincidentally, he owned a dump truck. "I'd like to come visit your place," he said.

"Great" said I. "Do you still own that dump truck?"

You can probably guess the rest of the story. If you guessed a new road and a big party celebrating the God who provides, you're right. We grossly overstate our capacities whenever we think we don't need God's help. Jesus said, "Apart from Me you can do nothing."[44]

"Nothing?" we say incredulously, as we look at our desks or houses or bookshelves. On them, or in them, is everything we need. Our connection to the Internet provides any bit of information on demand: marketing plans, financing plans, or stock market projections for our IRAs and kids' college funds. Web sites offer solutions for whatever is troubling us at this point in life, whether we need to find a mate or get rid of one, get healed of cancer, deal with aging parents or rebellious infants, or refinance the house because interest rates appear to have bottomed out. Many of us are too well educated for our own good. We've trained ourselves (and our culture has encouraged us) to depend on nobody but ourselves for our own well-being and getting on in the world. Don't depend on your neighbors; they come and go. These days, spouses do too. All you need is you.

That spirit has gotten us to where we are today. And where are we? We're in a world where the gap between the rich and poor continues to grow each year. The wealth of the world is increasingly concentrated in the hands of the few, while the many are living on less than two dollars a day. Most of the world's poor are having a hard time finding water to drink that won't kill them. We're in a world where, even among the successful elite, the marks of dysfunction are creating deep wounds. I don't need to mention them. Go to the self-help or sociology section of any bookstore, and you'll discover that we seem to be doing a poor job at intimacy, marriage, honesty, addiction control, raising polite children, educating a new generation, staying healthy, finding ways to care for the sick, keeping our populace housed, having good relationships with food, sex, and our own bodies, sleeping soundly at night, getting along with our parents, and reining in consumer spending, to name but a very few of our ailments. Really? We don't need prayer? It doesn't seem like we're doing fine on our own.

Assumption: Prayer Is for Getting Direction and Resources

This is a tricky one, because the temptation at this point is to say, "You know what, author? You're right. You've pointed out some things I hadn't thought of, and so from now on I'm going to spend time asking God for direction, and I'll be sure to throw in a word reminding Him how helpless I am without His intervention. That should do it, right?"

Well, yes, if God were some sort of filling station that also provided maps. But God isn't that utilitarian. He's not (and no disrespect is intended in this) a clerk, providing customer service for those humble enough to know that He alone, in all the universe, has what they need in order to live more successful lives. All they need do is come into His store and ask, and they will receive. That's what the Bible says, right[45]?

Yes, it's what the Bible says, but it's not *all* the Bible says, and so we can't blindly apply it as a promise. The Bible also says that God sometimes says no[46]. God isn't a store clerk. God isn't a store. God is a being who created us and longs to be in relationship with us. Unless you have a crush on the girl who works at that coffee shop on the corner, the primary reason you go in there and speak with her is because of what you want from her: coffee. If you know her only because you want coffee from her (or anything else from her, for that matter), it's not a real, vibrant, healthy relationship; it's just a transaction.

God won't be reduced to this kind of consumer-customer relationship with us. He wants intimacy. So even if God has revealed what I am supposed to do, even if I know that I don't have the resources to pull it off and have asked God for provision, I still have a reason to pray. Prayer is the intercourse between humanity and our Creator. The word *intercourse* isn't only a sexual word; it means contact and communication. I chose it carefully in this instance, to challenge our notions that prayer without intimacy is any healthier than sex without intimacy. Hosea invites people to know the Lord: "So let us know, let us press on to know the Lord. His going forth is as certain as the dawn; and He will come like the rain, like the spring rain watering the earth" (Hosea 6:3). That word for "know" is an invitation to intercourse, to intimacy. In the New Testament, Paul will go so far as to call us the "bride of Christ" and talk about the mystery of union[47].

There you have it. Once we challenge our assumptions, prayer doesn't seem such a foolish waste of time after all.

Intimacy Is Key

Of all the false assumptions that are lived out in a prayerless life, the worst one is our assumption that intimacy with God isn't really a big part of the story God is writing in our lives. In reality, intimacy is God's trump card, because we're not created physically or spiritually as automatons, mere cogs in a wheel that exists only in order to fulfill some grander purpose. This isn't *The Matrix*. It's not *1984*. And it certainly isn't much of *Brave New World* at this point. I may be made to spill the colors of hope into the world by teaching English to immigrants, developing water projects in Africa, fighting to reduce debt in developing nations, end human trafficking, cooking great meals, running a profitable business, making great art, or whatever else it is that I'm uniquely created to do. Still, the point is that if I find that calling for which I'm created and actually live it out, I might still be grossly dissatisfied. Why? Because whatever else I'm made for, I'm also made for intimacy. I may or may not be made for marital intimacy and sexual intimacy, but I'm made for intimacy with God.

When Adam and Eve were walking around with God in the garden of Eden, the intimacy was perfect; nothing was hidden. As soon as sin entered the picture, perfect intimacy ended, and we see running, hiding, covering, blaming, ignoring. The very first signs of sin on this earth after the initial act of disobedience had to do with a loss of intimacy, as we'll consider in greater depth in the final chapter.

We've been running and hiding ever since. Almost all of us have intimacy issues with God and with one another. We're made for intimacy, so we move toward relationship. But when relationship gets too threatening, we move away. We have lots of ways to move away: blame, busyness, duplicity, flattery, and dishonesty (with ourselves, the other, or both) to name a few. Closer, further away; closer, further away.

This brings back memories of standing around a big campfire. In the back rows, I'd get really cold, so I'd move to the front. But pretty soon, the front would be too warm, so I'd move to the back and then to the front again. (Once I moved to the back and Linda held my hand. No girl ever had, and I wasn't cold anymore. Terrified, but not cold. But I digress.) Too hot, too cold, too hot, too cold. That's the way it is with intimacy. We want transparency, vulnerability, searing honesty, perfect connection. Well, not really. We *think* we do, but when we approach those things, life gets perhaps a little too intense, and so we back off. To greater or lesser degrees, all of us do this dance with intimacy, moving closer and then backing off, as it suits us.

But even though our notions of intimacy have been distorted, the truth is that we're still made to love and be loved. This, after all, is the greatest commandment of all: Love God![48] Love God with every fiber of your being, which means that you'll be moving continually toward the vulnerability and transparency that are so hard for many of us. Hard though it may be, it's written into our DNA—born to love! And then again, the second commandment is just as challenging: Love people!

[49]As someone who's lived a while now, I can tell you that my most meaningful memories are of moments of intimacy. Outside on a windy night, four friends circled around a single candle stuck in a cupcake. We wanted to keep the flame lit until Marsha could blow it out to celebrate her twenty-first birthday. We knew we'd all be graduating soon and dispersing. We knew that this moment was the precious summation of some rich college friendships, some truly intimate relationships. We sang. She blew out her candle. We were

silent, hugging each other closely as tears welled in our eyes, profoundly grateful for the gift of love.

Does that happen with God, too? Oh yes! One day I walked out of a seminar at winter ski camp feeling that, in the room of 200 people, God had been talking only to me. I prayed, responding to what God was showing me. Another afternoon I was with friends, inhabiting an old fire lookout tower in the Cascades as the sun set. As the colors begin the bleed across the sky, all conversation stopped. After a long silence, we offered prayers of thanks to the One who gave us so much, so creatively, with such beauty. I'll never forget it. Another day I was at my dad's funeral, and I had a sense—that's the only way I can describe it—that God was with me, and would be with me. I wasn't too keen on God just then, and some dark days were yet ahead for me, a 17-year-old without a clue, but still, I won't forget that sense of God's presence. There are more, but they're too intimate to share.

Nurturing Intimacy

One thing is certain: God isn't inviting us to a perpetual honeymoon, as one might be led to believe from the candles, sunsets, and warm hugs of the previous paragraphs. These moments are glorious, but they aren't created on demand. They're born out of a larger context that includes confession, challenge, anger, hurt, celebration, lament, doubt, fear, boldness, laughter, tears. Are these experiences part of knowing God? Absolutely. Just read Psalms or the stories of Abraham, Jacob, Moses, Jeremiah, or anyone else who knew God.

Intimacy is nurtured by walking together on the long road of life. You don't waltz into a classroom on the last day of college and say, "Hey there, everyone, I'm looking for four people to go blow out a candle with. We'll sing a bit, hug, and shed some tears. Any takers?" The cupcake was meaningful because over the years, Marsha and Kate and Paul and I had sat around for hours and talked about life. They knew me during my own relationship meltdowns (yes—plural) and during my greatest joys. The same was true of me for them. Paul and I ran together. Kate and I went to Blochs for "after midnight" sandwiches. I helped her with music theory. She helped me with classical piano. That's the way intimacy works. Little by little, time after time. Today laughter, tomorrow tears, the day after that boredom, along with a dose of frustration maybe, maybe followed by trust earned. Do you know it? I pray you do, for it's the richest fabric of life.

But such intimacy is intended for both horizontal and vertical relationships. When was the last time you had a good cry with God, or a good laugh, or a good argument? Maybe it's been too long. You don't go looking for a good cry, any more than you go looking for a "cupcake moment." You just keep showing up honestly, talking, listening, and sharing life together. Intimacy is made of such stuff. How does that happen with God? I'm glad you asked.

The Many Voices of Prayer

When we think of prayer as the language of intimacy between us and God, we perhaps begin to see it in a different, more liberating light. We do ourselves a grave disservice if we limit our prayer language to any one particular form. Couples that only argue, only laugh, or only cry are sad to see. Every language is legitimate, but when any one of them becomes exclusive, some of the elements of true intimacy are missing.

Those who know God intimately are able to use several languages freely. Let's look at a few.

Requests

Early on, most relationships experience requests. While we were dating, the woman who is now my wife received a shipment of Alaskan king crab legs. They were sitting in a freezer in her dorm. In the course of conversation, I learned that she didn't care for king crab, and a verse from the Bible came to mind immediately: "You do not have because you do not ask." So I asked, and over the course of the next few days, I proceeded to finish off her gift from the North. It wasn't the last thing I've asked from her, and along the way, she's had a few requests of her own.

119

The Bible actually does say that "you do not have because you do not ask[50]." Jesus tells a story[51] commending a woman who kept harassing a judge to grant a request she had. He kept saying no, but she kept asking. He went home. She'd come over in the middle of the night and pound on the door until the judge finally granted her request, if only to get some sleep. (Please don't take this and run too far with it, either with the court judge who refuses to dismiss your speeding ticket, with your spouse, or with God.)

Jesus is a poet. He's not exalting nagging, making it the latest fruit of the Spirit. He's simply giving us permission to make requests of God, because that's the way healthy relationships work. You ask your friend if you can borrow his truck or if he can help you when your computer doesn't work. Your friend asks you for help sorting out a messy issue. You ask your neighbor for salt. You ask your spouse for a night of passion, for help with paying the bills, or "Can you find a ride tomorrow? I need the car." This is life in normal, healthy relationships.

Many of the people who came to Jesus came initially because they wanted something from Him. "I'd like to be healed." "Can You get rid of this demon?" "We, Your favorite disciples, want to sit at Your right and left in Your new kingdom." Jesus says yes to two out of three of the examples above. The point isn't that every request is met with an unqualified yes, but that one feels able to ask at all.

Asking has fallen on hard times these days. The "barn raising" culture of interdependency is harder to find than it once was. When we have a problem, we usually hire a specialist instead. We're isolated, and our culture teaches us to do things for ourselves, easily hindering our capacity to ask from God.

But of course, our lives are much the poorer for our lack of asking. We're poorer not only because we don't receive what we need, but also because our lack of asking is a sign that the relationship isn't healthy. After all, Jesus asks things of us! Maybe we're afraid to ask, because we're afraid of what to do if the answer is no. Maybe we're too proud to ask. When we pray, "Give us this day our daily bread," the very act of asking defines the relationship, because we are admitting who has the bread. I'm not certain of all the reasons we don't ask. All I know is that I've asked God to intervene in my life countless times, and the very act of asking challenges my faith and deepens my relationship. The fact that the road gets graveled is almost the least of it.

Intercessions

When you're in a position of authority, people ask you to do things on behalf of, or to, other people. Let's say you're the boss, and someone is underperforming. His friend comes to you and says, "You could help Mr. Jones be much more effective in his job if you'd heat his office and give him a phone that works. I hate to see him held back like this." That's intercession. It's asking of one in authority on behalf of another.

Jesus encounters this often in the Gospels. "Can you heal my son?" "My daughter has died." "Just say the word and I know she'll be healed." We can't forget the classic instance of some friends of a sick guy cutting a hole in the roof of a house so they could cut in line and get their friend healed. That's what might be called "graphic intercession." People are asking Jesus to do things for other people all the time.

When we step away from the Gospels and consider the larger scope of the Bible, we see that these intercessions are in no way limited to one person praying for another person's physical healing, though that often seems to be what comes up at the prayer meeting. Moses intercedes more than once for the people under his care, because their continual whining is likely to get them killed. At one point, we're even told that God was going to destroy them, and then Moses made the case for their preservation. What happened next confounds Calvinists and other forms of determinists everywhere (even as Calvinists everywhere can sling verses my way to confound me too): "So the Lord changed His mind about the harm which He said He would do to His people" (Exodus 32:14).

Do God's plans change because we intercede? I don't think we should go too far down that rabbit hole in this little book, but the encounter between Moses and God isn't the only place where God seems to change course because of the intercessions of His people. Look at Ezekiel 22:29-30:

> The people of the land have practiced oppression and committed robbery, and they have wronged the poor and needy and have oppressed the sojourner without justice. I searched for a man among them who would build up the wall and stand in the gap before Me for the land, so that I would not destroy it; but I found no one.

The text goes on to say that because no person was willing to intercede, judgment was poured out.

Texts such as these move intercession into a different realm for us. Because we're speaking with God, we might be tempted to develop a determinist mind-set, whereby we think to ourselves, *God is going to do what God is going to do, and there's nothing I can do to change that, so why bother asking?* On the contrary, the testimony of Scripture brings to light a mysterious interplay between God's sovereign activity and man's involvement. We can't systematize this mystery, but the role of intercessory prayer in God's ordering of the universe is large enough that we can't dismiss such prayers as being only for our own good.

Taken at face value, this can be quite a heavy burden to shoulder. "If my prayers are *that* important, why would I ever get up off my knees?" But you see, that's why it's a mystery. They aren't *that* important. When Jesus was coming into Jerusalem to begin His final week of ministry, people were shouting praises. When the leaders tried to silence them, Jesus said that the stones would cry out if the people didn't praise Him. There's the sovereignty card coming into play.

So we intercede for those people, places, and issues that God speaks to us about, and then we let it go. I intercede for Walter in Ghana, that God would continue to grant him opportunities to deliver girls, some as young as five, from their ritualistic sexual slavery. I pray for Heather and her work in Bolivia with women involved in prostitution. I pray for the leaders of our church and for various people facing overwhelming issues. I pray for my children and the needs of other family members. I pray for others too. But none of us can pray for everything.

Practically speaking, this means that not everyone will shoulder exactly the same burdens of intercession. If we're passionate about the needs of a nation, we can become frustrated when our passion meets someone else's apparent complacency. It might indeed be complacency. On the other hand, it might be that this other person already has a full plate of intercessions.

"A full plate of intercessions," though, is not the problem most of us face. We need to learn how to intercede regularly for the people, places, and ministries God has set before us, being persuaded that our prayers are part of our God-given assignment to spill the colors of hope across the globe. Get a little notebook and begin to write down your intercessions. You'll be surprised to see what consistent prayers for others will do in their lives and yours.

Wrestlings

Every relationship has its moments, and a healthy relationship with God is no exception. Here's Jacob, fearful of reuniting with the brother who, the last he'd heard, was planning to kill him. When he prayed, he reminded God of the promises made to him, and then he wrestled with God, refusing to let go until he received a blessing. Job expressed his disappointment to God regarding how his life had unfolded. Jeremiah accused God of tricking him. Gideon resisted God's call and argued a little bit about it. So did Jonah. So did Moses.

And then there's David, the man after God's own heart. What makes him that? Among other things, it was David's capacity for brutal honesty with God. After David got his neighbor pregnant and killed her husband, the child born to her and David became very sick. David prayed and fasted for seven days, interceding, wrestling, waiting. When the child died, David got up, took a bath, worshipped the Lord, and ate a meal. When his servants asked about this behavior, he said, "While the child was still alive, I fasted and wept; for I said, 'Who knows, the Lord may be gracious to me, that the child may live.' But now he has died; why should I fast? Can I bring him back again? I will go to him, but he will not return to me[52]."

Our life with God will include moments, seasons even, of deep wrestling. This may include intercession, requests, claiming the promises of God on our lives or the lives of others, seeking God for direction, mourning, and much more. It's all part of a healthy relationship with God. These are not the parts of the Bible, however, that we highlight with our pens. Nor do they ever become Precious Moments pictures. Can you see David all dressed up in a mauve robe, weeping for the sick child who is the illegitimate offspring of his affair? We secretly wish these parts that expose such raw humanity would go away. But they won't, thank God. They're there to remind us that our relationship with God is supposed to be a real one, not sanitized by formulas and easy answers.

I hope you wrestle with God. I know, by virtue of the fallen world you live in, that you'll have a reason to if you don't already.

Intimacy

All of this taken together, lived out with some measure of consistency, is what intimacy is all about. But it doesn't end there, or it shouldn't. Even if these encounters and experiences and forms of prayer blend together and become regular parts of our lives, we can still be missing something.

We've all known moments when words won't do, when words aren't needed. At the end of a long day, or after a season of challenge, or sometimes just in the midst of a very full life, when you find yourself alone with the one you love, no words are needed. Those moments of intimacy are the most precious of all. My wife and I will be sitting on the deck in our backyard. It might be the end of a busy day or week. So we'll cook up a little feast, pour some wine, and sit together as the sun goes down. We will undoubtedly share a little bit of everything: request ("Could you run inside and get the pepper?"), intercession ("Can you help the Smith family this weekend?"), wrestling ("Why didn't you...?"). But on the best of nights, after we talk it all through, all will become silent, and we'll sit and look at each other and simply enjoy being together. It is enough to know that we love each other.

We're invited to such moments with Christ as well. He invites us to come to Him and find rest. Among other things, He's offering the rest that comes in the context of intimacy. Through the history of the church, this kind of prayer has focused on silence, sitting with the conscious awareness of Christ's presence and listening for His voice[53]. In intimacy, we feel safe, sheltered, unafraid to be honest and vulnerable. We're invited to pursue just that kind of intimacy with God.

But make no mistake: God is not offering a frothy intimacy, a pseudo-intimacy that is available on demand. The invitation is to union with Christ, and such union will change us forever, exposing our darkest parts so they can be healed. It will force us to face the truth about ourselves and others honestly. It will move into wider circles of forgiveness, love, and honesty than we'd previously thought possible. Do we really want this?

Of course we *say* we do. But remember the campfire? I want just enough to feel warm. As soon as the heat is uncomfortable, I retreat. We don't do this only with God; we do it with each other as well. And we're the poorer for it. But God is still there, still inviting, still waiting to ravish us as the lover that He is, so that we will be able both to love and to be loved to the fullest extent of our destiny.

All this is wrapped up in the practice of prayer.

Chapter 9

Meditation and Truth Telling

When thou prayest, shut thy door; that is, the door of the senses. Keep them bolted against all phantasms and images. Nothing pleases God more than a mind free from all occupations and distractions.

Albert Magnus

Christians don't simply learn or study or use Scripture; we assimilate it, take it into our lives in such a way that it gets metabolized into acts of love, cups of cold water, missions into all the world, healing and evangelism and justice in Jesus' name, hands raised in adoration of the Father, feet washed in company with the Son.

Eugene Peterson

It was almost twenty years ago when, feeling the effects of leading a growing urban church, I withdrew for a couple of days for retreat. When I asked around, the same place kept coming up as "the best place to go when you're in need of some restoration," so I went. That it was a convent was irrelevant to me. Though I was raised in a protestant setting that was deeply suspicious of Catholicism, that fear had never gripped me, and in fact I often found more affinity with Catholic authors than evangelicals. Within a few short hours of leaving the city, I had unpacked my things in my small room tucked away in a thick old growth forest of fir and cedar trees and was eating supper with my hostess nuns and other guests there on personal retreat.

There were walking paths, massage therapists, spiritual directors, and counseling available, all at the ready to serve guests in need of restoration, but what changed the course of my life was a conversation with the nun who ran the library. I was perusing books when she asked if she could help, and this led to introductions, and a long conversation about the differences between Catholicism and Protestantism, and women in church leadership (she was all for it and had recently taken to boycotting mass as a result). After an hour of rich and memorable conversation (I can still, in my mind, see clearly where we were standing in the library), she asked me what I was looking for during my retreat time.

"I'm not certain," I said, adding that my life felt too fast and too fragmented. She smiled, guided me to a particular book, and said, "Read this." It was a book on meditation, and the result of that encounter eventually led to the development of a habit in my life that I now consider indispensable.

Meditation is viewed with suspicion in some Christian circles, because the word is used in many ways and in many cultures, with the result that most of us have preconceived notions of what meditation is. "I had a brother once who was into meditation, and he became Baha'i," someone claims, while someone else says, "Eastern religions mediate, so it must be wrong." Our heresy-detection antenna has sometimes become an overactive immune system, and we end up, in our fear of being identified with strange groups, missing truths and practices that are vital for our health, life, and calling. Meditation is a classic example of this problem.

While there are many forms of meditation in the world with stated goals of emptying the mind or transcending the mind, there is a form of meditation and goal for meditation that comes right out of the Bible: *"...his delight is in the law of the Lord, and on God's law he meditates day and night. He will be like a tree firmly planted by streams of living water, which yields its fruit in its season, and its leaf does not wither..."* (Psalm 1:2,3).

If you've traveled through arid lands, you understand the power of this word picture. The Central Valley of California, for example, is a

128

desert, save for the few rivers that flow down from the Sierra Nevada mountains. While driving the length of that region when I was a child, we could always tell where a river was, even if we couldn't see the water. Off in the distance, the stark, barren landscape would be broken by a density of trees. Eventually we'd cross a bridge, and a quick glance in either direction would confirm our suspicions. The trees were there because the river was there. They were firmly established, and their roots had access to the life giving water. This water meant fruitfulness, meant trees fulfilling the purpose for which they were created. Conversely, without the water, the trees would eventually die, as recent California droughts have shown.

If we're trees, then revelation from God is our water, and especially the revelation that comes from God's text, the Bible. We're told that stability, fruitfulness, and the life for which we're created are things which ripen as the result of drawing deeply and consistently on the wellspring of living water that comes from Christ himself.

Meditation: Osmosis for the Spirit, Soul, and Body

Trees receive water through osmosis, and we receive living water through mediation. The difference between Christian meditation and many other forms (each one also distinct) should be apparent right here. Our goal isn't emptiness; it's fullness. We are seeking to infuse our whole being with truth from God, and we do this by allowing God's revelation in the text to saturate us.

Meditation is needed today more than ever, because the notion of saturating our whole being with anything has fallen on hard times in our fragmented, technology-addicted, multi-tasking culture. Maggie Jackson, in her book *Distracted*, writes that "we are on the verge of losing our capacity as a society for deep, sustained focus. In short, we are slipping toward a new dark age."[54] The fragmentation of time, as we seek to multi-task and empower technology to interrupt us constantly, has resulted in literal rewiring of our brains. This rewiring leads to further fragmentation: of intimacy, friendships, of our relationship between faith and work, between nature and

129

culture, and between time and eternity. We are increasingly reactionary, increasingly tribal, increasingly anxious.

In reality, we're just thirsty. We're drinking, too often and too much, from the wrong sources, and our lives are drastically diminished as a result. Jesus' answer to this was articulated when He showed up on the last day of the Feast of Tabernacles, in the temple in Jerusalem. He stood in the middle of the courtyard and shouted, "If anyone is thirsty, let him come to me and drink," with the promise that those who did so would become rivers of living water for a terribly thirsty world.[55] The imagery would have had extra poignancy considering the Feast of Tabernacles celebrated Israel's wandering through the desert for 40 years, and God's amazing provision of water.

Is anyone thirsty? Of course. Thirsty for meaning, intimacy, joy, justice, peace, reconciliation, a good night's sleep. Jesus' audacious statement is that those who come to Him thirsting find not just water for their empty cups, but the transformative power to become, themselves, a source of blessing for others. All this, though, is predicated on assimilating the life-giving "water from the rock" that is Christ Himself.[56] How do we drink from that rock?

Meditation literally means "the act of focusing one's thoughts: to ponder, think on, muse." In contrast to the forms of meditation whose goal is to empty our minds, the goal of meditation in the Bible is to fill our minds with God's truth by displacing the false narratives, shaming voices, sanctified yet destructive ambitions, lustful longings, fears, boastings, and everything else, with "the mind of Christ," so that our lives increasingly reflect the character of Jesus.

We're not emptying ourselves. We're a water bottle, and it's filled with all manner of sediment, rot, and toxins. Other might drink from it if they must, but they'll look elsewhere first, in much the same manner that the world has sought "anything but the church" as the answer to grave dilemmas of our time. Then Christ comes along and says "drink from me," and it's tantamount to us allowing the pure, life-giving streams of Christ Himself to continually fill us, so that over time all the debris is flushed out and Christ's joyful, generous, healing life not only changes us, but empowers us to bless and serve the world. That's why we meditate.

How?

Meditation requires an intentional time of focus on receiving this pure water. This means turning off phones, walking away from computers, ignoring the news cycle, and committing, for a period, to simply absorbing God's revelation. These many distracting forces must be addressed, because their intrusion into the flow of our lives has become, for most, a point of surrender. "That's just the way it is," we say, as we respond to yet another urgent text message. Never mind that our conviction that a text message can't wait ten minutes, or an hour, is ludicrous. Our surrender here is a major contributor to the fragmentation that is our lives and culture.

To swim upstream against this current, it's vital that we learn to meditate on God's revelation and God's work in our lives. There are many ways to do this, and each of us must find contextually appropriate ways of meditating. The realities of raising a family, career responsibilities, aging parents, and many other circumstances will mean that each of us will find different ways of working meditation into our daily routines. Here, however, is mine:

I wake around six o'clock each morning and brew a cup of coffee. While I drink this glorious beverage, I drink from the scriptures. Though I've used many methods over the decades, ranging from reading through the whole Bible to Lectio Divina, I'm presently reading a daily devotional called "Seeking God's Face."[57] There's a weekly reading, along with a daily reading from the Psalms and another portion of the Bible. Every day, I'm encouraged to do this: *"Remind yourself that you are in God's presence and read again. Notice how God might be speaking to you through his Word - dwell on a word or phrase that jumps out at you..."* I do this, and then let the phrase on which I'm focusing sink deeply into my being by repeating it over and over again as I breathe, silently pondering what God is saying to me.

Most mornings by the end of that pondering time, the phrase has become embedded in my soul. After I've considered the phrase while inhaling and exhaling for a few minutes, I'll write it down in my journal. I'll know the degree of success of my mediation if I can recall the phrase or word later in that day. There are many days when I can't recall, and rather than falling prey to condemnation, I simply use these days as reminders of the value of deeper meditation and resolve to do better tomorrow.

I've found the overall effect to be remarkable, because there are certain words that have sunk into the deepest fibers of my being, even (I believe) beyond my conscious mind. Purposing to look at "no worthless thing," knowing that I'm "complete in Christ," remembering that "my days are numbered" are a few examples. These phrases from the Bible have not only sunk into my being; they've changed my priorities of time use and attitude. Movement away from shame and into purposeful living are the fruit, I believe, of allowing "the mind of Christ" to become purifying and life-giving water to my soul.

The Relationship of Meditation to Truth Telling

Often, the image of truth telling is this: "There's bad news out there, but nobody has the guts to talk about it. I'm going to be the 'honest' truth teller who will reveal the flaws and shortcomings." In the name of truth, they're eager to expose what's wrong. People for whom this is a fixation might think of themselves as truth tellers, but the problem is that it's not the whole truth. Their methods are tantamount to a surgeon cutting someone open to expose the tumor or infection, and then saying, "My work is finished here," without closing up the patient before heading off to happy hour for drinks.

The whole truth, as Jesus pointed out, doesn't "cut open" without also healing. It liberates rather than condemns, because it's a cord of revelation that includes the bad news of my brokenness, the good news of Jesus' provision to heal that brokenness, the good news of my identity in Christ, the good news that I am deeply loved and endowed with gifts given me by my creator so that I can live as a person of blessing, and the good news that history is heading toward an ending of justice and hope, healing and mercy, celebration and worship. The woven strands that create the cord of truth are filled with good news!

This is usually the way truth is presented in the Bible. For example, here's one of Paul's exhortations regarding how to live well:

> For the grace of God has appeared, bringing salvation to all men, instructing us to deny ungodliness and worldly desires and to live sensibly, righteously and godly in the present age, looking for the blessed hope and the appearing of the glory of our great God and Savior, Christ Jesus, who gave Himself for us to redeem us from every lawless deed... (Titus 2:11-14)

It's tempting to focus all our attention on the call to deny our darkest desires, as if that alone will lead us to the good life. In reality, self-denial taken alone only leads to a legalistic life, or a hypocritical life, or shame-filled life. This is because the exhortation to obedience and putting away destructive habits has been given to us by Jesus and His followers, not as ends in themselves, but as part of a means to an end. The goal isn't that you "avoid the bad stuff"; it's that you become a person overflowing with the vibrancy of life, fully present with people, with creation, and with your work, as a person of wisdom, blessing, and joy. That's the kind of life for which our world is starving, and for which we ourselves are starving. Self-destructive indulgences rob us of that life, dissipating our time and energy in pursuits like excess food, drink, sex, and shopping, all of which overpromise and under-deliver.

Looking at the second half of Paul's exhortation to Titus, it's clear that the truth that sets us free includes not only a self-denial, but a reorientation, a putting on of a new mindset by nurturing three virtues: sensibility, righteousness, and godliness. The simple act of meditating on this passage one day helped reorient my thought life away from some unhealthy indulgences, precisely because the imagery of these virtues is appealing to me. They've been embodied by people like Mother Teresa and Dietrich Bonhoeffer, George Mueller and William Wilberforce.

My understanding of words like "godliness" and "righteousness" came from meditation, though, and that has taken time. They were words in need of redemption because they'd been polluted culturally by legalism and constrictive, hypocritical religion. Until we're able to embrace a winsome view of the faith life, going through the valleys of self-denial will always be difficult. Meditation on truth will get us there, because we'll come to know two important truths at a level deeper than mere mental assent. First, we'll come to see that the world is darker than we'd ever imagined, as truth exposes us to systemic evils within our own hearts and in our world. Second, we'll see that the truth of what God is accomplishing through Christ is more profound, hopeful, and life-giving than we'd ever be able to fully grasp.

Identity Truths

When I was in seminary, a small group of friends began a lunchtime Bible study, trying to answer the question, "Why do Christians continue to sin after finding life in Christ?" It wasn't a theoretical question. Behind the academic curtain, seminary was a community with a healthy dose of struggling marriages, addictive behaviors, anger, and pride. We who gathered for this Bible study knew our community well enough to have seen these things not just in fellow students, but also in our faculty. Worse, we knew some of these things firsthand in our own lives. We were there because we loved God, felt some sort of call to share that love with with the world through some form of ministry in the future, and knew from the Bible that we each had unique gifts to share with the world. In spite all this, though, each of us also had our own valleys of darkness, sins that we couldn't seem to shake in spite of our best intentions.

A few years later, I'd encounter an intensified version of our Bible study group's problem when a person came to me for counseling. This person had a compulsive behavior that was destroying her, along with significant people in her life. She knew her behavior was wrong, hated herself for doing it, and had tried to free herself many times from this bondage without success. In tears, she expressed that she didn't know if she could continue on this path much longer. She was, in short, in search of freedom.

My answer to her came directly from what I'd received as a result of our little lunchtime Bible study in seminary. We'd invited our favorite professor to join us once, and in between bites had shared our dilemma with him. He smiled a sort of knowing smile and said, "It's simple, really. The only reason Christ followers sin is because we either forget, or fail to believe, the truth of who we are." That's most of what Jesus meant when He said, "You will know the truth and the truth will set you free."[58] He spoke of the reality that when people are "born again," they receive a new nature that is perfect, complete, and unable to sin. The old nature has been judged and condemned, and we're now invited to live out from the fullness and vitality of the new nature.

Our problems stem from both our failure to believe the reality of the new, and our failure to believe in the impotence and fatal destiny of the old. We are, in other words, believing lies. Our old life of lust, anger, greed, pettiness, and ugly self-righteousness is still alive and well, still our "go-to" source for decision making and meaning in our world, or at least, for self-comforting when life isn't working well.

As for our new life? The notion that there's a source within us that can choose purity, love, self-sacrifice, courage, and joy, every time— it's a little hard to swallow. Believing such incredible power is ours is even harder to the extent that we've been raised in an atmosphere of condemnation, shame, or verbal or physical abuse. We read the words on a page about being "complete in Christ" or being "blessed with every spiritual blessing" or having "rivers of living water" inside us just waiting to burst out and quench a thirsty and dying world. Yes. There they are. Words on a page. We might even, on our good days, give mental assent that they contain some measure of truth.

What we don't do is read them and say, "Yes! That's me! I'm complete, forgiven, empowered, deeply loved in spite of my past and future failures, gifted to bless the world, and unconditionally and eternally adopted into God's family. There are too many lies ricocheting around in the recesses of our souls for us to be able to actually believe these enabling declarations. So we're stuck, told we're complete but in practice we "still haven't found what we're looking for." Told we're able to overcome our self-destructive patterns and find real freedom because Christ has busted open the prison doors and broken our chains, we actually believe the chains are still on, the doors still locked. We are, in other words, stuck in the land of lies.

This brings us full circle, back to where we began this chapter, in Psalm 1. Remember the tree thriving in the desert? It's soaking up water, which enables us to enjoy everything necessary for life. You are that tree. That Bible on your shelf is water, filled with identity truths that can enable you to break out of the prison of lies holding you back.

Our little lunchtime Bible study in my seminary years was radically life-altering. I grew up in a legalistic church and a performance oriented family environment. These and other realities conspired to fill me with a grave sense of inadequacy, so that my default mode of thinking was "I can't." - "I can't overcome that sin." "I can't be generous." "I can't have the hard conversation." At various crossroads and facing various challenges, this mantra led to withdrawal, and I started college feeling stuck in nearly every area.

Reading an assigned textbook called *Birthright*[59] with my lunchtime Bible study group in seminary led to incorporating "identity truths" from the Bible into my mediation. I'd chew on a verse for a week, sometimes even a month! Imagine repeating "I can do all things through Christ who gives me strength" a few dozen times a day for a whole month, and after each articulation of the phrase prayerfully saying "thank you," whether I felt it or not, believed it or not, at the time.

Over time, the truth began to set me free. Though none of us will ever fully live into our freedom, I wish I could look you in the eye right now and say, "Learning to meditate on identity truths[60] is a practice in moving my faith from theory to reality, and moved Jesus from a historical figure to my best friend. Do it!"

Chapter 10

A Beautifully Woven Cord: Fasting and Service

"The greatest enemy of hunger for God is not poison but apple pie.

It is not the banquet of the wicked that dulls our appetite for heaven, but endless nibbling at the table of the world.

It is not the X-rated video, but the prime-time dribble of triviality we drink in every night."

John Piper

"Fasting is the first principle of medicine; fast and see the strength of the spirit reveal itself."

Rumi

Of all the disciplines that Christ followers are invited to engage in, none seems, on the surface, less relevant than fasting. An easy case can be made for all the others, but fasting? I'm writing this chapter while in Germany where foods are so much more than mere sustenance for me; they're pure pleasure! There's a fruit stand right across the street from the school where I'm teaching, and a bakery only a two-minute walk farther. Throw in bratwurst, the best sauerkraut on the planet, and chocolate that awakens a capacity for pleasure I didn't even know I had, and you can see why fasting is a challenge for me, at least in Germany. We in the West don't eat for sustenance merely; we eat for pleasure.

Why deny ourselves not just calories, but pleasure? Life is hard enough already. To answer that question, we need to step back a bit from fasting and answer a different question. "Why is the church growing far more rapidly in the developing world than in the West?"[61] Part of the answer comes from the manner in which the gospel is articulated in the developing world. We in the West tend to present Christ as the answer to our guilt question by teaching how the cross reconciles us to God. We're told that Christ moves us from guilt to innocence through his death. It's all good and all true; it's just not the whole story. In much of the developing world, a fear/power paradigm defines cultures, and Christ is offered as the source of power that will enable us to break the bonds of fear that shackle people. Both presentations are legitimate, as is the claim that Jesus enables us to move from living in shame to a place of honor, which prevails more in Eastern cultures. These movements are all vital, though emphasized differently in different contexts throughout the world. This is part of both the genius and malleability of the gospel. Innocence, honor, and power are all part of our inheritance in Christ![62]

For us in the West, though, the focus on our movement from guilt to innocence runs the risk of creating a distorted gospel, one where the power of Christ is lacking. This isn't a new problem. When Paul wrote one of his letters to the Corinthians, he told them that their intellectual ascent of Christ's identity was at risk of creating a community where they had the right words, but were lacking any display of God's power: "But I will come to you soon, if the Lord wills, and I shall find out, not the words of those who are arrogant, but their power. For the kingdom of God does not consist in words but in power[63]."

The reality of the 21st century is that the gospel is exploding in cultures where the fear/power paradigm prevails, because the power of God is being revealed in often indisputable ways. This paradigm taps into spiritual realities, as miracles happen and people are healed, liberated from addictions, transformed, and provided for, in ways that can only be attributed to supernatural intervention. We in the West, shaped by the Enlightenment, have too often reduced the gospel to a set of intellectual ascents. Just look at our Apostle's Creed:

I believe in God, the Father almighty,
    creator of heaven and earth.

I believe in Jesus Christ, his only Son, our Lord,
    who was conceived by the Holy Spirit
    and born of the virgin Mary.
    He suffered under Pontius Pilate,
    was crucified, died, and was buried;
    he descended to hell.
    The third day he rose again from the dead.
    He ascended to heaven
    and is seated at the right hand of God the Father
almighty.
    From there he will come to judge the living and the dead.

I believe in the Holy Spirit,
    the holy catholic church,
    the communion of saints,
    the forgiveness of sins,
    the resurrection of the body,
    and the life everlasting. Amen.

The tacit implication, too often, is that if you agree with these things you're "saved," and if you don't, then you need to "get right with God." As a result, we spend enormous amounts of energy seeking to prove the validity of these truths. We defend them, argue about them, divide over them, nuance them, and preach them. Words, words, and more words. How's that working out for us?

Our churches are filled with people who can recite and defend the creeds, but can't stop drinking. They can defend the historicity of the resurrection, but they can't stop eating in front of the television. They can happily agree that Jesus was born of a virgin, died, and rose again, but the bondage of materialism has so gripped them that they're overworked, overfed, overcommitted, under-rested, stressed, lonely, and deep down, afraid. It's not an animist fear of the forest, or other "little 'g'" gods. It's a fear that the gospel is nothing more than a Sunday joke because it's fundamentally not making any significant dent in their lives. They have the words. They have the doctrines. They even have the Sunday experience mostly, unless it's perfect weather, but transformation? Late at night, before drifting off to a fitful sleep, they wonder if it's true, this gospel, because it certainly doesn't appear to be working.

The problem is that we in the West have often only offered people one third of the gospel. We've spoken of the movement from guilt to innocence. But we've neglected the good news that Jesus also moves us, in spite of our failings, from shame to honor, because honor isn't a prized commodity in the West. We've also neglected the tremendous invitation to embrace the power of the gospel, an invitation that saturates the whole Bible. Moses displayed the power of God in parting the Red Sea, and God declared that it was the display of power that confirmed God's credibility[64]. Elijah displayed the power of God, again as a validating testimony regarding who the true God is, when he called down fire to consume an offering on the altar and so reveal Baal as nothing more than a mirage[65]. The display of power freed Israel from fear and focused her worship toward Jehovah, the all-powerful one. The ultimate display of power, of course, was Christ's resurrection from the dead[66].

Seeing God's power provide, heal, deliver, and transform is a central message of the gospel, in spite of the fact that this power has fallen on hard times in the developed world. As soon as we're able to see and acknowledge this, we come to see why fasting matters. There's an extensive story in Mark 9:14-29 regarding a young man who is demon possessed. There's a crowd, apparently watching an argument between some of Jesus' disciples and some religious leaders. When Jesus arrives on the scene, he's informed that the debate has to do with the disciples' failure to free this young man from his demon possession. When Jesus hears this, his frustration boils over as he says, "'O unbelieving generation, how long shall I be with you? How long shall I put up with you? Bring him to me.'"

Jesus proceeds, with a word, to free the man from the forces of darkness that had gripped him.

Afterward, when the disciples asked why they couldn't cast the demon out, Jesus said, "'this kind cannot come out except by prayer,'" and the version of the story in Matthew 17:21 reads "'this kind does not go out except by prayer and fasting.'" Why would fasting have anything to do with Jesus' disciples gaining the power to deliver someone from forces of darkness? The answer resides in what I call the fasting sequence.

Fasting Brings the Reality of Our Weakness to light

The original lie in the garden of Eden was that humans could live as free agents. Physically, we know that we live in dependency. Without air, water, food, we're dead. The same is true, though, spiritually. We were intended to live in intimate union with God so that the mind of God becomes our mind, the ethic of God becomes our ethic, the will of God becomes our will. Instead, humankind chose autonomy, and the results have been disastrous.

Before Jesus began his public ministry, he spent 40 days fasting in the wilderness. It was there, in the midst of experiencing the physical weakness brought on by fasting, that he overcame the temptations of Satan and was fortified to walk a path of perfect obedience for three years. For the rest of his days, a phrase that would characterize his ministry would be "not my own." Regarding his teaching, authority, judgement, works, will, and life, Jesus said of them all that they were "not my own." His was a posture of dependency, always empty enough to be filled with the teaching, authority, judgement, works, will, and life of the Father. He became the perfect channel of divine life, clearly displaying God's character at all times.

We're invited, of course, to live in that same posture of dependency, so the question we ask is, "How, practically speaking, do we live in this way?" Hints of an answer come from Jesus telling us that unless we receive the kingdom "like a little child" we can't enter it at all.

Children receive in a posture of abject dependency. Spending time with my two-year-old granddaughter recently reminded me of this. She woke from her nap and said, "Papa bring pants," which I translated as a request that I bring her some pants to put on. I handed her the pants and she said, "Papa put on," which I did. Then it was off to the living room, where she reached up toward a box of oranges and said "need orange," not for eating, but for playing catch, as I was soon to find out.

What if I'd said "Get your own pants! And don't think for a minute I'm gonna' help you put 'em on. Do it yourself!", and then "Why don't you show a little initiative and get your own orange?" Of course not. She's two! She's dependent, with an instinctive awareness that she can't provide for herself. Hers is a life of nearly continual, unapologetic receiving. She asks. She expects to receive. She receives. She shows gratitude.

It would be great if there were a way for us to embrace this same spirit of expectant, childlike dependency, so that we, knowing our own weakness, can look to God for resources we know we don't have. There is! At one point Paul shares how he had an affliction which was tormenting him and he asked God for relief. God's response was that Paul would receive something better than relief; he'd discover strength made perfect in weakness. "For when I am weak," says Paul, "then I am strong." Have you ever heard a declaration more contrary to conventional wisdom?

Walk into any interview for any position, and see if you can find someone boasting in their weakness. Do you ever say this in an interview? "I think you should know, almighty HR person, that I'm prone to melancholy, and I sort of have a mid-day crash between the hours of 2 and 4, when I'm basically worthless behind the desk. I'd be better off taking a nap." Ha! We only ever hear the very opposite of that. When an interviewer asks a candidate to share their weakness, they usually hear something like this: "My problem is that I'm a perfectionist, and can never be satisfied with mediocrity," or "I'm too committed to the well-being of the company," or "I try too hard to be a team player." We're good, very good, at branding ourselves, highlighting our strengths and maybe creating a few strengths we don't even have, while also minimizing and denying our weaknesses and liabilities. This is because we live in world that honors strength and punishes weakness. Along comes the gospel, switching the price tags, and we're not quite sure what to do!

This paradigm so saturates our thinking that we make every effort to present ourselves as "all strong, all the time." "Never be weak" translates into never be hungry, or tired, or sick, or vulnerable through confession. Fake it 'til you make it. Our efforts to stay strong at all costs have the effect of painting over our weaknesses, so that we become not only blind to them, but afraid of them. Sometimes the fear is paralyzing, so that when weakness arises we check out, preemptively pulling ourselves out of God's story because we fear we won't be worthy enough or strong enough.

The beauty of fasting is that it removes all facades of strength. When you step away from food, sex, media, or anything else you consume on a regular basis, you quickly discover how weak you are. You begin to see how easily your appetites control you, how addicted you are to comfort and pleasure. Beyond the exposure of our addictive tendencies, there's also the simple reality that when we skip food our blood sugar plummets and we feel weak, especially in those first hours and days[67]. Some of us become a visible expression of that new word, "hangry," that unique kind of ill-temper that only shows up when we're hungry. At least for most of us, fasting doesn't, on the surface of things, make us better people. Instead, it just reveals the (poetically speaking) devils we're capable of being when we don't drink the milkshake.

If fasting exposes weakness, why does Jesus fast before facing the devil, or Moses fast during his intense encounter with God? Wouldn't they want the strength of all their resources and faculties at those critical moments? Don't weaken yourself; strengthen yourself! So goes conventional wisdom, at least. All of us have our own version of carb-loading prior to the big race, but whatever the race, and whatever the form of pre-loading, the principle is this: When you're on, you need to bring your very best self to the stage, or arena, or boardroom. So eat a nice meal, get a good night's sleep, study, psyche up, and then you'll be ready to take on the world as the strong winner you are.

Instead, Jesus prepares to fight Satan by fasting for 40 body-weakening, hunger-inducing days. Why? The answer gets to the core of the gospel. A message that has echoed down through the ages among Christ followers is that the Christian life isn't difficult. It's impossible. This sounds like a cute saying for putting on a poster, but it's much more. The Bible is filled with stories of people doing things people can't do. They're walking on water. They're parting oceans like some scene out of *The Lord of the Rings*. They're raising the dead, shutting the mouths of hungry lions, and calling fire down from heaven to consume an offering that's been saturated with water. People doing the impossible is, or should be, a major thread in the fabric of Christianity.

When you look at all those stories, it becomes clear that the participants have no "plan B." If God doesn't do the deed in God's supernatural way, with God's supernatural power, nothing's going to happen. This sort of "shoot the moon" emptiness is completely counterintuitive to we in the West, with our "can-do" spirits, and our ambitions to plan, innovate, and create. It's also, though, vital to real faith. God is wanting to write stories in and through our lives that are explicable only by the supernatural hand of God. To get there, we need to let go of plan B, and C, and D, and all the way down to ZZZ, because God knows if we have a plan other than naked dependency on God, we'll find a way to use it. Fasting exposes our weakness, strips us down to nearly pure spirit. As a result, our soul moves into a posture of dependency. "I can't go on…" you say, and yet you must, so you pray, and only then discover a strength you didn't know you had, to do a job you didn't think you could! This is the beauty, mystery, adventure, and hilarity of the gospel.

Knowing Our Weakness Leads Us to Using Christ's Strength

In Matthew 17, Jesus cast a demon out of a man who was perpetually lapsing into self-destructive behavior. The man's parents said, "I brought him to Your disciples, and they could not cure him," and this led Jesus to cry out in exasperation, "You unbelieving and perverted generation, how long shall I be with you?" He then called for the man, confronted the demon, "and the boy was cured at once."

I'm intrigued by the story for a couple of reasons. First, it's almost amusing to me that Jesus was so perturbed with his disciples. He was fed up with their lack of faith, and they were the good guys! As I ponder this, I realize that Jesus walked through this earthly life on an entirely different plane than the rest of us. He's this vessel that's always filled with nothing less than the life of God, so that power, and healing, and wisdom, and strength pour through him like water, spilling onto the parched souls of human hearts who are literally dying for a drink.

The rest of us are, to put it politely, "not that way." We leak out a little bit of authentic spiritual power now and again, but just look at the Internet; most of what Christ followers have to say is rubbish. We're blathering on about how this or that political party is the devil, or fighting about who gets to own what kind of guns, or bragging about our kids, or church, or favorite sports team. We're not much better face-to-face, as we vex and worry over the state of things, whether physical, economic, political, or global. Our behavior reminds me of Jesus' disciples. They were discouraged when a few people didn't believe and they wanted to rain fire down on them. They argued about who got to be the greatest. They boasted about their abilities and were easily offended, easily despondent, easily frightened. They were, in every way, weighed down with their fallenness. Just like us.

Jesus' frustration is right there. He knew that each of these disciples was sitting on a mountain of potential, knew that they had the capacity to change the world, and knew that in spite of this, they were playing small ball on a small field that meant nothing to anyone. It's as if Jesus was looking at a team of world-class athletes who decided to stay off the field because they'd rather go drinking and play video games at a pub. What a waste! His desire was to see

145

them filled like He is full, powerful like He is powerful, liberating like He is liberating.

For any of that to happen though, they needed to be "dependent as He is dependent." That required them to come to the dramatic realization that for all their education, verbal skills, management strategies, vision-casting ability, change management plans, vocational aptitudes, and grand funding mechanisms, they were still lacking the one thing that can turn them into rivers which can quench the desert. They needed God's power! That realization came when they saw that in spite of it all, they were weak. What took them to that space of dependency where power is born? Fasting.

We should more accurately say, fasting *can* take them there. It doesn't always work out that way, though, because fasting itself has mutated into a mere ritual, a means of ostensibly gaining access to God's power. If your reason for fasting is that you want to tap into the power of God, you're still missing the point. This becomes clear when the prophet Isaiah exposes the folly of fasting for personal gain. Listen to what he wrote.

"Why have we fasted and you do not see? Why have we humbled ourselves and you do not notice?" (Isaiah 53:3a) Apparently, people were doing the right things, fasting and humbling themselves. In spite of this, nothing seemed to be changing in their lives, and so they were seeking to understand why. Isaiah had an answer:

"Behold, on the day of your fast you find your desire, and drive hard all your workers. Behold, you fast for contention and strife and to strike with a wicked fist. You do not fast like you do today to make your voice heard on high" (Isaiah 53:3b,4). There they were; fasting, "humbling" themselves, seeking God - on one hand. And also, they were driving their workers too hard, and were unwilling to take steps that would address the rampant contention and strife that existed among God's people. In this case, the strife was over economic matters and vast divides between the rich and the poor, divides which apparently don't only go unaddressed, but are actually intensified by the choices of God's people. In essence, with superpowers knocking at the door of Israel, about to conquer her,

God's people were obsessed with personal wealth and comfort. Yes, they were fasting, but only because they, already being rich, wanted even more!

Fasting as a means of knowing the reality of God's power is only a good thing if we know the end to which that power will be used. If we fast for more personal peace and prosperity, it's a sham. God wants none of it, and says so. This warning applies to all spiritual disciplines, because none of them were ever given to us as either ends in themselves, or as means to personal power and well-being. Those who teach otherwise are, to say the least, misguided. Until we come to grips with the truth that God's left us here on earth for the express purpose of serving, we'll miss the point of our spiritual practices. We'll think that they're for our personal well-being. Period. They *are* for our well-being, but only so that we, being filled, can pour out our lives in service to others.

Isaiah frames this beautifully:

> Is this not the fast which I choose, to loosen the bonds of wickedness, to undo the bands of the yoke and to let the oppressed go free and break every yoke? Is it not to divide your bread with the hungry, and bring the homeless poor into the house; when you see the naked, to cover him; and not to hide yourself from your own flesh? (Isaiah 58:6,7)

God's vision is that our fasting always be yoked with our active pursuit of justice, mercy, and hospitality. This makes sense, because we who fast are choosing to forego what others, less fortunate, must forego out of necessity. When we abstain, and turn our energies towards God's kingdom values while we do, we're aligning our entire lives with God's heart. By fasting, our works and service will be forced to draw on deeper, supernatural resources. By serving as we do, those supernatural resources are released to bless and heal parts of our broken world in ways that they never would, had we chosen to continue on the basis of our human strength. The results are amazing:

"Then your light will break out like the dawn, and your recovery will speedily spring forth; and your righteousness will go before you. The glory of the Lord will be your rear guard. Then you will call, and the Lord will answer. You will cry, and He will say, 'Here I am.' If you remove the yoke from your midst, the pointing of the finger and speaking wickedness, and if you give yourself to the hungry and satisfy the desire of the afflicted. Then your light will rise in the darkness and your gloom will become like midday." (Isaiah 58:10)

Isaiah paints a glorious picture of God's people at work serving, blessing, reconciling. This, he says, is where you'll find life. The implication should be obvious. Quit taking pride in your religious rituals, because without a commitment to pour hope, justice, healing, and hospitality into the world through your actions and priorities, your pious activities are a waste of time. Paul said the same thing when, speaking of empty asceticism, he warned that, "these matters have, to be sure, the appearance of wisdom…but are of no value against fleshly indulgence[68]."

Spiritual disciplines without a commitment to service create nothing more than hollow religion. Commitments to service without spiritual disciplines creates nothing more than wishful thinking among a crowd of activists. When spiritual disciplines and a commitment to bless and serve those on the margins are woven together as a cord of gospel reality, very good things happen. How good? Here's what God promises:

> I will always show you where to go, I'll give you a full life in the emptiest of places - firm muscles, strong bones. You'll be like a well-watered garden, a gurgling spring that never runs dry. You'll use the old rubble of past lives to build anew, rebuild foundations from out of your past. You'll be known as those who can fix anything, restore old ruins, rebuild and

renovate, make community livable again. Isaiah 58:10-12
The Message

If ever there was a time to restore, rebuild, and renovate our world, it's now. So let's get on with it, God's strength pouring through us as we consciously choose weakness through fasting. Who's in?

Chapter 11

Simplicity and Generosity

Behold, this was the guilt of your sister Sodom:
she and her daughters had arrogance, abundant
food and careless ease,
but she did not help the poor and needy.

Ezekiel 16:49

But whoever has the world's goods, and sees his
brother in need and closes his heart against him,
how
does the love of God abide in him?

1 John 3:17

But godliness actually is a means of great gain
when accompanied by contentment. For we have
brought nothing into the world, so we cannot take
anything out of it either.

1 Timothy 6:6-7

Sometimes the word picture of oxygen and breathing breaks down, because the inhaling disciplines aren't wholly energizing or healing, and the exhaling disciplines aren't completely consumptive or exhausting. Rather, one finds in nearly each element that which might create fatigue at one level and energize at another. The discipline of generosity seems at once to be challenging and easy, tiring and energizing, inhaling and exhaling. Yet it falls into the category of exhaling, because it requires that we divest ourselves of resources, that we let them go so that they might give life to others. Of course, what we find in the letting go is that we're richer than ever, for in the letting go of ourselves in the right ways and for the right reasons, we come to discover the truer, deeper self that we were all along.

Show Me the Money

In Romans 12, Paul challenges followers of Christ to be shaped in their thinking by the revelation that comes from God rather than by the prevailing structures of the world in which we live. But that's easier said than done, as the structures that shape our culture are omnipresent and powerful, and those who seek to live counter to them must swim upstream against an incredibly strong current.

These currents aren't always recognizable, because we're simply being carried along effortlessly by their forces. Boats drifting in a tidal current or hot air balloons that move along with the wind both carry passengers who can be blissfully unaware of their own movement, because their motion is in harmony with all that's around them. This is how it is with the predominant economic model, which has engulfed the developed world and is rapidly conquering the remainder. We can't afford to be unaware of these forces that are shaping us. Our passive drifting along the currents of prevailing economic models is moving us further from the life to which Christ invites us, diminishing our humanness, and hurting other people.

When you wake up in the morning and listen to the news, you hear about many different things: global warming, wars and rumors of wars, energy crises, food shortages, droughts and famines, political oppression, and terrorist threats. Then comes a commercial break (or, if you get your news via the Internet, you close that page), after which you receive the business news. This is where you hear stock prices and learn whether the Dow Jones average is trending upward or downward. If it's up, productivity has increased, or more goods and services have been purchased, or both. Downward trends happen when a piece of the model doesn't appear to be working; productivity is down, or people aren't buying enough.

What does *any* of this have to do with following Jesus? I can hear the question, because I've asked it myself. The answer is that our ship is drifting in an economic current, and this current is also carrying the rest of the news. Should we go with the current, or should we turn around and swim upstream? After all, we may be heading toward a waterfall that will kill us all. We can only decide whether or not to let the current sweep us along by discerning whether it's in keeping with God's desire and His direction for His people and His kingdom. And God has a few things to say about economics.

The current in which we're drifting has its roots in eighteenth-century Enlightenment thinking, especially the teachings of Adam Smith.[69] Smith's view was that people made whatever economic decisions they made because those decisions furthered their own self-interests. This foundational assumption explains why superstores are crushing local shops. When someone has to choose whether to walk up the hill to their local grocer (if one still exists) and pay $9.00 a pound for their fish or drive some distance to a superstore where the same fish is available for $5.00 a pound, Smith posits that most people will pay $5.00 instead of $9.00 because it's in their self-interest to do so. The other $4.00 can help the buyer acquire more fish or some beer to go with it or a Lotto ticket. Or perhaps the buyer will simply walk home with the $4.00, a richer man for having lived out the gospel of Adam Smith.

"Gospel?" you ask? Yes, because *gospel* means "good news," and Smith wasn't merely making an observation. He went on to moralize and explain that this reality of acting in our own economic self-interest is a very good thing. His argument was that if this system is left to function on its own, producers will continue to innovate in order to increase production, and consumers will continue to benefit from this innovation as goods become cheaper. Thus everyone wins as the economic tide of prosperity rolls in. Admittedly, it brings more wealth to some than to others, but eventually, everyone is better off than they were before.

The drive to pursue efficiency has led to assembly-line production and specialization. Why have one person make one chair every two days, when ten people can make fifty chairs in two days? This, of course, dramatically increases productivity, so the manufacturer runs the risk of making more of a product than he can sell. The manufacturer must continually look for new markets, and thus we see the birth of advertising and a global economy. This is a vast oversimplification, but it can fairly be said to be the essence of the situation.

But is this really good news? At some levels, yes. Consider the average life span of someone born in 1831 (42 years) compared to someone living today (76.9 years). Consider that cultures that reward hard work, innovation, and productivity have been at the forefront of educational, artistic, and humanitarian endeavors. The world has shrunk through globalization, the Internet, and easy access to travel, so we can now clearly see where in the world we might best invest our time and money to bring hope, healing, and blessing. These are good things.

But this gospel isn't all good news. Our increases in productivity won't result in prosperity unless enough people are willing to buy the stuff. Growth of the amount of goods and services produced and consumed is the gold standard by which the health of economies are measured. And as former British prime minister Margaret Thatcher said while in office, "There is no alternative" to economic growth. How can our global economy assure such growth? Welcome the advertising industry into your life, and not into yours only but into the lives of people across the globe, even in deeply impoverished areas. This industry works hard at creating a sense of both dissatisfaction and entitlement, a "gotta have it" mentality that leads us down a path of reckless consumerism.

Thus do we find ourselves facing mountains of debt, forcing us to work longer hours, because our lives are filled with stuff we don't really need. We just thought we needed it. And why did we think we needed a third Styrofoam ice chest, that latest CD, or (fill in the blank)? We thought we needed it because, whether directly or indirectly, we were told by our culture that we needed it, that we deserved it, that it was in our own best interests to buy a beautiful, gigantic car that costs three times as much as a smaller one that will get us from here to there. We're acting in our own self-interest, right?

Visible Costs

Manufacturers use a great deal of advertising to convince us that we're acting in self-interest. Left to our own ways of thinking, we might come to our senses and realize that we can live a very good life with far, far less stuff than we have right now. The stuff with which we've surrounded ourselves has come at a high cost. Some of the cost is visible, some hidden.

The visible cost includes the harsh realities of debt. The average credit card debt per American household in 2016 was calculated at over $8,300. This debt, and the many social pathologies that stem from it, has continued to grow, because somehow we've come to believe that we need more things than we're able to afford, and so we've overextended ourselves. This overextension is a theological problem. It stems from our failure to recognize that the current of consumerism carries us away from our Christian calling. As a result, all of us, to varying extents, have been drifting along in the wrong current, buying and selling as if there were no tomorrow. But tomorrow comes, and with it a big bill from VISA in the mail.

The choices at such a point become painful. Will I take on extra work to dig out from the debt? That will require a loss somewhere else, in time spent with friends and family, in physical energy, and in the margins that enable me to breathe. Any or all of these become the price we pay for "acting in our own self-interest," and so we come to the conclusion that perhaps it's not in our self-interest after all to see every new movie that comes out, drive a huge car, have season tickets to the local sports team, or whatever else we happen to be thinking will make us happy. Such "happiness" might not be worth the price of admission. Even if we have the means to pay for it all, we might ask ourselves if this money couldn't be spent in a better way by investing in God's kingdom rather than another personal pleasure.

Counting the Costs

The visible price of relentless consumerism is clearly too high for some people. I have a friend who ran a successful medical practice until the report that his heart had been weakened by stress caused him to rethink his life and make some dramatic changes. He sold his practice and moved to a farm in the middle of nowhere. Not content merely to exist, he and his wife have become deeply involved in helping the desperately poor of the world as they travel to refugee camps in the wake of disasters and use their talents to help in any way possible. They've never been happier.

Other people have cut back on both expenses and working hours in order to have more time to invest in relationships, hobbies, or service to their communities. Creative co-housing movements are growing across the country, as people realize that by sharing housing costs they can free up immense time to do things other than work. May their tribe increase!

Still, the prevailing model of Adam Smith's gospel is a powerful current, and relatively few people are swimming upstream, even among people of faith. Part of the reason for that might be that for many people the visible cost of consumerism just isn't that high. We've worked hard, received good educations, climbed the ranks or made our own ways, and tasted the fruits of success. We have enough money to buy what we need and then some, and we live generously, giving to our faith community and the poor. God and Adam Smith have been very good to us, and we're giving back *and* enjoying the fruits of success at the same time.

Those of us in this boat would do well to consider the *hidden* costs to our consumerism before we rent a third storage space for our stuff. These are the costs that we don't see readily. In fact, to see them at all requires close scrutiny and an open mind. Still, these must be considered as we develop our practice of generosity. What are these hidden costs?

Let's begin by considering the loss of community. Nowhere in the Bible are we encouraged to operate out of a paradigm that considers our own self-interest as the highest good. To the contrary, the great weight of the Bible's teaching, both through the Old Testament prophets and the instruction of Jesus, is that the good life is to be found not in consuming more, but in caring for those who don't have enough. Jesus, in fact, made an interesting statement about this. He said, "No one can serve two masters; for either he will hate the one and love the other, or he will be devoted to one and despise the other. You cannot serve God and wealth" (Matthew 6:24). Put another way, Jesus seems to be offering us a prophetic assault on Adam Smith's model. He challenges the assumption that our choices, if made on the basis of financial expediency and personal benefit, will result in the good of all and the furtherance of God's purposes.

In fact, history has borne out the fact that Jesus was right on this one and Adam Smith was wrong. Surprised? When I buy the cheapest coffee on the market, I buy coffee that keeps those who pick it in a state of perpetual economic oppression, as some of these pickers work for only 60 cents a week. Of course, the long hours that these workers are in the fields does little for their health or well-being, either spiritually or physically, and the work is oppressive for their family life as well, usually forcing the children to work from young ages and keeping them illiterate.

The same could be said of those shoes that I purchase with the fancy logo on the side. The logo not only lets everyone know that I'm as good an athlete as the person endorsing the shoe, it also provides a wage to some workers in Indonesia of only two dollars a day. Or the diamond I buy my wife—if it was mined by a child who was taken by force from his or her family in order to fund a rebellion, then my purchase of it, though it might be the cheapest diamond and thus in my own best interest, also had the effect of breaking up a family and harming a small child. I don't think this is what Jesus had in mind when He talked about coming to bring us life. The point is simple: Every economic choice has a hidden cost, and I'd do well, at least with the major purchases of my life, to consider the hidden cost before putting my money down.

Perhaps the biggest hidden cost isn't really even hidden if we'll just stop and look around. For all the increases in productivity, disposable income and recreational choices—all the larger houses, cars, boats, and TVs—prosperous Americans are simply no happier today than they were in 1950. As Bill McKibben documents and articulates so well, since 1946 "there have been steady decreases in the percentage of Americans who say that their marriages are happy, that they are satisfied with their jobs, that they find a great deal of pleasure in the place they live.[70]"

A second and perhaps deeper flaw in Smith's model is that it ignores the price of increased production that creation itself must pay. When a manufacturer buys raw materials, he weighs the cost of those materials and finds the cheapest ones available. That's the way Adam would do it (Smith, not the first man in Genesis, though he too might think the same way after his sin entered the scene). Coffee grown on land that has been slashed and burned is more productive, and therefore cheaper than that which is grown in ways that preserve the forest. Coal taken from strip-mined hills is cheaper than coal mined with deference to environmental costs. Lumber from clear-cut hillsides is cheaper than selectively logged lumber, but the clear-cut will often result in the streams of the hill's watershed being filled with soil that washes off in the rains, destroying spawning beds for fish. You get the picture. In nearly every case, the cheapest way is also the most degrading to the environment. This model fails to consider the long-range impact of its actions.

None of this is a problem if you view the earth as some storehouse of goods to be plundered until Christ returns at the end of history to clean house. But such a view of history fails to embrace our calling to care for the earth and all life therein. God has charged us to sustain creation, to care for it and maintain its well-being in a similar way to that which we as parents are called to care for our children. Our goal with children is to feed and sustain them so that they thrive, recognizing that they will give us many blessings along the way. So it is with creation. God has shown us various ways to do this through the Scriptures, and it is now up to us to take these principles and apply them in our situation at this dawn of a new millennium[71].

Once we see sustainable economic models that move away from oppression and toward the well-being of both humanity and creation as the goal, we can no longer embrace our existing economic models with unreserved enthusiasm. Smith's model has always had a definition of success that was primarily material, failing to take into account communitarian and environmental costs. But in the past, the consequences of this model were smaller and localized. Today, the consequences are global and often catastrophic. And we're feeling the pain already.

If the acquisition of raw materials is fraught with problems on the front end of consumerism, the waste created by excessive consumption is equally problematic on the back end. One of the tenets of our current economic model is that we'll all be better off if everyone continues to buy. Thus the planned life of that product you bought is short so that you'll buy again. Our landfills are growing as they accommodate the things we absolutely had to have, along with the packaging in which those things were wrapped, protected, and shipped.

The environmental results of our excessive consumption are numerous. Landfills, toxic waste sites, the loss of huge aquifer pools underground, the extinction of species, the pollution of our food supply, loss of watersheds and stream beds, and the pollution of the ocean are just a few of the many effects that exist so that we can enjoy our lifestyle of abundance. Adam Smith was right. We will operate according to our best economic interests. But when we consider all the costs and embrace our calling to spill colors of hope into an oppressed and polluted world, this observation ceases to be wholly good news.

Seeing—the First Step Toward Generosity

The story of David and Bathsheba comes to mind as we consider these matters. David, king of Israel, brazenly stole the attractive wife of another man, a soldier. Once she discovered she was pregnant, David sought to cover it up by inviting the soldier husband home for leave. But in his devotion to the cause, the husband-soldier refused to sleep with his own wife. David continued the cover-up by sending him back to the front line and having him placed in the fiercest battle so that he was killed. David knew God, loved God, and wanted to serve God. Yet in this scene in his life, he acted entirely out of his own self-interest, and such actions result in the destruction of a man whose power and available options were less than his own.

When David was confronted about this sin, he was set up by Nathan the prophet. Rather than speaking directly, Nathan asked for a ruling on an economic matter. What should the punishment be for a man with many sheep, who stole the one lamb his neighbor owned and killed it for a meal? David was infuriated and called for swift justice, and only when Nathan made the connection did David see that the story was about him (2 Samuel 11:1–12:15).

But it's not just about him. It's about us too. Perhaps in these days we should reverse the parable so that we'll get it. Perhaps we need our *economic* sins framed as a *sexual* story. Suppose a man comes into the coffee shop where we're meeting with a couple of friends for a Bible study. He tells us about someone he knows who is married to arguably the most beautiful woman on the planet. She's not only stunning of form and face, but she's healthy, witty, articulate, immensely rich, and sexually creative. What's more, she adores her husband and is utterly faithful to him, continually forsaking all other offers just to be faithful to this lucky chap. This man, whose wife is the envy of every man, sees that his neighbor has a wife, too, lovely in her own right. He uses his wealth and power (both of which were derived from his lucky marriage to his wife) to seduce her, breaking up the man's home and leaving him lonely and embittered the rest of his days. What kind of judgment would you recommend for this home-wrecker?

Evangelicals would know what to do. Because it's sexual sin, there's no room for error here. He's to be confronted, excommunicated from the church, and marked the rest of his days as one lacking self-control. We'll feel justified indignation, because he plundered another man to feed his own excessive appetites.

The prophet who relayed the story to us simply stares at us, and an eerie silence hangs in the air. Before he arrived to share the story, we'd finished our Bible study. We were just sitting there, sipping our three-dollar lattes and dipping our two-dollar biscotti into it as we checked the Internet on our laptops for a shoe deal we heard about through an Internet company that undercut the local stores by at least 30 percent. We picked up our cell phones and told someone else about the deal. The shirts we were wearing were made in a factory in Indonesia; our pants came from Malaysia. Neither piece of clothing provides a living wage for the factory workers who make them. Our coffee has come at the cost of a rain forest in Central America, and it kept the pickers economically oppressed, their children lacking basic health care and education. Before leaving the shop, we get an e-mail from our electronic superstore, telling us that the latest HDTV has arrived and is now on sale, cheaper than ever. Wow! We ponder the reality that our present TV, though only three years old, isn't HD. Yes, we decide we'll drive out to the suburbs and check it out. "That's pretty disgusting," we say as we ponder the playboy's sins while we polish off our last sips of coffee.

But the prophet continues to stare at us and then points his bony finger our way and says the same simple four words he said to David so many centuries ago: "You are the man!" (2 Samuel 12:7). Will the scales fall from our eyes? Will we begin to see the possibility that economic sins can be just as damaging as sexual sins?

Until I begin to see the real costs of the "most goods for the cheapest price" model, I have no reason to change my ways. But seeing the price requires some searching, because it's in many people's best interest to keep the rest of the story hidden from the buying public. Adding to the challenge is the reality that when pastors try to address these issues, they're often told to "stick to the Bible" or "stay out of politics," as if Jesus' message wasn't political. Strangely, the people who resist economic conversations as too political are often the same ones who want to be sure we're mobilizing our congregations and getting out the vote when issues surrounding abortion or the definition of a family are in the legislative halls.

The truth is that it's *all* political and *all* gospel, because the gospel is political; it's just that the gospel's politics are not beholden to any one party. If life in the womb is political because it affects the well-being of the unborn, then certainly the structures that support my consumerist habits are political too, because they affect family farms, manufacturing communities, the state of the air and water, the economic condition of billions of people, and our dependence on oil that fuels terrorist agendas and makes us an increasingly fearful, armed people. The reality is that Jesus *is* interested in these things because the kingdom of God is about making all things new[72].

Limits

To move toward generosity, I can begin by structuring my life around God's financial priorities. The Bible clearly lays out several of these priorities.

I need to define my life in terms of what I give rather than what I consume.[73] Jesus warns consistently against a life that is anxious over its pursuit of material well-being. He says that in reality this is how most of the world will live. History has shown that this preoccupation leaves multiple social maladies in its wake, including bankruptcy, oppression and class wars, fear and isolation, and a commensurate destruction of much that is beautiful in this world along the way.

But Jesus also offers an alternative, contrasting the prevailing paradigm with a consideration of the flowers of the field, which draw on the resources that God generously provides. These flowers then become creations of great beauty, and they offer generous provision for others to know and enjoy life. It's a marvelous system, and Jesus says that it's not reserved for flowers, but can be ours as well if we'll swim upstream against the prevailing economic models. Jesus seems to envision little communities that embody this alternative, communities that will bear witness to hope.

When I decide that giving is better than consuming, I begin to reorder my priorities. I take seriously God's instructions to live generously, by giving first and then building my life around what's left. The rarely read book of Haggai provides insights into this whole matter. There God points out that the people who are stuck in a state of perpetual discontent were there precisely because they'd failed to order their financial lives according to God's priorities. These people said, "We care about giving. We care about God's priorities. We care about the poor. It's just that right now there's a leak in our roof, and we're still paying off that vacation to the islands last summer. Then there's the matter of braces, and we're putting away for college. And we bought a bigger car because SUVs are important in places where it snows one day in every 862, blah blah blah. Yes, we care about giving, just not right now. As soon as..."

There's the problem. When we say, "as soon as," we kid ourselves into thinking that we agree with God's priorities, even though we're not living them out. We'd never get away with that kind of justification in our sexual ethic, would we? "Yes, I intend to limit my sexual expressions to my spouse as soon as he wakes up to my emotional needs. For the time being the mailman makes an extra stop at my house a few times a week for a special delivery, first-class. I'm working on getting my emotional needs[74] met, so I can have something to give to my husband someday. I really do believe in what God says about fidelity, but for now...blah blah blah. I'll stop sleeping around as soon as..." Try telling that to your small group.

If that reasoning doesn't fly sexually, it probably doesn't fly economically either. The best thing we can do is sit down with a list of our expenses and income, existing and anticipated debts, and commit to giving the first portion of that to the work of God's kingdom. This will give us a new, smaller number to work with when deciding how to live.

If Adam Smith had been *absolutely* right, we could now try to sustain our previous lifestyle by simply buying the same stuff, only cheaper. But as we've peeled back the curtain and seen the true costs of goods, our choices become more complex than that. Perhaps we should eat more local food so as to reduce the amount of pollution generated by transport. That would also support small local farms, which use far less energy and take better care of the soil than industrial farming operations. But the local farmer's food will cost more, so we might need to change our diet and eat some protein a bit further down on the food chain, or at the very least buy less prepackaged food and more raw ingredients, from which we can prepare our own delicious meals. Ironically, we'll find that such dietary changes make us healthier. The fresh vegetables, higher fiber, and better quality foods might decrease our odds of contracting some diseases.

Entertainment, transportation, housing, energy use—every element of our consumption should come under the same scrutiny. Which choices will be best for humanity, contributing to the well-being of producers and minimizing impact on the earth?

Whew! This sounds like a lot of work—but it's not, actually. It's more like swimming. I need to stop standing where I am, on the shore thinking about it all, and jump in. Once I'm in the water, I'll begin to adapt to the new environment, learning little by little to make choices on the basis of blessing and stewardship questions, rather than simply seeking the most goods and services for the least amount of money.

Turning my economic choices over to God's reign seems to be almost impossible if I live in isolation. In order to enjoy the simple things of life, I need to have enough space in my life to actually gain pleasure from noticing creation or cooking a wonderful meal with friends. My inhaling habits of solitude and silence will help ground me in what's really important so that I can choose wisely among the multitude of options in my life that have to do with gaining, investing, and consuming resources.

A family in our church had come under the conviction that they needed to reorder their financial priorities, which led them to cancel their cable TV and eat out less often. These two choices combined to create much more time for this couple to spend talking together. Nights of *American Idol* were replaced by candles and lingering conversation at the supper table long after the children had left. These conversations eventually exposed some very intimate issues, which led to a profound transformation of their marriage. Now they're looking for more ways to shift their priorities from consumption to generosity, convinced as they are that this new paradigm will lead to increased riches of the heart. And after all, those riches give life the most meaning anyway.

Let me put it another way:

> fresh, vine-ripened tomatoes—$1.50

organic pasta—$.75

handful of pine nuts and romano cheese—$2.00

olive oil—$.50

salad and fixins'—$3.50

California merlot—$5.00

Cooking with my spouse, turning the TV off, and eating together in the backyard as the evening sky darkens and the candles light our faces, conversing about matters of the heart and touching hands, cherishing God's gifts of creation and companionship, all the while knowing that this lifestyle enables us to provide basic support for children in the developing world—**PRICELESS!**

Chapter 12

Solitude

There should be at least a room, or some corner where no one will find you and disturb you. You should be able to untether yourself from the world and set yourself free, loosing all the fine strings and strands of tension that bind you, by sight, by sound, by thought, to the presence of other men.

Once you have found such a place, be content with it,

and do not be disturbed if a good reason takes you out of it. Love it, and return to it as soon as you can, and do not be too quick to change it for another.

Thomas Merton

All the unhappiness of men arises from one single fact,

that they cannot stay quietly in their own rooms.

Pascal

One of life's baseline realities is that we're alone. Each of us comes into the world out of the womb and becomes a distinct person. We're connected with people along the way. Some connections are close and strengthening, others hurtful and draining. We'll have acquaintances, friends, and close friends, but none of these relationships will be static. Look back on your high school yearbook. How many of those people for whom you wrote "friends forever" are still your friends? And of those, how many are still close friends? Even in our family, with our spouse, parents, and children, relationships will change. Eventually, some of these people will depart from our lives because they depart from this world. And of course, our day will come too. We'll die. And though, if we're fortunate, we might die with some friends or family at our side, we'll ultimately die alone.

Why is this author depressing me? I don't like this chapter. At first glance, I'll agree. The reality of our aloneness seems dark. Maybe it's best not to think of it, best to fill our lives with parties and connections and relationships. At all costs, let's avoid settling in with our uniqueness and the reality of our solitude. This might appear to be wise, but those who have traveled that path have diminished their lives, and in spite of their best efforts, they still died alone. Instead of avoiding this reality, I'm going to suggest that if you'll press through this with me, you'll come to see that this apparently depressing news is the vital foundation upon which we can build a life of intimate relationships, deep inner security, great joy, and lasting peace. But it all starts with letting this reality settle into our hearts and accepting it: *We're ultimately alone.*

As I've already noted, many people, including most of those in our faith-based world, seek to avoid this truth by filling life with people, activities, socialization, projects, entertainment, to-do lists, and all manner of noise. The tragedy of this is that we are in danger of forever insulating ourselves from the one reality that will propel us toward intimacy with our Creator, for it is out of my aloneness that I turn to God, who then becomes, literally, *enough.*

Henri Nouwen points the way for our intimidating journey into solitude:

> In discussing solitude and the need for it, three words are important: aloneness, loneliness, and solitude. You and I and all people are alone. Aloneness is a natural fact. No one else in the world is like me: I am unique. No one else feels and experiences the world the way I do: I am alone.

Now, how do I deal with my aloneness? Many people deal with it through loneliness. That means you experience your aloneness as a wound, as something that hurts you, makes you miserable. It makes you cry out, "Is there anyone who can help me?" Loneliness is one of the greatest sources of suffering today. It is the disease of our time.

But, as Christians, we are called to convert our loneliness into solitude. We are called to experience our aloneness not as a wound but as a gift—as God's gift—so that in our aloneness we might discover how deeply we are loved by God[75].

In my own story, the untimely loss of my dad created the existential awareness that indeed we are, all of us, alone in the world. Painful? Excruciating. But right here, in our emptiness, we are enabled to turn to Christ and find the source of all that we need in order to become whole people—people marked by hope, joy, healing, mercy, honesty, grace, service, and generosity.

A Short History of Solitude

Turning to God, who is invisible, usually requires an intentional removal of that which is visible, because given a choice, we'll choose the visible over the invisible almost every time. For this reason, God leads people away from the crowds, away from the noise and distraction of the material world, so that we might encounter the invisible, hidden realities. Abraham was to become the father of a nation, a special nation whose vocation would be to display God's character for the world. But the beginning of his call was a call into solitude: "Go forth from your...relatives and from your father's house[76]." Abraham happened to ignore this simple command, and this disregard created untold grief and complexities for his journey and the fulfillment of his destiny. God's intention had been that Abraham would be leaning into God alone as the source. But for most of us, it's more tempting to look elsewhere for companionship.

Later in the same book, Abraham's grandson Jacob is shaped through solitude as he faces God alone in the desert—twice. These solitudes were forced, because Jacob had cheated his brother, who was therefore intent on killing him. Later still, Jacob's son Joseph was shaped by solitude, again a solitude not of his own choosing. Hated by his brothers, he was sold into slavery and then later framed for sexual assault and put in prison, where he was forgotten for years.

Moses? Alone in the wilderness, partially because of some bad choices, but alone nevertheless. Later, Moses was once again alone with God, this time on a mountaintop for 40 days to receive the revelation of God's heart, all that He desired for His people, Israel. Up there, alone with God, his heart was shaped for all that was to follow.

David spent large chunks of time in solitude, and we have Psalms as a result. Elijah, Job, Jeremiah, John the Baptist, Jesus, Paul—each of them experienced solitude, a time away from other people, as a means of drawing near to and learning to depend on God more wholly as their only true source of strength, wisdom, and direction.

Let's take Jesus as our primary example. Based on His calmness in every circumstance, boldness in confronting the powers of the day, and capacity to perform great feats of strength (like raising people from the dead and walking on water), He seems like a decent role model, someone worth emulating, someone that you'd perhaps want to invite over for dinner. And if you could ever muster the courage, you might ask Him, "Jesus, how is it that You're so secure, so centered, so solid?"

His answer might surprise you though, for a quick survey of His own words would indicate that Jesus didn't view Himself as inherently secure or centered at all. Instead, He saw Himself as a conduit through which the life of His heavenly Father could find expression. That's why He made each of the following statements:

My will is not my own:
> "My food is to do the will of Him who sent me and to accomplish His work" (John 4:34).

My power is not my own:
> "Truly, truly, I say to you, the Son can do nothing of Himself,
>> unless it is something He sees the Father doing" (John 5:19).

My life is not my own:
> "As the living Father sent Me, and I live because of the Father,
>> so he who eats Me, he also will live because of Me" (John 6:57).

My teaching is not my own:
> "My teaching is not Mine, but His who sent Me" (John 7:16).

My initiative is not my own:
> "I do nothing on My own initiative, but I speak these things
>> as the Father taught me" (John 8:28).

Is there a pattern to any of this, any recurring theme? If Jesus were to summarize these things, He might make a statement like this: "My calling in life is to be a living, visible expression of the living, invisible God. Therefore all that I do, I do because I live my life in utter dependency on the Father, looking to Him to be in and through me, that which I am incapable of being on my own."

Wow. It's a good thing that was *His* calling and not yours and mine. But no! If we keep reading we come to the startling realization that

His calling and our calling are actually the same. "Truly, truly, I say to you, he who believes in Me, the works that I do, he will do also; and greater works than these he will do; because I go to the Father" (John 14:12). Maybe we need to just sit for a moment or two and ponder that, to let it sink in before proceeding. If we lower the bar here, settling for some shabby imitation of Christ rather than a real manifestation of His power, all we're considering is a colossal waste of time, a house of cards, a sham. We're called to be the very presence of Christ, and that is the vital vision that motivates us to breathe deeply, for shallow breaths won't give us enough strength for the journey.

So we're to live in the same posture of dependency on Christ as Christ demonstrated when He walked on the earth, living in perfect dependency on God the Father.

The principle that Christ's life finds expression through our available humanity is more significant than we might realize at first glance. It shifts the weight of our faith life from the primacy of obedience to the primacy of dependency. We eventually realize that the only One capable of living a life that expresses the heart of our Creator is Jesus Himself. This would be bad news, except for the incredibly powerful and liberating truth that this One lives within us, enabling us to do and be all that we are incapable of doing and being on our own.

A problem remains however, and I hear about it often when I travel and teach these truths. "Yes, Mr. Dahlstrom—we've heard this many times: Christ lives in us. We need to depend on Him to express His life through us. But how?"

This is where solitude comes into play. When we look at the One who did a very good job of maintaining this posture of dependency, we find a recurring theme: "alone," "alone," "alone." God's life found expression in Christ because Christ was available to the Father. This availability grew out of, among other things, a conscious, periodic withdrawal from the crowds in order to maintain His posture of dependency.

The Why of Solitude

Why would Jesus, God in the flesh, need to get away from the noisy crowds and spend some time alone? There are several reasons why solitude was important for Jesus and is important for us.

We Hear the Right Voice

In the first chapter of Mark's Gospel, we're introduced immediately to the very active life of Jesus. After being baptized, He began a preaching and teaching ministry that brought Him into contact with countless people. He cast a demon out of a man in the synagogue. He healed Simon's mother-in-law. Quickly the word about His healing powers was out, and we read that "they began bringing to Him all who were ill and those who were demon-possessed. And the whole city had gathered at the door. And He healed many who were ill with various diseases, and cast out many demons[77]."

"They began bringing *to* him." Most of us have multiple roles in our lives, and each role demands that we be something for some certain group of people. I'm a teacher for my congregation and for others when I travel to various places. I'm a pastor (in the classical, one-on-one shepherding sense) for a smaller subset of that group, different people at different times, depending on a variety of factors. I'm a husband to my wife, a father to my children. I'm a friend. Each of these dimensions to my life has its own set of demands, and when those demands converge, I feel as if everything is coming *at* me. When that happens, I lose all sense of purposefulness and control, and I simply begin reacting.

It's as if I'm in a video game, driving a race car. I watch the screen, and here comes the terrain. A turn appears and I react, a pedestrian and I react again, a hill with a curve at the bottom and I react again. In order to stay competitive, I accelerate, which simply means that all of this is coming at me faster and faster. Soon I'm doing nothing more than reacting to everything that's coming my way.

In real life, I walk into the office and find a set of data to which I'm supposed to react: 150 e-mails, appointments, meetings, supervision responsibilities, meetings to plan meetings, and even (yes, this is true) meetings to plan meetings to plan meetings.

Oh, and don't forget about the other roles. Teacher: Okay, time to study, prepare, write because I need to preach, and Sunday comes around with surprising regularity. Father: Invest in your kids, go to their events. Homeowner: What should I do about the siding that appears to be rotting on the front of the house? Husband: Date night, flowers, words of encouragement because that's her love language.

I love all of it, actually (with the exception, perhaps, of the siding), but sometimes it's all coming at me so quickly that I lose sight of the point of any of it. At those times, I feel as if I'm preaching not because I have something to say, but because I have to say something. At those times, I check my family off my list in some pathetic way, as if they are tasks rather than people. I'm not proud of it, but at times I succumb.

This is where the story with Jesus gets interesting and powerfully relevant. When life was coming at Him like a video game, He did something nobody would have expected. Read with me: "In the early morning, while it was still dark, Jesus got up, left the house, and went away to a secluded place, and was praying there" (Mark 1:35). This is certainly counterintuitive. When life is coming at you quickly, your instinct isn't to drop everything and go to the mountains alone. Yet that's exactly what Jesus did.

The reason for this counterintuitive move is seen by its results: "Simon and his companions searched for Him; they found Him, and said to Him, 'Everyone is looking for you.' He said to them, 'Let us go somewhere else to the towns nearby, so that I may preach there also; for that is what I came for'" (Mark 1:36-37).

Do you notice the great refusal skills Jesus has? Where do you think these come from? It's not too hard to see. In the solitude of the morning, praying and listening for the voice of the Father, Jesus received direction to move on to a different city. It would be very difficult to miss the causal link between Jesus' early rising and solitude and His moving out of Capernaum to a different city. He could have stayed right where He was. Some people certainly thought He *should* have stayed right there; after all, the market demand was huge. Not every disease had been healed there. Not every demon had been cast out. There was more to do, and if the people of Capernaum had controlled the agenda, if Jesus had been an approval addict, He would have stayed there the rest of His days.

Instead, He was secure enough, centered enough, called enough to say no to "the whole city" gathered at the door and to move elsewhere. Each of us needs to ask this fundamental question: Whose voice is determining the agenda of my days and my hours? We need to be aware of at least two kinds of wrong voices.

The Voice of the Other

We live in a performance-oriented world. Please people, and they will shower you with gratitude and affirmation. Disappoint them, and they'll make you pay. This is a generalization, of course, but it's often the truth. We've learned that this is the way it is, to greater or lesser degrees, through our families, our education, our friendships, and our employment. Desperate to fill the void in our souls that longs for love, we begin performing for others everywhere we go, in hopes of getting the affirmation we long for in return.

Life quickly becomes that video game again. Mine felt that way before those games were even invented. I was a musician in high school, a good one. People told me I was good. And it felt good to be told that I was good. So anytime someone asked me to play for something, I would say yes. Band? Yes. Orchestra? Yes. Honor Band? Yes. Pep Band? Yes. Band to play at ice hockey games so that you can bring a date to the game for free? Of course yes. Everything was yes, and for the most part it was also enjoyable. What concerns me looking back isn't what I was doing, but the reasons for the doing. When you boil away all the fluff, the bottom line is that I had poor refusal skills, and as a result other people were writing the script of my life rather than God. In fact, any agenda God might have had for those years was quickly pushed to the margins unless it had something to do with playing percussion or piano.

If the wrong voices continue to govern, many of us will spend our entire lives busily working for the approval of others by involving ourselves in a far more scattered and stressful agenda than the one God has for us. The results of this reactive living are apparent everywhere: sleeplessness, various aches and pains, defensiveness, the phrase "I'm too busy" that appears every time we run into an acquaintance, cars and houses that are broken because we neglected basic maintenance. Though none of these are absolute indicators that we're living reactionary lives (other things can cause insomnia and backaches, for example), when these symptoms constantly recur, they might indicate we're driven by the voice of the other rather than the voice of God.

The Voice of the World

Even if no other voices are talking to us, another voice is talking to us that is more subtle, more powerful, perhaps more insidious than all the voices of our well-meaning friends and acquaintances. The Scriptures say that this voice comes in three pitches: the lust of the eyes, the lust of the flesh, and boastful pride of life[78]. These are the voices that are always lurking, rising up at inopportune times, calling us to make choices that will lead to loss and perhaps even destruction.

When our family lived in the mountains, we ran a ropes course, and one of the fun things we'd occasionally do was send someone up blindfolded. She couldn't possibly navigate the course without a voice down on the ground shouting instructions. But just to make things interesting, we'd have not only the voice of truth shouting up to the little adventurer; we'd also throw in four or five voices intent on bringing her down. They'd shout their lies as convincingly and loudly as possible, and the person had to learn to listen carefully and discern among all the voices, sifting truth from lie, wheat from chaff.

Of course, that's the way life is. The voice of lust leads us to fornicate, or eat, or shop, when we've already had enough to be satisfied. The voice of pride leads us to boast, get defensive, or lash out in anger when our reputation is threatened, even though God has already promised to be our vindication. The voice of pride also compares our own lifestyle to that of our friends and neighbors, which leads us to take on debt in order to enjoy the same things they do, which leads us to work longer hours, which leads to loss of health and intimacy with our friends and family. Why do we listen to these voices? Perhaps because we've never trained ourselves to listen to the voice of truth, a training that even Jesus Himself demonstrated could not be acquired apart from the discipline of solitude.

Solitude is an important context because of the valuable things that happen there. Let's look at a couple of them.

We Learn That We're Loved

In solitude, we become rooted in that which is most true about ourselves, our identity, and our relationship with God. In John 13, Jesus did something that obliterates all our categories and hierarchies of human relationships. He laid aside His garment, wrapped Himself in a towel, got on His knees, and began to wash the feet of His disciples. He was the teacher; they were the students. He was the leader; they were the followers. The whole thing was an assault to propriety and the senses, breaking social mores and taboos. One of Jesus' students was so offended by this that He said, "Never shall you wash my feet[79]!"

By serving His followers, He turned the social and political power structures upside down, as we've already seen in the chapter on fasting and service. But there's more. Consider the context in which He was doing this. It was happening when Jesus was about to be betrayed by one of His own, arrested, unjustly tried, beaten, and executed. He would also endure the wrath of God, poured out on Him as a means of breaking the dark curse that hung over the whole world. Being omniscient, Jesus knew all this ahead of time. Psychologists would say that such knowledge of a disastrous, painful impending future might cause Him to score high on a stress test. In such a time, a short fuse would be understandable, a breakdown defensible, an outburst of anger acceptable. Imagine the disciples' surprise when Jesus, instead of any of those things, simply began serving them by washing their feet.

Where did Jesus get this capacity to serve those He knew were about to betray and abandon Him? The answer is rooted in what He knew.

He knew about the impending suffering, but He also knew that He was about to be with His Father, that He'd come from the Father in the first place, and that He was going home. Further, He knew that the Father had given all things into His hands. It's true. You can read about it in John 13:1-3. It's the rationale given for why He put on the towel and began to wash the feet of His followers.

We might call this model of serving others "ministry from a full cup." Jesus' cup was filled by His relationship with the Father. He was at rest in the Father's love. He was committed to doing the Father's will. He was secure in His eternal destiny, knowing that He would forever be at home with the Father. What more did He need? Because of this fullness, He was able to serve.

Without a secure identity in my relationship with God, the only place I can go to have my cup filled is the world in which I live. This makes me a person in need of being served. My cup, after all, is empty, and I'm in need of the affirmation, encouragement, friendship, acceptance, guidance, and so much more that you might have to offer me. Thus do I run from relationship to relationship, seeking the fullness that I will never receive because I am asking more of people than they are capable of giving. They too have empty cups. My cup has a hole in it, as does yours, and they will never be filled until the healer of our souls plugs the leaks. Jeremiah spoke of this: "They have forsaken Me, the fountain of living waters, to hew for themselves cisterns, broken cisterns that can hold no water[80]."

Maybe that's why I spent the first two years after my dad's death in a frenzy of social and musical activity. Who would fill the cup now that Dad was gone? I was never busier, never had a fuller social calendar, and never more depressed. A year later, I would leave a worship service at a retreat and go for a walk alone in the snow. It was, looking back, my first attempt at solitude. Once I was away from the chapel I started crying. I didn't even know why. There were no words. I only knew I was needy. And there, in the snowy woods of the Sierra Nevada mountains, I felt the powerful and healing embrace of Jesus. He would come to be a friend, a source of living water, and the One I turn to again and again when my cup is empty.

I discovered that solitude is the best context in which to receive the embrace of God.

> Hear my cry, O God;
> Give heed to my prayer.
> From the end of the earth I call to You when my heart is faint;
> Lead me to the rock that is higher than I.
> For you have been a refuge for me,
> A tower of strength against the enemy (Psalm 61:1-4).

> My soul waits in silence for God only;
> From Him is my salvation.
> He only is my rock and my salvation (Psalm 62:1-2).

> Whom have I in heaven but You?
> And besides You, I desire nothing on earth.
> My flesh and my heart may fail,
> But God is the strength of my heart and my portion forever (Psalm 73:25-26).

Can you grasp the genuine joy and delight that these authors found in being consciously intimate with God? For them, at least in the moments when these words were penned, it was enough. David failed often, but he always and ultimately seemed to come back to the primacy of his relationship with God as the foundational source of joy and meaning. He who had ruled as king said that he would rather be a doorkeeper in the Lord's house for a mere day than spend ten thousand days somewhere else. Such sentiment was formed not through a didactic Bible study class but through time, lots of time, spent alone with God.

I know the glory of sleeping by myself out under the stars and gazing into the heavens, pondering infinity and learning intimacy with my Creator. In forest cathedrals my most profound cries of worship and praise have ascended to God, and on top of mountains the clearest sense of God's majesty has become real in my heart. But I needn't go that far to gain solitude. Powerful moments of worship also come as I simply sit with the Scriptures and a cup of coffee, reading and listening for the voice of Jesus.

We Hear What Needs to Be Heard

In our busy culture, we can easily misrepresent the purpose of silence. Henri Nouwen highlights this:

> We say to each other that we need some solitude in our lives. What we really are thinking of, however, is a time and place for ourselves in which we are not bothered by other people, can think our own thoughts, express our own complaints, and do our own thing, whatever it may be. For us, solitude most often means privacy...we also think of solitude as a station where we can recharge our batteries, or as the corner of the boxing ring where our wounds are oiled, our muscles massaged, and our courage restored by fitting slogans. In short, we think of solitude as a place where we gather new strength to continue the ongoing competition in life[81].

This really isn't the point, though. Consider that Jacob, in solitude, wrestled with God until he became a broken yet healed man. Or that Jesus, in solitude, sweat drops of blood and agonized over the internal conflict between His own will and that of God until finally yielding. The vision that Isaiah received in solitude led him to cry out, "Woe is me!" as he saw, perhaps for the first time, the sins of his own heart. Solitude is more than a little break from the daily grind; it's a context for transformation.

Once we stop listening to all the other voices that are out there and in there, once we come face-to-face with God, we will probably have some work to do. God will reveal things to us that we need to see. Some of them will be comforting, like the warm embrace and the assurance that we are loved. Other things will be painful, like the revelation of our misguided loyalties and those areas of life where we are refusing to trust God.

In real solitude, the scaffolding of our lives is dismantled, and without the manifold distractions that normally drown out God's voice, we are left standing naked before God. Like Adam, we're tempted to run and hide. That's one of the reasons that people who begin the disciplines of solitude and silence usually begin with five minutes a day. It's hard to handle much more than that.

Looking back, I can see that I spent a good bit of time running away from God after the death of my dad. His death seemed utterly senseless to me, and the loss was so painful that I could hardly trust that God could have good things for me. But then came that night in the Sierras, when I walked away from the crowd and wept. It was a turning point for me, because I stopped turning away from God and began turning toward Him. I needed to pour my heart out to God and share my loneliness, anger, and frustration if I was ever to experience healing. I did pour it out, and healing began. Now, solitude has become an increasingly important part of my life, both in daily rhythm and in seasonal times of intentional movement away from all noise, all media, and all agendas, simply to be with God.

And ironically, in the solitude, my cup is filled with more than enough.

Chapter 13

Hospitality

If more of us valued food and cheer and song
above hoarded gold, it would be a merrier world.
Thorin Oakenshield
The Hobbit

The 1980s brought the death of polyester leisure suits and disco, but they brought the beginning of that ubiquitous entity known as "religious broadcasting." The birth of cable TV led to an explosion in televised church services and Bible teachers, with Christianity, for the very first time, having its own channels. This phenomenon gave a few preachers and Bible teachers access to millions of homes and millions of dollars. But the power and wealth in this new industry carried the seeds of corruption, and before the decade was over, gigantic scandals surfaced. Sexual and financial meltdowns became front-page news regularly, adding fuel to the fires of skeptics and cynics everywhere.

During these days, an incident occurred while I was golfing on the small island where I was a pastor[82]. When I came into the clubhouse, the locals all stood and opened their wallets. "Hey Pastor, have you heard a message from God about how badly He needs our money?" They were mocking the scandals, but they were also making it clear that, in their minds, all of us who proclaimed Jesus' message fell into the same camp: corrupt, greedy, irrelevant hucksters.

Who could blame them? How many people hear Bible teaching, buy into what's being taught, and later discover that the teacher, isolated from his listeners, doesn't even come close to living the message he proclaims? In many cases, in fact, these celebrities' failures are the same sins they decry most in their teachings. Preaching generosity and sacrificial giving, they flit across the country in their private jets;

preaching moral purity, they seduce women and use them for their own pleasures, leaving enormous emotional wreckage in their wake.

Because of this cesspool of hypocrisy and a growing credibility crisis in the church at large, my wife and I began pursuing a different path. We were reminded of the message Paul wrote to the Thessalonian believers: "Having so fond an affection for you, we were well-pleased to impart to you not only the gospel of God but also our own lives, because you had become very dear to us" (1 Thessalonians 2:8). Do we really need more Bible teaching? It's easy to find in books, on the Internet, and on television. But in an age of cynicism, the teaching rings hollow for millions, because no one knows if or how the teachers themselves apply their publicly declared precepts in their own homes, with their own spouse, and with their own dollars.

Sensing the need to share not just teaching "but also our own lives" with people, we moved to the mountains with another couple and began a ministry of intense hospitality. We envisioned a place where people could not only study and digest teaching but also eat, work, pray, laugh, weep, and celebrate with our family. We purchased a large chalet in the Cascade Mountains and would eventually come to have 20 or 30 people around our supper table on a regular basis.

Some of our first guests included people from Switzerland I'd met while teaching at Capernwray Harbor Bible Centre in Canada. Thomas and Kathy were a delightful couple, newly married, who had devoted the first year of their marriage to traveling throughout North America. I had prepared individualized courses of study to help them work through particular issues, and these things occupied their morning hours. The afternoons consisted of either hiking or working on the property, and then they would spend each evening at the Dahlstrom family table for supper. After the meal, family and guests would linger together at the table, learning about each other's cultures and interacting regarding Christ and His role in our lives and in the world. There would also be jokes, arguments, weary kids, weary parents, tense moments, laughter that lasted until we cried, and everything else that marks family normality. This kind of pattern would be replicated hundreds of times over the next six years, as our family made hospitality a centerpiece of our lives.

At this table, our young children met people from Vietnam, Japan, Australia, China, Sweden, Germany, Austria, Switzerland, England, New Zealand, and even such distant places as Mississippi and Maryland.

One of the most difficult nights of my life was the one spent in our chalet before moving to the city to do pastoral work. I sat down at the piano to relax. As I began to play, the music brought a flood of deeply buried memories to the surface. We'd been privileged to offer hospitality to countless people during our years in the mountains, and the faces of many of them began to pass through my mind's eye: Christians, skeptics, Europeans, Asians, Americans, communists, capitalists, modernists, postmodernists, and people in the midst of finding deliverance from such diverse prisons as drug addiction, eating disorders, sexual addictions, and the effects of growing up in the midst of Satan worship. As the memories came with the music, I realized what a privilege sharing our home with so many people had been—how richly it had shaped our lives, our faith, our children. I didn't want it to end.

Hospitality. The word stems from the Latin root *hospit,* which means "guest room." In ancient days, throughout the world, the practice of hospitality made travel and trade possible and was generally expected among anyone with room and means. But hospitality has fallen on hard times these days. I gained an insight into one of the reasons for this when I met Ilke in 1993.

Ilke had grown up in former East Germany and was attending the Bible college where I was teaching. We quickly became friends and would often stay in the dining hall, talking long after the meal was over. The whole communism thing was intriguing to me, and I wanted to hear her insider's perspective. She spoke of what it was like to be a person of faith living in the midst of atheism and totalitarianism. She spoke of her surprise and the initial euphoria surrounding the dismantling of the Iron Curtain. It was, no doubt, an amazing time to be a young adult. I asked her how things were now, three years into the full-blown pursuit of the Western European lifestyle and economy.

"It's a mixture," she said without hesitating. "The freedom to worship and talk about God is awesome. And it's nice to have access to newer things and freedom to travel. But not everything has changed for the better." There was a longing in her eyes as she continued. "Under communism, our village lost power at seven each night. So all of our neighbors would go outside and gather in the streets to talk. Because of this, we knew each other, loved each other, helped each other.

"Now the power is on all the time. Each person comes home and goes inside her own house. We don't see our neighbors anymore, and it's becoming more common that we don't even know them. I guess that is what it means to be rich and free. I'd never want to go back, but there are things I desperately miss."

Of course you'll understand that this isn't about vilifying Western culture or democracy. Totalitarianism was and is one of the most destructive forces in history. But it is vitally important to understand that every blessing carries with it the possibility of becoming a curse. The blessing of wealth and freedom carries within its DNA the potential curse of isolation and loneliness. Consider the movement from neighbors convening together for conversation to the isolation of each family within their own domicile, brought to you by your local utility company.

But don't stop there. The family moves indoors and eats together around the table until they can afford a television. This new luxury dispenses with the need for conversation, even among family members. We can all watch "the tube" together, collectively numbed and isolated, even as we sit in proximity. We're still not finished. A few more dollars will buy media centers for each member of the family, with headphones! Now, no one need ever bother conversing because each person can pursue his own private world of entertainment to distract him from the inconvenience of reality.

The adults in the house needn't worry about the trials and trauma of reality either, for prosperity brings with it all sorts of diversions from the blessings and challenges of real relationships: fantasy football, soap operas, pornography, and a dozen magazines for women and

186

men to "help you be your very best self." This wealth of material at our disposal is, in reality, a great source of discouragement for millions, as they seek to measure up to culturally imposed ideals about wealth, health, education, and skin tone. Social media often contributes to the problem, filling us with a vague sense of inadequacy as we compare ourselves to these mirages. Life can often be much simpler, when connecting with real people is a priority.

Some of the best memories I have as a wealthy North American are rooted in those hours when the lights went out. I was teaching on an island in Canada one winter when a snowstorm brought not only a loss of power but a loss of phone contact too. There was nothing. My lectures were moved down to the dining hall, where we studied by candlelight and wood heat. Then there was a meal, served on paper plates. The students' cabins had only electric heat, so nobody left the room. We stayed and talked for hours and hours in the warmth of the woodstove and the glow of candlelight.

The event stands out in my mind because our culture doesn't linger well after supper. We all have important places to go, important television shows to watch, important e-mails to check, important virtual relationships to maintain. Yes, wealth has its blessings. I love having clean water, access to health care, and some space to call my own. But after a few conversations with people who've lived in poverty, I have an easier time understanding James's words: "Come now, you rich, weep and howl for your miseries which are coming upon you" (James 5:1). Maybe those miseries include isolation, depression, and the loss of relationship that comes when hospitality is displaced by the pursuit of wealth. Our faith has mutated from a communitarian experience to an individualistic pursuit, shopping for God at many churches the same way we shop for shoes at the mall. It's time to consider a better way.

The Exhortation to Hospitality

"Let love of the brethren continue. Do not neglect to show hospitality to strangers, for by this some have entertained angels without knowing it" (Hebrews 13:1-2). The hospitality theme runs deep throughout the Scriptures, because the good news, before it is anything else, is intensely relational. Everyone, it seems, is invited to share their lives with each other: Father with Son, God with us, we with each other. This promotes a vision of all creation joining together in celebration, passionate love, feasting, and worship. And none of it could occur without genuine hospitality and a spirit of generous sharing.

Consider Abraham. In the heat of the day, he sees three men passing by his tent, and he runs to meet them and asks them to stay for lunch. I love the language. "If now I have found favor in Your sight, please do not pass Your servant by" (Genesis 18:3). He goes on to tell them what a privilege it would be to give them water, wash their feet, and refresh them with some bread. I realize that the cultural differences are vast, but try to remember the last time you considered inviting strangers into your house. Okay, maybe that's too hard. When was the last time you invited your literal, physical neighbors into your home just because they're your neighbors and you want to share your life with them? Still looking for an answer? When was the last time you invited your extended family over? And was that a privilege or a burden?

Let's face it. Our driven, consumerist, modernist culture doesn't create conditions in which hospitality will come naturally. The classic movie *Christmas Vacation* reveals just how far we've traveled from the days of Abraham. The family is at rest, awaiting the arrival of relatives for the holidays. They're all lost in their individual worlds— listening to music, watching TV, slicing vegetables—when the doorbell rings. The first ring is the cheery tone that says, "The guests are finally here—now the fun can begin." But nobody answers, and so the doorbell rings again, this time at a lower pitch, less cheerful, more foreboding. This continues until the last ominous ring, which seems to say, "Ask not for whom the bell tolls, it tolls for thee." All the chaos, selfishness, greed, addiction, and passive-aggressive behaviors that mark this family are about to surface, because everyone is home for the holidays. And relief won't come until everyone goes home, sometime after January 1. No wonder we'd rather be alone.

But the Bible invites us to hospitality because to make room for others is to make visible a deep characteristic of our generous, hospitable God. We're told over and over again that "the earth is the Lord's, and all it contains," and yet we're invited to inhabit it with God[83]. We're given rains to water the earth, food to eat, sunrises, an infinity of stars to ponder, the power of thunder, the peace of a mountain stream. God has freely shared all things with us, with the intent to share not only the earth but also intimacy and love—humanity with its Creator. Now God says to us, "Freely you received, freely give[84]."

Hospitality is also vital because serving others and sharing our lives with them is an act of worship, a means whereby we serve Christ. Jesus reminds us that if we give even a "cup of cold water to drink," we won't lose our reward[85].

The Mutuality of Hospitality

I was teaching at a ski chalet one winter. The conference ended on Christmas Eve morning. Once breakfast was over, our family piled into the car and began the three-hour drive home. We hadn't traveled two miles from the camp when I attempted to drive around some snow that had avalanched off the hillside. Our car hit some black ice and began fishtailing out of control down the road. We were heading straight toward a Volvo that had also run into the black ice and was fishtailing *up* the hill.

Both cars were going slow enough that we could see the inevitable ahead as we braced for the impact, pondering our collision deductibles and preparing our stories for the police, all before we collided. But collide we did, with the result that my engine compartment was crushed, my windshield cracked, my steering column bent, and my wheel wells so twisted around the tires that the car couldn't even be pushed to the side of the road. The Volvo's grill covering its headlights fell off, marking the extent of its damage and yet another triumph for the Vikings. After a brief meeting with the police, the driver left, wishing us all a merry Christmas.

We, on the other hand, needed to wait for a tow truck to come and haul our car down the mountain, where, thankfully, we had another car. Planning to be home by noon, we were disappointed to be getting into our other car at about four in the afternoon, yet we were thankful we had a second car and would be home in time for supper. At least that's what we thought, until our alternator stopped functioning, as evidenced by the dimming of our headlights. When I opened the hood, the repair appeared easy, a simple tightening of the alternator belt with a screwdriver...*Wait, where is that screwdriver? Oh that's right, it's in the other car. The totaled car. No problem, Richard, you can buy yourself a screwdriver at the next car shop or borrow one from a mechanic or maybe stop at a grocery store for one.* These are all good plans on any night except Christmas Eve, the one night when everyone is home drinking warm beverages and singing songs about having a merry little Christmas.

It's a long story, but we finally arrived home about 11:00 p.m., mortified that we'd ruined Christmas Eve for our guests. As we pulled into the driveway, we saw the lights of our Christmas tree in our chalet window and knew that our guests were still awake. How kind of them. As I walked upstairs, hungry, humbled, and bone tired, I wondered if I could get to the bedroom without saying hello to anyone.

But it was not to be. Instead, we opened the door and walked into a room fully prepared for a Christmas Eve feast. The table was set, candles lit, and food warm, having just been prepared by our friends from Australia and Sweden (she had a good laugh about the Volvo), who were there to enjoy an American Christmas. *Are you kidding? You waited for us? You cooked for us? You held off your own celebration so that you could celebrate with us?* In an instant, the grime of the day was washed away, as we settled down and enjoyed an incredible meal with our friends before going to bed early Christmas morning.

I don't keep score, but my instinct tells me that when people get in the habit of practicing hospitality, they will say they receive far more from their guests than they give out. Nearly every guest at the table has a story, has special gifts to bless others, has hurts that need healing, has battles being fought, has storehouses of laughter and pain, and so much more. One of the things I love about Jesus is the way He seems to flatten out the hierarchies in our lives, so that instead of vacillating between feelings of pride when we're on top and shame when we're on the bottom, we sense the humble mutuality that pervades wholesome relationships. We're aware that we're giving and serving, but also we have this sneaking suspicion that on the whole, we're receiving more than we give. This is as it should be.

The Challenge of Hospitality

On the other hand, not every Christmas with guests looks like a Budweiser commercial or Currier and Ives painting. Francis and Edith Schaeffer were a generation ahead of the rest in seeing the desperate need for hospitality as the richest soil in which the invisible God is made visible. But they didn't romanticize the cost:

> L'Abri is costly. If you think what God has done here is easy, you don't understand. It's a costly business to have a sense of community. L'Abri cannot be explained merely by the clear doctrine that is preached; it cannot be explained by the fact that it has been giving answers to questions. I think those two things are important, but L'Abri cannot be explained if you remove the third. And that is there has been some community here. And it has been costly.

> In about the first three years of L'Abri, almost all our wedding presents were wiped out. Our sheets were torn. Holes were burned in our rugs. Indeed once a whole curtain almost burned up from somebody smoking in our living room[86].

In our years of hospitality, we too have seen the cost. A young woman who stayed with us was tormented by the forces of darkness and often woke us up in the middle of the night. Sometimes she was screaming. Sometimes she was banging her head against the concrete walls in the basement. Carrying her pain and battling with her for her freedom was wearying but worth every breath, every interruption of sleep.

Other guests were greedy or overly critical. One woman, at the end of her stay, sat at the table with our entire staff and offered harsh criticism of our ministry team, articulating details of how she'd been mistreated by each of them. Then she summarized her life by saying, "I've found that I only really get along well with plants and animals." Frankly, though we felt sympathy for this bitter and broken woman, we struggled to keep from laughing. Yes, plants and animals suited her well, the former having no discernible will of their own, the latter too wild to be tamed. She left, and we all sat at the table looking at each other, realizing that her presence had been some sort of emotional hypodermic, drawing down our stores of energy. Hospitality means making space for these ones too.

Jesus said that if you invite to your house only people who you know will invite you to their house in return, you really haven't accomplished very much, though perhaps it's a start (Luke 14:12-13). The real challenge and real blessing come from offering hospitality to those who can never repay you. But that, of course, is right where the rub comes, because you don't really know how to gear up for such hospitality.

We also had church in our living room, so our home had a de facto reputation among some of the upper river valley residents as being open 24/7. It wasn't really true, but it felt that way for some. One Christmas Eve morning, I was hanging out with my nephews and niece from California, when a man came roaring up the driveway in his old car. He got out, slammed the car door shut, and ran upstairs to the area that served as our living room and dining room and sanctuary, where our Christmas tree stood. He had a crazed, stoned look, wearing shades and carrying a gun. I knew he wasn't out caroling.

He informed us that our Christmas tree was a phallic symbol, and the fact that we had one proved that we were idol worshippers. I was a little worried that he'd do something with the weapon that would spoil Christmas for everyone (poke his eye out, perhaps), so I invited

192

him to go with me for a walk. We went outside and talked, and eventually he calmed down a little bit, apologized, and drove down the road. He came back often in ensuing months and eventually told us that the hospitality he found at our house was one of the few safe places in his life.

We must all take steps to open up our lives to people who are outside our normal sphere of comfort. Paul says that one of the dramatic effects of Christ's new way of living is that it will tear down the walls between people that exist in this fallen world[87]. This kind of deep hospitality pushes all of us out of our comfort zone. It includes risk and inconvenience.

On the other hand, a fullness comes to our lives when we take Jesus' exhortations regarding hospitality literally. We meet people whose gifts will bless and strengthen us. We learn about how big our God is and how beautiful and broken is our world.

Do You Want Room with That?

When I first moved to Seattle, I didn't know that people who drink coffee have their own special vocabulary. Short, double shot, tall, skinny, grande, venti. The whole thing seemed ridiculous to me, and I always order plain black coffee anyway, so I wasn't worried. But then, when I ordered my coffee, the barista said, "Do you want room with that?"

Room? What is that supposed to mean? I quickly shook my head in the negative as if I knew the implications. When the coffee arrived, filled to within a millimeter of the cup's top, I divined that "room," had I asked for it, would have provided room for a little cream.

Yes, I thought, *room would be nice.* I wasn't thinking of my coffee, though. I was thinking of life in the city. Families scatter to the wind as their children consume activities and their parents produce dollars and consume even more activities. Then they all gather at home, dropping into their separate worlds, exhausted, only to begin the same routine again the next day. I don't think the jury's still out on this lifestyle. Isolation, depression, heart disease, addictive behavior—these are the fruits of our driven, individualistic lives. So why do we continue down this road?

Perhaps we continue because making room for relationship necessitates moving into terrifying space. Real hospitality leads to real relationships, and these lead us to places where our pain and shame are exposed, where truth telling and forgiveness are vital, where intimacy becomes real. Skipping all that is far easier, and one of the most popular roads bypassing the practice of hospitality is busyness. If we're busy, we can convince ourselves that we'd like to be hospitable, but we simply don't have time.

Try making time. Try reserving one night a week for hospitality. Try providing enough space in your life to listen between the lines to people's stories, hearing not only their words but their hearts as well. Try it. You'll find much more than you were seeking.

Chapter 14

Silence

The purpose of a fish trap is to catch fish and when the fish are caught, the trap is forgotten. The purpose of a rabbit snare is to catch rabbits. When the rabbits are caught, the snare is forgotten. The purpose of the word is to convey ideas. When the ideas are grasped, the words are forgotten. Where can I find a man who has forgotten words? He is the one I would like to talk to.

Chuang Tzu[88]

For many of us, solitude comes easier than silence. After all, people are sometimes a bother, and our personalities shy away from the inevitable conflict that honest relationships bring. Besides, we have jobs that surround us with people, so some of us welcome solitude as a gift. "Yes. Of course I like solitude. I need those times to recharge my battery and get my bearings again." I've heard many people say this.

Silence, on the other hand, doesn't come so easily. I have a commitment to regular times away from people in order to pray, write, and study. These times are refreshing indeed. The place I go has no Internet access, no radio, and no TV. I'm in solitude, and this comes naturally to me. But the same cannot be said of silence. In fact, when I go into seclusion, the first thing I want to do is turn on some music. I always bring music, my companion in solitude. On the way to the mountains, I'll stop and pick up a copy of the local newspaper. I always bring a bag or two of books. And I'll often watch a movie or two, just in case God has nothing to say to me through the entire Bible, prayer, and the wonders of creation.

What is the value of silence? Why do the wisdom of Proverbs, the warnings of James, and the classic teachings of the church ranging from the desert fathers to the Quakers all invite us to nurture this forgotten discipline?[89] Why is silence so threatening to me, to us?

The threat, in part, lies in the flood of words in our modern world. From the moment we wake until the final seconds before the lights go out—and even sometimes long after that—our lives are filled with words and noise: magazines, television, radio, the Internet, e-mail, billboards, an avalanche of advertising, movies, plays, books.

This ocean of words has become our native environment. We have adapted to it so well that silence is no longer golden, but threatening. Our hand instinctively reaches for the radio when we get in the car. When we sit to eat a meal alone, we instinctively reach for something to read. To just be, alone and in silence, is a distinctly foreign posture these days.

Words are the norm in our time and place. Digesting, filtering, and disseminating them is what many of us do with most of our waking moments. But when the market is flooded with words, as with any commodity, they lose their value. So we stop listening. When we stop listening, words are stripped of their power to do the one thing for which they exist: communicate.

We find ourselves, as result of this flood, in a moment of history when there is a great deal of noise, but very little effective communication. Simon and Garfunkel alluded to this a generation ago, when they sang of the "sounds of silence." They invited us to notice the multitudes of people who were talking without speaking, hearing without listening. Too many words will do that to you.

This same discomfort with silence is revealed in our propensity to speak too quickly. I know that many are uncomfortable with any gaps of silence in a conversation. Thus we feel the need to fuel the fires with words, anecdotes, questions, factoids, observations, and subtle boastings. We're always talking, and even when other people are talking, we're often busy concocting what we're going to say next. This is true in spite of the fact that the Bible wisely declares "everyone must be quick to hear, slow to speak and slow to anger" (James 1:19).

"Quick to hear" implies that the inner noise of my own heart must be quiet so I can actually enter into what the other person is saying, listening with my whole being in order to gain the real meaning of what is being communicated. "Slow to speak" implies that even when the other is finished using words, I need feel no obligation to let spill out the first thing that rises to the surface. But in order to move into this way of relating to others, I must become comfortable with silence.

And comfortable is the one thing I fear I will never be. The reasons go deeper than modernity's flood of words. They have to do with the nature of the human heart. If you'll try something for a moment, you'll discover what I mean. When you're finished reading this paragraph, set this book down and sit upright, making yourself comfortable. Turn off all music, phones, and other noise makers. Begin to pay attention to your breath as you slowly inhale and then exhale. Count your breaths. Your first exhale is number one. Your first inhale is number two, and so on. Keep going until you reach 50. Quiet your mind, so that your only focus is on this single phrase: *The Lord is my shepherd.*

Did you even do it, or did you skip the exercise altogether? And if you did it, was it comfortable? I didn't think so. Your mind may have gone something like this: *The Lord is my shepherd. Sheep. I remember that my in-laws' neighbors had sheep when they lived in northern California. They ate them! I haven't been to northern California in a long time. The last time I was there I went bass fishing. I want to learn fly fishing. Scott fly fishes. I'd better talk with him today. I wonder how he's doing? I know a dentist named Scott. I need to get my teeth cleaned. Wait, wasn't I supposed to be doing an exercise in silence? I'm not sure I like this book. I know another book I need to read, but I haven't ordered it yet because my Internet's down and my phone battery is running low. How will I get my e-mail? Wait, wasn't I supposed to be doing an exercise in silence?* Isn't this fun?

We have a thousand reasons not to engage in the discipline of silence. It's too Eastern. It's too Catholic. It's too mystical. It's too impractical. But these excuses are all rubbish. The vacuous silence of Eastern mysticism is different from the kind of silence to which we're invited through the Bible. In contrast to seeking an absolute vacuum, we are carving out space to listen for the voice of our Creator, who will speak to us, is speaking to us frequently, if we'll but stop the whirlwind of words long enough to receive. We seek God's voice and a conscious awareness of His presence. This is a common undertaking throughout the whole span of church history. To neglect it because we have a major disagreement with some group that happens to practice it is illogical, narrow-minded, and dangerous to our own maturity. The real reason why so many of us don't practice the discipline of silence is usually less theological and more practical: It's too difficult, too counter to our addiction to productivity.

My car sometimes makes a clicking noise. It's sporadic, so I've never bothered to discover what the real problem is. But it still bothers me. I don't like hearing strange noises coming from under the hood. Not being mechanically inclined, I like to turn the radio up when the clicking noise begins. Presto! Problem solved! This seems be the paradigm we use in our relationship with God as well, and it is why we're prone to shy away from silence.

We have a track record of running from God. It stretches all the way back to the garden, where Adam heard God's voice and was afraid, so he ran and hid. We've been running ever since, and one of the best ways of running is to simply turn up the volume of everything else in my life so that we can't hear His voice. This dynamic kicks on all by itself, as the previous exercise reveals. Even when I'm sitting alone in a room in absolute silence, the volume of noise in my mind spontaneously gets louder, which absolves me from responding to God's calling. I can't respond to what I don't hear, right?

Actually, *not* right. Jesus' prevailing complaint during His day was that even though people had ears, they weren't listening to what God was saying. Though they had eyes, they weren't seeing. We can go through life in such a way that the revelation God is offering us is drowned out by a sea of white noise. Our ambivalence toward intimacy creates this tendency in us to run when things get too exposed, too vulnerable, too honest. We're afraid that the searing honesty will hurt us. Actually, exposure to such a flame will only burn away the dross, but we don't necessarily believe that. So we remain afraid to listen and fill the void into which God speaks with a million other things.

"More volume" was my paradigm until a few years ago when, by God's grace, a couple began attending our church who took the discipline of silence seriously. They'd invited me to their home, and I will never forget the first time I walked through their door. They were gracious, hospitable, and very kind, and a sense of peace filled their home. As we began to talk, I realized that this couple practiced the discipline of silence on a regular basis. They invited me to join them. I resisted at first for all the reasons I've already articulated. But they were persistent, and their thorough understanding of the role of silence and contemplation in church history was compelling. I eventually gave in and agreed to come and sit with them for five minutes of silence.

It didn't feel like five minutes. It felt like five hours. My mind wandered in a million different directions. In our debrief, they assured me that this was normal and that when the mind wandered, it was best to quietly call it back to a conscious awareness of Christ. They told me learning to sit silently is a discipline, and as with any discipline, I would gain skill through consistent practice. I'm sad to say that I wasn't very consistent in meeting with them. But I created a space at home for the practice of silence, a little alcove in the attic. And since that time, I've tried to develop a consistent practice of silence. It has been both the most rewarding and most challenging discipline of all.

The rewards come because in these moments when I seek to make myself consciously aware of Christ's presence, God speaks to me most powerfully, peeling away layers of defense in order to reveal the areas where I'm most in need of transformation. Sometimes I'm reminded that I'm loved, whole, and secure in my relationship with God, and the silence is encouraging, affirming, healing. Other times I'm offered a word of challenge or correction or rebuke, and I need to repent, to break the bonds of some sin that has a grip on me. Still other times, I find needed direction and wisdom.

The challenge comes because sometimes nothing at all seems to happen. At other times, I battle with a flood of lies, the voices of condemnation that I so easily believe. And I always struggle with distraction. Every time I try to be quiet, my mind wanders down enticing side roads, distracting me from the still small voice that I need to hear. Because of this, I sometimes feel as if I'm wasting my time. But stepping back and looking at the larger picture, I see clearly that this little discipline is never a waste of time. These five, ten, or—on a good day—fifteen minutes have become some of the most important moments in my day. I'm providing space in my life to listen to what God is saying to me all day long: that I'm loved by God, forgiven, accepted, and blessed. In these silent moments, I see once again that life isn't just a whirlwind of consumption, fear, and anger. Rather, life is about stepping into God's invitation to be a blessing, using the gifts we've been given to offer hope, beauty, healing, justice, reconciliation, truth, and celebration to all.

Nurturing the Sounds of Silence

We swim in a sea of noise, so the development of silent spaces in our lives won't come without intentionality. But intentionality doesn't require complexity or bigness. We can start by turning off the radio in the car, drinking our morning coffee or walking slowly in silence. In the silence, we can pray for our friends and family as God brings them to mind. In our praying, we offer God space to bring a sense of conviction or direction regarding our involvement in their lives.

Simple steps such as these, when done consistently, often become valuable enough that we find ourselves wanting to create still more silent spaces. Perhaps this entails the creation of a place in your home devoted to prayer and waiting on God, or simply an increased commitment to the silent spaces you've already created. (*All right then. I'll keep the radio off on the way* home *from work too.*) The addition of silent spaces and intentional listening for God's voice should become an increasingly natural part of your journey and transformation.

Eventually, you'll want to spend an hour in silence and solitude, or even a whole day. The silence isn't really a total vacuum. It's more of what the psalmist calls *selah*, a space into which you allow the revelation of God to settle. This revelation penetrates into the deeper recesses of your being and changes your life at the most foundational levels. Because of this, silence should be interspersed with Scripture reading and prayer, both of which become contexts for God to speak to you.

When I was preaching a series on spiritual disciplines, I decided it would be the height of irony to talk for 40 minutes about silence. So we had a silent sermon instead, whereby congregants sat in the chapel while various scriptures were displayed on a screen for their meditation. Such a large race of silence was difficult for everyone in the room. Make no mistake. It was also, for many, transformative. Giving God space to speak, though, will change us.

The regular practice of silence seems to create in us some very different ways of living:

A different way of being with people. Practitioners of silence are often better listeners, as the habits that have enabled them to listen to God better also make them more effective in listening to people. I have a friend with whom I meet every six weeks or so. We share what's going on in our ministries and what God has been teaching us, and I always feel heard when I'm with this man. He listens thoroughly and thoughtfully, asking questions and absorbing matters deeply before he responds. Such friendships are golden, and I seek wise counsel from such people. I don't want to hear the answers people have for me unless I'm convinced they've taken the time to really listen for the question. Such listening skills are forged in the discipline of silence, which my friend practices on a regular basis.

A different way of organizing. We've already seen that Jesus' ministry agenda was constructed according to something other than conventional wisdom. More than once He made choices that could be described as spectacularly inefficient. The only explanation for this was that He was marching to the beat of a different drummer. As we listen for the rhythms of grace, we too will make decisions that defy the norms. Some such decisions will lead to downward mobility, nonviolence, or lavish generosity. Who voluntarily moves into the inner city, living in the same condition as impoverished neighbors?

Who settles in contested neighborhoods in the Middle East, offering hospitality to both warring factions in hopes of being a voice for peace? Who spends their vacation working in an orphanage in Albania? In every case, the answer is the same: those who have ears to hear what God is saying to them. A cacophony of voices are shouting at us, "Taste me. Buy me. Use me. Sleep with me." Only with disciplined silence can we hear the voice that matters most.

A different way of responding. Revelation and response are separated by a moment. The difficulty is that for many of us the moment is nothing more than a nanosecond. *React* is often a more accurate word than *respond* in many of our lives. To the extent that I'm uncomfortable with that empty space, uncomfortable with waiting, I will move to fill the space with words or actions prematurely. But of course that space, that waiting, is where more wisdom and revelation from God are often gained. That's why those who are comfortable with silence speak less and more slowly. But when they speak, people listen.

A group of us were considering various members of a task force, and when one person's name came up someone said, "He's so quiet. I rarely hear him say anything." But someone else quickly added, "Yes. But when he speaks, people actually listen, unlike…" Well, you don't really want to hear the rest of that sentence. The point is that those of us who have flooded the market with our own words have diminished the value of the commodity. Those who choose their words carefully, on the other hand, are honored in the highest places. That's why Proverbs says, "When there are many words, transgression is unavoidable, but he who restrains his lips is wise" (Proverbs 10:19).

The Warning Label

Perhaps no discipline practiced by the church has been more fraught with misunderstanding than silence. I have mentioned many of these charges, and I responded with the sweeping generalization that to practice silence is to stand in the same stream as the great saints of the Bible and church history. Unfortunately, the full answer is not quite that simple.

Each of us have recordings that play in our head and, even deeper, at some subconscious level. These recordings tell us who we are and what we can do to make our lives better, or at least less painful. The trouble with these recordings is that many of them include a pile of lies. We have messages telling us that we can never be loved because…(insert your list of failures here). We have messages telling us that we can be loved but only if we…(again, insert a list of things you must do, ranging from making more money, to having larger breasts, to praying more, to…the choices are nearly infinite, as are the ways to feel inadequate). We have recordings telling us that we're just fine, that all of our problems are caused by…(insert a list of people who have failed you in both significant and insignificant ways over the course of a lifetime. The list can be long and quite detailed). These messages are all lies, but somewhere along the way, many of us picked them up and began playing them as a means of coping with the darker portions of our lives.

The problem with the discipline of silence is that it can be quite fertile ground for these recordings to play, loud and unhindered, cementing these lies ever more deeply into the foundations of our soul. That they are lies leaves me with little doubt regarding their origin. That the antidote is truth is also plain to see. We're told that we are transformed by the renewing of our mind[90].

That's why silence and solitude aren't recommended as stand-alone disciplines. They clear the decks of our mind and heart so that God's Word can bathe us, heal us, and empower us to live freely. But all of that is predicated on God's Word being available as a ready resource so that God can bring to mind the truths we need and fill the silent places with them. It's kind of like, "You shouldn't take vitamin Y until you've been taking vitamin X for a little while." Silence is vitamin Y. Immersion in the Word is vitamin X. Any questions?

Chapter 15

Gathered Worship

Worship is a way of seeing the world in the light of God.

Abraham Heschel

The evidence shows that religious people—as defined by regular attendance at a place of worship—actually do make better neighbors.

Jonathan Sacks

The core of the person is what he or she loves, and that is bound up with what they worship.

Dallas Willard

When I was in college, I had a job as the office manager in a warehouse for a little while. I was surrounded by truck drivers, welders, forklift operators, and machinists, all of whom worked with steel. I'd receive orders and push them out to "the floor" where they were dealt with, eventually ending up on trucks for delivery throughout the valley. As with any job, I learned as much from the work friendships formed as I did from doing my actual job. Take Pete, for example.

He was my supervisor, hardworking, just, funny, and as foul-mouthed as anyone I'd ever met. He made the warehouse thrive, bringing order where there should have been chaos, teamwork where there should have been backbiting and gossip, and fun where summer heat and winter cold should have alternately melted or frozen any sense of joy in the midst of what was largely a cacophony of mundane tasks.

Pete and I became decent friends over time, enough that I learned about his family, kids, and hopes for the future. He knew about me, too; my studies in architecture, the death of my dad, my loneliness and depression that seemed to have me in a vice grip at the time. We had lots of hours together in the office, so we talked. Most of the conversations have long since evaporated, forgotten in the ether of time and space. There's one, though, that remains. Pete spent some time one afternoon, not trying to understand my faith, or my declarations about Jesus. "Those things" he said, "I can see how people believe them. But," he continued, his brow furrowed with real confusion, "I'll never understand why you people go to church. Why would you waste an entire day each week to go sit and listen to someone tell you how bad you are and how you need to live better, and then what? Don't they make you pay before you leave? Why the hell would anyone do that?" He wasn't being sarcastic. He really wanted to know.

Why indeed. Lots of people on the inside are asking the same questions as Pete, only they maybe leave the swearing out of the question. They wonder why we gather, in part because we're living in a time when we expect more from gathered worship than it was ever intended to deliver. At the same time, our gatherings themselves are often failing to deliver the very things they're intended to provide, things for which our souls rightly thirst.

While working at that warehouse, I was in the midst of a bit of a faith desert. Numerous deaths in the family had led to depression and a bit of cynicism, which led to some health issues, too. Still, I usually managed to find my way to Sunday worship most weeks. It was boring more often than meaningful, and the dissonance between the doubts and discouragements of my own life and the smooth flowing easy answers that rolled off the tongues of my peers left me feeling isolated. In spite of those things, for reasons I don't fully understand, I continued to go, continued to gather with other people and sing "Amazing Grace," and then open my Bible and listen to the old pastor explain whatever it was he was trying so hard to convey on any given Sunday. At night, at the end of the service, the room would go dark, leaving visible only the big cross up front, backlit with blue neon lights for effect. Then, once the darkness had settled, we'd all sing "Beneath the Cross of Jesus," and I'd think about the words, wondering if "God on the cross" really happened or not, while at the same time being thankful for the sense that, in all the universe, perhaps someone cared enough about humanity, in fact, even cared enough about me, to die for us. Doubt and faith intermingled in my soul nearly every time we sang, and I was haunted, in the best sense of the word, by the beauty of it. Then I'd walk out into the night, maybe get ice cream with friends, before hitting the reset button on Monday morning, and starting life over yet again.

I never thought about why I was doing this. I can say definitively that I wasn't doing it for the "wow factor" or the social connections. The best way to describe the gravitational pull of gathered worship for me is found in a little phrase in Psalm 42 where I'm told that "deep calls to deep." Though I'm a pastor, I'm not astute enough to know what that idiomatic language might have meant to the original Hebrew hearers, but I know my own soul well enough to know what it means to me. The space where gathered worship happened for me during those dark years after my dad's death was the same space where I'd "gone to church" since before I could walk. Because of this, things had happened in that space which were significant in shaping me.

"Significant" might be a misleading word, for you might end up thinking that I'd walked in some Sundays and the earth shook, if not literally, then at least metaphorically, and I came out knowing I'd been changed. Maybe you'd think people were weeping, and there were powerful prayer moments with demons being cast out, or miracles even. That sounds significant, and it would be. Except we were baptists. The most excitement inside the walls that I can recall was when drums were allowed in the sanctuary on youth Sunday.

What I mean by significant things happened in that space, was that over time I became grounded in something bigger than me—bigger than our church even. I'd marveled, even back then, that people had been gathering like this in order to celebrate, worship, talk about, and remember Jesus since the first century. It was astonishing to me. Through the fall of the Roman empire and Europe's descent into darkness, through the Renaissance and Europe's flowering of the arts and intellect, through religious wars and the Black Plague, the rise and fall of kings and emperors, the invention of the printing press, and the first steps on the moon—no matter what, people kept gathering to remember Jesus. When I gathered, knowing that I was doing something that had been done for 2,000 years gave me a sense of rootedness. After all, my personal world was imploding through the death of many family members and my graduation from the cocoon of high school. The bigger world had lost its anchor, too. Watergate. Cambodia. Long lines at the gas pumps. Polyester leisure suits. Nothing was certain anymore.

Nothing except for this: People of faith gather weekly to remind each other of Jesus. I did it, even during my darkest moments of doubt, because even in the midst of my unbelief, I still wanted to believe. The "deep" of my longing to believe—of my longing for a better world, of my longing to be a better person—that "deep" was calling out to the "deep" of Christ with every song, every recitation of prayer, every hearing of every word spoken, however imperfectly, about Jesus. Deep calls to deep. So we gather.

In particular though, certain things happen when we gather that can *only* happen when we gather. These are worth pondering, because they invite us to swim upstream against the streams of hyper individualism and consumerism that are robbing so many of the rich life of community, intimacy, and interdependence for which we're all created.

Gathering Encourages Others

We suffer under the misunderstanding that our withdrawal from a community is our loss alone. This is often because we both fear we have nothing to give, and because we've approached the community as consumers, seeking ultimately to gain something from our participation. In reality, our physical presence is enough, even if we never speak to another person, to encourage. I've gathered with saints on five continents, and every time, I'm encouraged. Sometimes the music in these gatherings is sub-par, or at the least not according to my tastes. The preaching is often in a language I don't understand, and the cultural variations range from what appears to be such sterile formality that I wonder if the congregants have died during worship, all the way to dancing in the aisles, copious tears, and uproarious joy. Cut through all of the variety though, and all the issues of personal taste ("too big," "too slick," "too sloppy," "too long," "too traditional," "too post-modern") and one common thread that is the same everywhere is this: people are encouraged (or should be) by the reality that others are worshipping too.

Let's face it. There's a sense in which we're shooting the moon in our pursuit of this Jesus stuff. We're staking our lives on the belief that, because of what happened on a cross, and later in a tomb, two millennia ago, the entire course of history has changed its trajectory. Love will, in the end, win. Peace will reign, and death, disease, war, human trafficking, slavery, racism, plague, drought, famine, and all the rest that is ugly will eventually come crashing down, falling into the fires of Mt. Doom to be destroyed forever. We stake our lives on this, but then wake up to another report of a car driven through the middle of a plaza in Europe, or a bomb exploding at a marathon, or sarin gas here, or a nuclear bomb test there. "Really?" we ask ourselves, wondering if the whole enterprise is nothing more than a joke after all. At least some of us wonder, some of the time.

But then we gather, and we run into a friend that's moved to Central America to help empower women trapped in prostitution. Someone else is grieving as their spouse grows weary with chemotherapy. All of us are world-weary because of race riots and political cynicism, financial uncertainty and relationship tensions. Then we stand and say the Lord's Prayer, or maybe recite the Apostle's Creed. There's Millie, unable to stand because of her illness, eyes closed, facing heavenward and saying, "for Yours is the kingdom, and the power, and glory forever—Amen" and I shiver with joy because Millie believes it, along with Don, Janice, Hakeem, and all the others in this room and a hundred thousand more like it. I'm not alone.

Not being alone doesn't make my beliefs true, of course. But the reality is that we're shaped by those in our circles. Spend time with marathoners and you'll start running, with hikers and you'll start looking at polar fleece jackets, with vegans and you'll give up bacon. It's an almost inviolable principle that we both shape and are shaped by the communities to which we belong. But only if we show up.

This is what the author meant by "encouraging one another" in Hebrews 11. We tend to think that encouragement comes through profound words, but usually it comes through the simple act of presence.

Can you see how this flies in the face of our increasing involvement in virtual communities, including virtual church? "I get fed by listening to podcasts while I run, so I don't really 'go to church' anymore." Congratulations. You're fed. If eating were the goal of your faith, you'd be done. The truth, though, is that you're wired to bless and encourage others, and that happens through the ministry of presence, just plain showing up as a means of saying "this matters in my life; it's worth the effort."

Gathering Makes Christ Visible

While Jesus walked on the earth, he offered humanity a perfect display of human potential. Humans, Jesus taught us, can cross social divides, be instruments of healing and reconciliation, challenge others to choose the high road, lay down their lives as a means of loving and blessing others, and live courageously, generously, and joyfully, always allowing nothing less than the life of God to pour through us into like a river in desert lands of despair and darkness.

Jesus departed, though. His followers were left staring at the sky, in all likelihood perplexed, but not without guidance. Jesus had hinted that, after His physical departure, He'd keep showing up in this tired world. "Wherever two or three are gathered in my name, there I am in the midst[91]." Then Paul the apostle developed the concept further, explaining that even though Jesus' body left the earth physically, He still has a body here on earth. That body, containing nothing less than the resurrected spirit of Christ, is healing, serving, reconciling, inviting, advocating for justice, giving generously to those in need, blessing, forgiving those who have failed, and laying down his life in millions of small ways.

Paul explained that each Christ follower is a unique, yet partial, expression of the resurrected Jesus. One excels at hospitality, another at leadership. One has a heart for the downtrodden and gifts of mercy, while another has a knack for telling the truth in ways that people will receive. One can teach, another can serve. Stated positively, this means that we're better together, that Christ is seen with more and more clarity as each person uses their unique gifts to express Christ in ways that only they can.

Maybe you're old enough to remember dial-up Internet and modems? If so, you remember that when you downloaded a picture, your first viewings of it would be tragically distorted, nothing more than a few boxes of various color shades thrown together, seemingly randomly. But as your phone chattered unintelligibly, more and more pixels would be added and the picture would slowly gain clarity. It was a sort of visual version of "wheel of fortune," with every added pixel granting more certainty until you were finally able to see: it's a picture of Jesus!

This, friends, is not only an apt description of church life, it's an apt description of why churches have consistently failed to represent Christ accurately. The church's tragic caricatures of Jesus can be summarized this way: not enough pixels. When the justice and love Christ has for all people was removed from the church, great travesties were carried out in his name. Racism, colonialism, anti-Semitism, and unspeakable violence were perpetrated and what the world saw looked nothing like the real Jesus. Take Jesus' servant heart out of the picture, and you create a classist church. Take away Jesus' commitment to non-violence, and you create a church that carries out countless wars in Jesus' name. Take away any particular pixel, and the picture of Christ that ought to be the church suffers distortion.

The crux of the matter is simple then. Each of us is a pixel. As such we're utterly inadequate to represent Christ on our own. Equally true is the reality that without our contribution, the entire picture is distorted, which is a way of saying that the failure of any single individual to show up, serve, and use their gifts for the good of the whole becomes a loss, not just for that person, but for the whole church. It becomes, as Paul would say, like a body without an eye, or an ear, or a hand, or, God forbid, a liver. You and I both have important parts to play in making Christ visible in our world, and playing our parts requires showing up.

Gathering Builds Community

Dan Buettner, in his groundbreaking work studying those places in the world that boast the highest percentage of healthy, long-living people, made the discovery that, of the 263 centenarians he interviewed, scattered across four continents, only five didn't belong to a faith community. While "faith community" can mean many things, including faiths outside of Christianity, what's apparent is that all faiths invoke regular gatherings as part of their culture, and with at least one good reason that runs like a common thread through them all. Relationships.

When we gather, we form relationships. It doesn't matter if the gathering is a few people in someone's house, or thousands in a cathedral; those who continue to gather regularly form relationships, and relationships, when they function as they should, are like oxygen. They're life-giving.

When I was in Rwanda, we interviewed a woman who'd been through immense darkness during the genocide of 1994, leaving her with physical, spiritual, and emotional scars that were still in the process of healing, decades after the events. She shared that some days the darkness of soul created such a weight and depth of despair in her that she found it impossible to get out of bed. She was a single mother with small children, though, and both they and the village needed what she had to offer, since the water purification system for her neighbors was in her living room. When I asked her what happened when she felt so overwhelmed, she simply said, "My church friends come through the front door, walk into my bedroom, and get me out of bed" adding, "I don't know where I'd be without them." She said this matter-of-factly, as if walking into your friend's house and compelling them out of bed were somehow normal.

It might be normal there, but we suffer in our land of great wealth from immense relational poverty and isolation. Mother Teresa said that the deepest poverty is relational, not material, and that America, according to such a criteria, is one of most impoverished places in the world. What seeps into relationally impoverished cultures is a sense that our lives don't matter to anyone and that our presence or absence doesn't make a difference in the lives of others.

Armed with such a mindset, we withdraw, and our withdrawal furthers our sense of isolation which increases our tendency to withdraw. A vicious cycle is set in place that makes isolation the default position. Those who gather regularly, though, become known by others, if not in the first week of participation, at least over time if the church community is anything more than a worship-dispensing machine. We begin to believe that others need us, that we have something to give. We begin, also, to believe that we need others. We slowly embrace the truth that sharing life together, praying together, raising children together, and growing old together in the context of weekly reminding each other of the things that matter most, is worth the investment of time, even though some weeks it's a hassle, or boring, or "not meeting my needs." We become weaned from our lust for the spectacular, and learn to value the unseen fabric of shared life that is invisible, woven week after week simply by the ministry of presence.

Just Do It

Jesus began speaking publicly when, according to Luke 3, he went to the synagogue on the Sabbath day, "as was his custom." The practice of gathering with others on a weekly basis has not only been around a long time, it was a regular practice for Jesus. All of us build our lives around big activities, and then fit everything of secondary value in the cracks. For some, football is the big thing on Sunday, or outdoor activities, if the weather's nice. I know this because I'm a pastor, and I see our attendance for weekly worship fluctuate based on football and weather, indications that perhaps gathering with others for worship is a secondary activity, something to fill in the gaps when gaps are available.

Jesus, by example, suggests otherwise. He suggests that the regular weekly gathering is God's idea, instituted because every person has both something to give and something to receive through worshipping together. Because of this, there's a real loss when we fail to gather regularly. What's difficult, though, is that the loss isn't always palpable, any more than there's a real sense of loss when I indulge and have ice cream for supper instead of a balanced meal, or when I stay up until the middle of the night because of a party. You might not notice any immediate effects from making bad choices, at least not for a while. In fact, skipping the regular gathering might feel really good in the moment, like a bowl of ice cream for supper, or choosing TV and chips instead of the gym. The impact over time, however, is real. Others miss out on your presence, which is priceless in itself, even if you don't do or say anything. You also miss out on what others have to offer.

Missing out on the eternal perspective and the unspoken reality that there are others who also believe will, over time, have a subtle corroding effect. In the Psalms, Asaph notes that, lacking the eternal perspective, a skewed view of the world began taking root, a view that says that seeking God and living by faith are a waste of time. Asaph declares that this increasingly dark view of the world that had taken hold was "troublesome in my sight" but then adds, "until I came into the sanctuary of God[92]." He's not saying that gathering in a building with others in various states of faith is magic. He's not saying its always easy. What he is saying is that gathering regularly makes a big difference over time, but it takes time, like changing your eating habits. You don't eat a single salad and watch your cholesterol level drop overnight. Most changes happen slowly.

I attended a small church in the mountains where I live during a recent weekend when I was on holiday. There were, at most, 30 people in the room. The music was from an old songbook, and other than the internal speakers in the electric piano, there was no sound system. No "latest and greatest" anything, just local people gathering to declare what they believe to be true, and in so doing, reminding whoever happened to be harboring doubts, or found themselves in a valley, that Jesus lived, died, and rose again.

During the reciting of the Lord's Prayer, I couldn't help but hear that the women in front of me was speaking German. During the next section of our worship time, when we greeted each other, she introduced herself to me, so I asked her when she left Germany. She was likely in her mid-eighties, but vibrant, with a strong handshake and quick wit. "A short time after the war," she said, adding that she'd come from Garmish, a Bavarian ski town in southern Germany, and that she and her husband had taught skiing here on our little ski hill in "the sixties, seventies, and eighties." I asked her how long she'd been attending St. Bernard chapel and she said, "Since we moved here in 1964."

It was apparent, without asking, that she didn't do a weekly cost/benefit analysis of gathering with others for worship. She gathered with others for worship because that's what Christ followers do. Everywhere. Around the world. Every week. She shared that her husband had just died a year ago, but that he had made all the ornate wood carvings in this beautiful little chapel. He contributed his own beauty of Christ. She was continuing to contribute with her presence, and will, I have no doubt, until her final breath.

Why?

It's what Christ followers do.

Chapter 16

Soil Care For the Soul

The soil is the great connector of lives, the source and destination of all. It is the healer and restorer and resurrector, by which disease passes into health, age into youth, death into life. Without proper care for it we can have no community, because without proper care for it, we can have no life.

Wendell Berry

Meet Lisa Allen. According to her file, she was thirty-four years old at the time of the interview. She started smoking and drinking when she was sixteen, and had struggled with obesity for most of her life. At one point, in her mid-twenties, collection agencies were hounding her to recover $10,000 in debts. An old résumé listed her longest job as lasting less than a year. In spite of these deficiencies, researchers were studying her because she had completely turned her life around in a very short period of time. When the team of researchers met her, she was lean and vibrant, with the toned legs of a runner. She looked a decade younger than the photos in her chart and appeared to be able to out-exercise anyone in the room. She'd lost sixty pounds and had just completed a marathon, along with a master's degree. According to the most recent report in her file, Lisa had no outstanding debts, didn't drink, hadn't smoked in four years and was in her thirty-ninth month at a graphic design firm. Lisa's story was a story of movement from destructive behaviors to productivity, and who doesn't enjoy a good story of transformation?

We all do. Whether it's *Beauty and the Beast* and the transformation of relationship, *A Christmas Carol* and the transformation of values, or *The King's Speech* and a king's movement from fear to courage, stories of change for the better inspire and resonate with our deepest longings. This is because something deep inside all of us realizes that the world can get better, and that we ourselves can be better, too. At

217

an even more fundamental level, these desires for upward movement resonate because transformation is the central good news that Jesus brings us. "I have come that you might have life, and that you might have it more abundantly" is how Jesus put it one day when talking with a crowd[93]. Later, Paul would say it this way: "He [God] made him [Christ] who knew no sin to be sin on our behalf, in order that we might become the very righteousness of God" (II Corinthians 5:21). Did you catch the weight of that? God's desire for you and me isn't that we simply settle for sobriety, a touch of generosity, and paying our taxes. Our destiny is to become nothing less than "the righteousness of God," which means that God's desire is that justice, mercy, hospitality, peacemaking, generosity, and hope pour through our very being so that those in our lives can be blessed. That same Paul would tell us that we're called to swim upstream against the prevailing currents of culture, not being conformed to the dominant taboos and mores, but being "transformed by the renewing of [our] minds" (Romans 12:2).

How do we get there? We'll start by saying that the narrative of culture won't get us there. We're increasingly stressed out, addicted, anxious, lonely, and afraid. It appears that wealth and hyper-connectivity aren't providing a pathway to the lives of peace, intimacy, and meaning. Such things won't be found by passively embracing the values of Western culture, or any other culture, for that matter. Jesus compared our life journeys to walking, and suggested that we're often standing in front of two doors. One door is huge, well-lit, inviting, and the masses are clamoring to get through it. The other door is small, unassuming, and a bit "out of the way." Jesus has an opinion about this choice: *"Enter through the narrow gate. For wide is the gate and broad is the road that leads to destruction, and many enter through it. But small is the gate and narrow the road that leads to life, and only a few find it"* (Matthew 7:13,14). It's as if Jesus is telling us that defaulting to conventional assumptions won't get us to where we want to go, and won't enable us to build the life for which we're created.

A crusty prophet of old hinted at the same mentality, using a road metaphor, rather than gates or doors. *"Stand at the crossroads and look;*

ask for the ancient paths, ask where the good way is, and walk in it, and you will find rest for your souls" (Jeremiah 6:16)

All of us could use a little more rest in our lives, or so it seems at least. This picture is painted by Jeremiah and Jesus, who shares a similar message, when he says, "Come to me, all who are weary and heavy laden, and I will give you rest."[94] The promise is that those who are weighed down by carrying heavy burdens will be able to find rest if they can develop a consistent and real relationship with Christ (hence the phrase "learn from me" in the same invitation). A consistent and real relationship with Christ, though, is like any relationship that's going to be consistent and real. Relationships take time and require the development of habits.

Naming these relationship habits and working at moving into them is what this book is about, and the reason I believe it is so important that we work at this is because without such habits, our faith journey becomes little more than sporadic episodes of spiritual experiences. We might enjoy a beautiful worship service one Sunday and we're moved in the moment, but not changed. We might pray a bit more, or a lot more, because of a personal health crisis, or a global terror attack, but then slip back into a default mode, passively embracing the values of the broader culture, even as we continue to do so-called "Christian" things. Deep down, though, this sort of living is as ineffective for transforming our spirits as running to the mailbox a few days a month is for marathon training. We can be more, enjoy more, love more, but this requires the development of spiritual habits.

The process of developing spiritual habits has been called the creation of a *rule of life* by many throughout the history of the church. At the end of this book, there's a tool that will help you in creating your own rule of life, and such a creation is precisely where everything we've considered has been leading. So let's dive in and consider the what, why, and how, of that ancient path called "the rule of life."

What is a rule of life?

It's simple, really. A rule of life is your declared intention regarding the habits you seek to make real in your daily life. Jesus, for example, gathered with other worshippers on the sabbath, not just when he felt like it, or if the weather was just right (not good enough for sailing, but not bad enough to make getting there inconvenient). According to Luke 4:16, Jesus gathered with others "as was his custom." He had a habit of worshipping with others. Similarly, God invited God's people to make a habit of pondering God's revelation.[95] Paul says something similar when he says, "Let the word of Christ dwell richly within you"[96] Similar exhortations are offered around developing habits of simplicity, generosity, and hospitality, as we've already seen. Habits are brilliant, because once they become a natural part of our lives, they bring both order to our time use, and free our minds for other pursuits, as mental energy is no longer wasted on seeking to bring order out of chaos every day. Order exists already, because you've developed habits!

God is simply telling us that what we already know to be true physiologically is also true spiritually: "use it or lose it!" The challenge is that we also know from history that the default for us as fallen humans is to stop using it. We stop exercising. We stop eating mindfully. We stop praying. We stop taking the stairs. We stop. Develop life-giving practices so that they become habits, and they strengthen and multiply. Neglect them, and they atrophy and decay. This was the story of God's people, Israel, in days of old. They knew God, loved God, had been blessed by God. Then, in all their blessedness, they became busy, preoccupied with their own private lives and as a result, the life-giving habits of worship and justice, sabbath and forgiveness, slowly evaporated until they lost their distinctive life-giving capacity. This drift is just as real for us, as inevitable in the realm of the spirit as in the body. All we need do to drift is live a life without intention. The good news is that it's also just as repairable. How? By building a few simple habits into your life that feed and strengthen the spiritual soil.

In addition to habits, your rule of life will consist of an intention to fan certain attitudes from a tiny spark into a full, raging fire. Attitudes are different than habits, in that they're more a way of looking at and responding to the world. They could almost be called values, and they're fanned into flame by putting them in front of you on a regular basis. Our minds are renewed and transformed by choosing wisely day after day: contentment over consumerism, hospitality over isolation, silence over noise. For example, by being mindful of Christ's hospitality and care for people who are weary and downtrodden, I'm sensitized to the practice of hospitality, and this changes the way I relate to people. Maybe I volunteer in a ministry that builds relationships across social divides. Maybe I engage with homeless people differently. By being mindful of my call to generosity, maybe I change my giving habits. With a "pilgrimage" mindset and willingness to journey, I choose obedience over safety and predictability. A truth telling mindset refuses to believe lies of shame, and also refuses to whitewash problems.

Intentionally choosing to build certain habits and affirm certain attitudes is what it means to build a rule of life. One author writes that a rule of life serves as a framework for freedom - not as a set of rules that restrict or deny life, but as a way of living our vocation alone and in community. It is rooted in Scripture, pointing always to Christ, and in the words of Saint Benedict, it is "simply a handbook to make the very radical demands of the gospel a practical reality in daily life."[97]

Why is a rule of life important?

One of the most famous parables in the Bible is the story about the seed and the sower. "A farmer went out to sow his seed" is how it begins, and by the end of the tale we discover that not all the seeds reached their full potential. The seed, though, was never the problem; it was the soil. Too many rocks. Too many thorns. Not enough depth. It's a powerful tale, because later in the Bible we're told that "His seed abides in us."[98] The astonishing reality is that nothing less than the life of the resurrected Jesus has found a home "in us." This means that His seed, if allowed to grow, will find unique expression through each of our lives, so that the joy, hope, mercy, justice, sacrifice, love, and generosity of Christ can continue to be revealed in this dark and broken world. Each of us has a part to play, and when we do this, we're living the lives for which we're created!

Some people recoil at the word "rule," because they believe that since we're saved by grace, there's actually nothing we need to do other than receive what God has freely given. My response: "Yes. Just receive the seed, the same way soil receives the seed." What farmer do you know who plants seeds without preparing the soil? The reality is that the seed of Christ's life is God's rich gift to us; the life is in the seed, the growth is in the seed, and the fruit is in the seed. Farmers don't randomly toss seeds out from the window of their houses and say, "There's really nothing more I can do, because it's all about the seed." Rubbish. Of course there's no fruit without the seed. But there's no fruit in your life without the union of seed and soil, and who needs to take responsibility for the soil that is your soul? You do! Your habits and attitudes will determine the quality of the soil, and hence the fruitfulness of Christ's seed flowering in your life, so that you can enjoy the kind of life for which you were created, a life overflowing with meaning, joy, and love.

Soil care happens. Either we're fortifying the soil through life-giving habits and attitudes, or we're allowing rocks, weeds, and thorns to choke the seed by neglecting soil care habits. The whole project is a lot like exercise; sometimes energizing, sometimes not so much. And yet, by faith, I've come to believe that it's always valuable. Now the question is much less "How was my time of Bible reading?" because I know, through experience, that what matters isn't the particular experience of any single day. It's the trend line that counts, and the trend line of life-giving soil care habits is remarkably positive. I know it. Saint Benedict knew it. The Celtic church knew it, and so did the vast majority of life-giving movements in church history. Hope and life have been poured into the world through people who had life-giving soil care habits. Do you want a strong heart? Then do some aerobic exercise every day, not too much or too little, not too hard or too easy. Find your sweet spot and do it. Over time, your heart's capacity to pump life-giving oxygen will increase, though on any given day, the progress won't be noticeable. The same exact process awaits you as you train yourself to be a person of hope in this world, using your gifts to bless and serve others. Yes, "physical training is of some value, but godliness has value for all things, holding promise for both the present life and the life to come."[99]

Those who farm or garden know that there's a rhythm to every year as harvest turns to winter, turns to planting, turns to harvest. Throughout, though, the matter of soil care is never far from the heart of the those dealing with the life of plants. The reasons are obvious, and yet, the reality is that we face a soil crisis of epic proportion. As an article in *Scientific American* states:

> …Unless new approaches are adopted, the global amount of arable and productive land per person in 2050 will be only a quarter of the level in 1960…soils play a key role in absorbing carbon and filtering water, (and) soil destruction creates a vicious cycle, in which less carbon is stored, the world gets hotter, and the land is further degraded. "We are losing 30 soccer fields of soil every minute," says Volkert Engelsman, of the Federation of Organic Agriculture Movements.[100]

Our soil problems stem from neglect of the elements that produce long-term value in the soil in favor of policies and practices that provide instant gratification and short-term profit. The results are clear to everyone, yet everyone keeps neglecting the future in favor of the immediate. Sound familiar? It's not just a soil problem. It's a soul problem.

How do we care for the soil of our souls? I'm glad you asked!

Chapter 17

Rule of Life: Developing a Breathing Practice

Do or don't do; there is no try.

Yoda

I don't remember my parents ever teaching me to breathe. Somehow it came naturally to me. It's a good thing, too, because there's no time. Breathing needs to come first, before we learn to speak, use the toilet, use a knife and fork, read, or ride a bicycle. Breathing comes early, from the first moments after a baby is born.

All the rest of it needs to be learned. So while I don't recall breathing lessons, I do recall lessons in learning to ride a bike. Dad was the teacher, and I had training wheels. We'd go outside, and I'd pedal around a bit, getting comfortable with the notion of sitting on this thin contraption, this interplay of rubber, steel, and plastic (the plastic was for the streamers that flowed out of the handlebars). Several days were devoted to simply learning to exert force; first one leg, then the other. Then I learned to steer by turning the handlebars to the left and then the right, staying on the machine rather than on the ground. These skills are not easily learned, even with training wheels. Perhaps you've forgotten how difficult, how complex the whole endeavor is, because you've become a regular pedaler; you've mastered the art. But back in the day, even the rudimentary skills were challenging.

The vast majority of us who read this book have learned to ride a bike, but we probably never learned the framework for practicing spiritual disciplines that the church has often called a *rule of life*. We have already addressed some of the many reasons for this. And we've also discovered that diagnosing why we don't do something is never quite enough, because unless diagnosis moves beyond itself to prescribe a solution to the problem, all we have is blame. "I don't ride my bike because my dad was too busy to teach me…because we were too poor...because I fell once or twice or ten times...because it's hard to learn." You can fill in the blank with any number of things.

Great. You can articulate why you don't, but so far you've only provided a reason why you didn't ride your bike in the past, right up until this present moment. But let's say that you're standing in front of the bicycle that you never learned to ride. Gas is $12 a gallon, or your doctor has told you that your heart is getting clogged with bacon fat and you need to exercise. You're seeing the need to make a change, and you're pondering taking up bike riding. All the reasons you didn't ride yesterday are now irrelevant. Those failures, phobias, and family of origin issues, real as they are, don't change the fact that today you can make a choice to get on the bicycle and learn to ride it. And either you will or you won't.

Developing our rule of life begins with seeing the need for one. The need has perhaps been hard to see in our culture because we've placed a huge premium on believing the right information, thinking that somehow giving intellectual assent to certain statements constitutes belief. Jesus doesn't see it that way. He ties belief to our practices, to what we actually do. And I don't know about you, but when I hold my practices up against the vision Jesus cast of what constitutes right living, I find myself falling short continually.

That's because His vision is considerably different from prevailing visions of both religious and secular cultures. His vision includes loving our enemies, praying for those who are mistreating us, living generously, caring for the least of these, breaking down social barriers, throwing parties for people who have nowhere to go, and so much more that is contrary to our consumerism, individualism, racism, isolationism, and any other "ism" that so easily seduces us away from God's purposes. When I begin to understand my calling, I see two things: (1) I'm not yet fulfilling it, and (2) I can't fulfill it alone. If you can at least see these two things, thank God for where you're standing. You've been delivered from self-righteousness and pride, and you are ready for transformative adventure available only to humble people. Let the adventure begin!

If I buy into Jesus' vision and admit my need for His strength and guidance (two very big ifs, by the way), I'm motivated to learn how to ride. I may have tried and failed in the past, but now, seeing through a different lens, I realize I'm at a crossroads, where either I'll learn the new skills needed or I won't. Yoda was right: there is no try. My faith is not a set of beliefs divorced from living. My faith is the continual interplay of believing and living, learning to integrate the two so that I am able to fulfill my destiny as an artisan of hope. And this requires the development of practices that have contributed to that goal throughout history. They are the breathing practices described in this book, given shape by a rule of life.

We may recoil at the notion of developing a set of practices and commitments as a means of giving expression to our life in Christ. The very word *rule* smacks of all that we thought we had escaped by finding liberty in Christ, or if not liberty in Christ, at least liberty, the freedom to wake up each morning and order our day according to the need or desire of the moment. Why should we force ourselves into some regimen of practices? If we feel the need to sleep in, let's sleep in; no need for a rule of life to wake us up. We've all known people who were addicted to rules. They're not at the top of your guest list when you're throwing a party.

We can make two important observations here. The first is that you already have a rule of life. Maybe you live by your appetites, so that sex, food, sleep, exercise, the acquisition of money or clothes, or some other need or desire controls how you order things. Maybe your commitment to avoiding pain predominates, and so you sleep too much, eat too much, read too little, watch too much TV, and don't even realize how far you are from God's best. Perhaps you're living for the acquisition of power, for your family, or for the approval of your parents, spouse, or friends. Certainly, more than one value can shape your decisions. But values they are, and they shape you, directing your choices. You have a rule of life. The question you must ask is, do I want to be governed by my present value system, or would I rather be more deeply infused with the mind and heart of Christ? It's not a trick question. There's one right answer.

The second observation is simply this: Jesus went to parties, loved parties, was invited to parties. Apparently, His commitment to doing the will of God didn't result in His becoming a bore. The rule of life about which we're speaking is not an invitation to self-imposed asceticism, suffering, and the negation of all that is good and beautiful in the world. Rather, gaining the mind and heart of Christ allows us to increasingly manifest the life and character of the One who knew how to live fully, embracing mourning and laughter, feasting and fasting, serving and celebrating. The only One who does it right is available to shape our hearts. Why not learn from the best?

Best Learned with Others

I find it interesting that a child's first solo journey on a bicycle, even if only for a few dozen feet, is one of those markers, not only in her life but also in the lives of her parents. "Suzie just rode her bike alone!" one parent runs into the house and shouts to the other. Perhaps the whole scene is captured on video and posted to social media for the whole world to see, especially the parents' friends and relatives. Up until that moment, the learning to ride was something that required help, required a teacher, a mentor, a friend.

"You therefore, my son, be strong in the grace that is in Christ Jesus. The things which you have heard from me in the presence of many witnesses, entrust these to faithful men who will be able to teach others also" (2 Timothy 2:1-2). Thus did Paul remind Timothy that faith is much more than a set of propositions one signs off on, as if you were reading an employee handbook and then signing your initials to say you agree. It's more like riding a bike; if you're to live it effectively, you will have to intentionally develop certain skills, skills which are best learned in the context of relationship.

Perhaps you've heard of the self-help movement. Born in a culture of fierce independence and individualism, this movement posits that there are few things in life that you can't learn on your own with just the input of a book, Web site, podcast, or DVD. In this information age, there's no shortage of data. Simply go out and get the facts, teach yourself, and get on with it.

This seems adequate for some things, but it's never the best way to learn how to live the Christian life. And it is always unacceptable when it comes to the things that matter most. I want to know that my surgeon didn't study surgery through an online course, or that my mountain guide didn't learn their skills from *The Idiot's Guide to Climbing Mount Everest*. Most things are best passed down through human contact rather than a book.

This is certainly the case when it comes to the development of a rule of life. The Celtic church, which existed in Ireland and Scotland, was not controlled by the Roman Empire as was the rest of Great Britain, and it developed its own unique ways of embodying the faith. One of its essential practices was to establish a relationship with someone who would function as a confidant, resource, and support in the development of the faith life. This tradition called such a person a *soul friend*, and it was said that a Christian without a soul friend was like a body without a head.

Jesus would agree. He called His disciples not simply to impart information but to be with them. It's good to spend time with someone who is a bit further down the road, who already knows how to ride, because that's the kind of person who can listen to you, watch you, offer specific responses to your particular situation, and even show you how it is to be done.

In our individualism, we're tempted to skip this step. "We don't need anybody but Jesus!" we shout. True enough. But the real question is this: How do we hear from Jesus? Through His Word, certainly. But Jesus has a body here on earth right now, made up of people who are committed to making the invisible God visible through words and actions. When we look for Jesus, we see Him not only in the Bible; we also see Him in His followers, who are His hands and voice on earth today.

Of course, skipping any human intermediaries and always going directly to the Bible has many advantages. I'm able to bypass all the untidiness of human relationships, the complexities of communication, the disappointments of misunderstandings, the need for discernment when sifting through counsel. I'm relieved of all of that. I'll just go straight to Jesus. The trouble is that Jesus expresses His life not only through His Word but also through His body. This body of His, called the church, is intended to be an interrelated community, and so my attempts at developing a rule of life all by myself will invariably create a mutation that falls far short of what God has in mind. In other words, I don't have what it takes to live the Christian life in isolation. I'm called to a community of interdependency.

I have a friend who is committed to living out his rule of life as a means of growing in Christ. We meet regularly. I've shared my intentions with him regarding the various breathing practices in this book, and when we're together we pray, share about our lives, and gauge progress in our spiritual practices. These are valuable times, as he is able to offer specific encouragement, counsel, and resources for the issues I face. Whether you become part of a group of people committed to developing a rule of life or you meet with one other person, it is far better, if possible, to learn to ride with others.

Training Wheels

We do well to address the gap that exists between what we say we believe and how we actually live. In other words, we need not only orthodoxy (correct beliefs) but also orthopraxy (correct practices). In a culture where prominence is achieved through intellectual advancement, we're tempted to conclude that the maturing of one's faith is merely a matter of accumulating information. In such a model, where emphasis is placed on content, little children may participate in clubs devoted solely to the memorization of Scripture, earning badges by reciting verses. At first glance, the merits of this system seem obvious. If I fill the minds of little children with Bible content, they will be more likely to order their lives according to God's Word rather than any of the many other prevailing options. We are, after all, transformed by the renewing of our minds[101]. All this is good to a point, but there are limits.

The problem with this paradigm is that Jesus' greatest antagonists were those who studied, memorized, dissected, debated, defended, and taught their Bible[102]. So Bible study apparently isn't enough.

230

Jesus finishes His powerful Sermon on the Mount by declaring that the wise ones are those who not only hear the words of Jesus (or we might add by extension—study them, memorize them, teach them) but also *do* them. Those are the ones whose lives will be able to weather storms.

I think of Sophie Scholl, the young woman who was part of the movement known as the White Rose, a resistance work against the Nazis in World War II. I knew nothing about her or this movement until I watched the movie whose title bears her name. It remains one of the most powerful films I've ever seen. These young people lived robust lives of faithfulness to Christ, standing against the tide of darkness sweeping through Europe. It cost them their lives. One of Sophie's companions wrote, "Belief is no simple thing. It demands constant strain and struggle. It has to be mastered over and over again. And to be a true Christian: that is the most difficult thing of all, because we are never, ever able to truly follow Christ—except perhaps through death[103]."

"No simple thing." Giving genuine expression to our faith is not a matter of mastering the content of a doctrinal statement, giving mental assent to it, and purposing to avoid the sins that are socially unfashionable at the moment. Rather, I'm called to be the very real presence of Christ Himself, bringing to bear all the resources of His life in every situation.

And this is why developing a rule of life is so valuable. The various inhaling and exhaling disciplines articulated in this book work together to create a healthy body, a body responsive to the Spirit of Christ, so that whatever is needed in a given moment might find expression, whether that be generosity, confrontation of injustice, care for creation, the loving of one's neighbor, or the holding up of a situation in prayer. If we're regularly developing the skills and resources that sensitize us to Christ's Spirit, we will be more responsive as He calls us to respond in all the varied circumstances of our lives.

A good way to begin practicing these things is to consider your breathing habits prayerfully and to make some commitments to express them in your life. This is exactly what is meant by developing a rule of life. As we prayerfully consider the disciplines to which we are invited, each one should establish practices that are hard enough to be challenging and lead to growth, but not so daunting as to assure failure.

What does this mean practically? It means that I look at the breathing habits that I need to sustain life, and rather than just ponder them, I name my intentions to practice them. For example, I might look at hospitality and write down, "I will host a neighborhood party every three months," or "I will join a book club," or "I will tell my faith community that our spare bedroom is available for visitors." I'll do something similar with solitude. "I will rise 15 minutes earlier for time alone with God," or "I will spend one Saturday morning a month alone, journaling and praying." I prayerfully develop my unique commitments with the support of a friend or friends who share a commitment to breathing. I post mine on the bulletin board by my desk, a constant reminder of the commitments I intend to keep in the living out of my faith.

Contrary to what some might say, the development of a rule of life is neither a formulaic approach to Christianity nor legalism. It's not legalism because these practices are not a way of gaining acceptance from God or forgiveness for failures. Those things are already ours because of Christ's gifts of love to us and because of our acceptance of His invitation to join Him in participating in God's reign. Rather, the rule of life is simply the declaration of our intention to practice those disciplines that will result in the colors of hope being poured into the world.

You didn't practice pedaling as a way of gaining acceptance. Nor did it feel like a legalistic imposition. "Not again, Dad! I'm sick of pedaling. Can't I just ride my bike today without worrying about pedaling?" Or maybe you're sick of steering, or balance, or leaning when turning. Yes. Just dispense with whichever habits you don't like, deeming them to be too heavy-handed, so you can get on with riding. I have a name for you: Scabby.

Why put your plans in writing? Why nail it to your bulletin board or magnetize it on your refrigerator? Think of the particular naming for each habit as training wheels. Until the habits of faith become second nature, having a reminder in front of us is helpful. We wake up in the morning and stumble to the kitchen, looking for the coffee grinder. Right there, above the beans, is our rule of life. Under "Word" it says, "I will read the online daily verse on my home page while the coffee is brewing." There's the paper waiting to be read. There's my computer. This is my moment of truth. Remember the journey? Do I turn around in search of food or continue upward to the summit? Every journey is a million steps like this one. The reminder of my commitment is staring me in the face while I grind my beans. That isn't legalism. The training wheels are intended to bring me freedom.

It's important that none of the disciplines become legalistic structures, for such forms can tighten and become a noose that chokes all breath and life out of a person. That's why we need to embrace the next reality with equal force.

Falling

I love watching babies learn to walk. The other night I was in a meeting, and two baby sisters were in the room. The younger of the two was just learning to walk. She would stand up and take a couple of faltering steps, and then her sister would sneak up from behind and give her a gentle yet forceful push, sort of like a nursery version of a football player whacking the guy who just caught the ball. The younger one would fall down, cry for about two seconds, and then get up. Then the whole thing would happen again and again and again. It was fun to watch. The little one kept getting up until the older sister grew tired of the pushing and got lost in a different diversion.

As the younger girl kept getting up and trying again, I watched and wondered what happens to us, so that the day comes when some sort of failure leads to disengagement from activities? Why do we become so careful? When do our egos, our bodies, and our lives become so brittle and fragile that one loss, one failure in an area causes us to quit trying? We get hurt in relationships and decide to stay alone. A church lets us down, and we drop out of the community of faith. We fall in a crevasse and decide to never walk on a glacier again. We lose in a risky investment and lock our money away in a bank or under a mattress forever.

Why are we surprised that we have failed and made mistakes? The Bible says that "we all stumble in many ways[104]." That's the reality of it. So failure shouldn't be such a big deal. It also says that we will never be fruitful without risk, and if you know anything about investing, you know that the guy who parlayed one talent into five almost certainly suffered losses in the process of achieving gain. On the other hand, the one who was afraid of failing did nothing. Safe? Predictable? Yes. And he was also the one who received a scathing indictment from Jesus[105].

We achieve maturity through trying and failing. The hockey great Wayne Gretzky said it well: "You miss 100 percent of the shots you don't take." When it comes to the breathing habits so vital to our faith life, many of us take a few shots, miss some of them, and then quit. But this is where Jesus' invitation for us to have faith like a child once again becomes so vital for us. Children who are learning to ride a bike don't quit trying when they fall. They get up again and again, hundreds of times, until they become riders.

A strong force is pulling me down, inviting me to fail. That force is called the flesh, and I'm told in the Bible that it is my ever-present invitation to failure and to something far worse: a disengagement from even trying. I've given in more times than I can count, choosing isolation over hospitality, anxiety over the rest of prayer, selfish indulgence over kingdom generosity. Oh well. Today is a new day. God made it. I'm alive. It's another chance to get it right. Paul said it this way:

> Not that I have already obtained it or have already become perfect, but I press on so that I may lay hold of that for which also I was laid hold of by Christ Jesus. Brethren, I do not regard myself as having laid hold of it yet; but one thing I do:

forgetting what lies behind and reaching forward to what lies ahead, I press on (Philippians 3:12-14).

Balance

I met with a friend who has more experience with a rule of life than I do. I wanted to talk about how my breathing habits were developing. I told him that I was discouraged because I had too many things to learn and because trying to develop all of these things at the same time was too complex. To use the bicycle analogy, I always seemed to be leaning too far one way (toward the inhaling practices at the expense of exhaling), and so I was often falling down. He provided some much-needed objectivity by helping me see that different elements prevail in different seasons and that what constitutes balance is unique for each person. One is built to lean more naturally toward exhaling. Another toward inhaling. Don't let the realities of temperament, tendencies, gifts, and seasons become the basis for some false shame or condemnation, some sense of not measuring up. And don't let those things become license for neglecting the disciplines needed for maturity either.

I don't need to learn everything at the same time, and that is both comforting and liberating. When we lived in the mountains, hospitality and Bible study were my main breathing elements. Most of my days during that season consisted of studying or teaching the Bible, or spending time with guests in our home. Yes, there was prayer, time in creation, a nod to kingdom ethics and generosity, and even a little celebration once in a while. But largely, two elements dominated the landscape of my life.

Today I still study and teach, and we occasionally open our home to guests, but those elements don't occupy the same space in my life anymore. Instead, prayer, intentional solitude, and generosity are in the forefront. As artisans of hope, we are continually adding colors to our palette through the development and refining of the various disciplines, and that will enable Christ to be seen more clearly. The colors we are developing at any given time are contingent on many factors. Parents with young children often don't study much, and they might laugh at any notion of solitude. But they're learning more about service than could be written in ten books, and those busy, blessed, tiring years will increase their capacity to serve others during the rest of their lives.

That's how it works. God is shaping us, like a potter shapes clay, so that we become vessels able to pour out hope! Our responsibility is always to be mindful of the forces that are shaping our vessel so that we grow according to the flow of God in our lives, not against it.

Practice

Finding the balanced posture in these things is tricky. Some of us grew up in structures that forced these breathing habits on us, along with other habits like Lent, fasting, wearing choking neckties on Sunday mornings and sitting motionless in a large building with opaque windows. Living faithfully was reduced to developing these habits (especially the inhaling ones). Christianity became nothing more than doing a few things (go to church, read your Bible, give some money to the church) and avoiding a few other things (deny yourself some pleasures before Easter, don't eat certain meats on certain days, don't smoke or drink), as if these things had any power whatsoever to make you holy[106]. The Christian culture imposed rules like this without explaining the larger context of our calling, and that's why many people walked away from the faith without looking back.

However, in many cases the pendulum of reaction has swung too far the other way. Seeing both the danger of rules and reality of our liberty in Christ, *authenticity* has become the word of the day. Afraid of empty form or ritual without reality, we've declared that we need do nothing, indeed should do nothing, unless the doing of it is authentic. We've seen marriages where people stay married but aren't in love anymore, and we're frightened that the same thing might happen to us, either in our human relationships or our relationship with God. We don't want to settle for anything less than the real deal, so we throw away any devotional guides that would call us to daily Bible reading or prayer, and we resist any commitments to practice inhaling and exhaling disciplines in some sort of systematic way, as if ritual invariably destroys relationship.

236

This, to put it mildly, is rubbish. I know this because I'm married to someone I love deeply and know well. Yet, in spite of both my love and my commitment, the past four decades have included a day or two when I was disillusioned with being married, when I didn't feel like carrying out the responsibilities that fidelity and commitment require. But I'm glad to say I carried them out anyway, kept showing up at the supper table, kept coming home from the airport, kept offering words of encouragement. There have been other actions in my marriage as well, actions born out of frustration, anger, confession, fear, and disappointment. But to take such emotions or moments as signs that I should disengage from relationship, ostensibly because my love is no longer authentic, would have been very shortsighted. I'm glad I kept showing up, even when it didn't feel natural or comfortable.

This human analogy offers a close parallel to our relationship with God. The breathing disciplines we're considering are the inward and outward expressions that are common among people who love God. Thus, if we truly love God, we should be intentional about doing them, even when we don't feel like it.

Challenge

There's a bike race near the Canadian border called Ride 542—Mt. Baker Hill Climb. It's about 25 miles, 24 of which are uphill! Who does this? Recently, I found out. My wife and I were hiking in the Cascades when we came upon four women in their fifties who were out picking blueberries. When we stopped to talk with them, I learned that one of them had not only entered the race, but won—both for her own age category and the category below hers!

I didn't interview her and ask about her training techniques, but I'm fairly certain that she didn't learn to ride her bike the week before the race or the month before or the year before. People who win races likes this one have been riding around more than a little bit for quite some time. They've developed such efficient habits of balance and breathing that they can ride uphill, nearly nonstop, gaining thousands of feet in elevation, with grace, strength, and beauty.

For those of us who stopped riding a long time ago, or who get on our bicycles only when our car battery is dead, feats such as these aren't doable at all, let alone with such grace and beauty. Such is the case as well for those who do or don't practice the habits of spiritual breathing. We needn't begin with any sort of hill climb. I fear that biographies of missionaries and famous Christians have the effect of discouraging most of us from even starting. This one was martyred in Central America. He rose at six each morning for prayer and journaling. That one moved to Hong Kong and worked with drug addicts. This one speaks four languages and runs a clinic in Indonesia. That one has a miraculous story about God's provision to build a school in India. Each story can either inspire or mock us. Taken wrong, they become challenges to ride our bikes uphill for 25 miles, when we're still struggling to find the pedals and keep our balance.

Here we are, back down in the valley, going to school, trying to get out of debt, seeking to resolve a messy relationship or overcome an addiction. What do these hill climbers have to teach me? If I'm prone to comparison and the horrible vacillation between pride and self-condemnation that goes with it, I avoid their stories. They discourage me. But their stories aren't intended to shame or discourage; they're intended to inspire us to respond to God's call in *our* setting, *our* time, *our* lot in life.

Years ago, a good friend of mine died. He was an associate pastor at our church for many years, and had an uncanny ability to help people step up to new challenges and grow in their faith. He did this by inviting them to take a step just outside of their comfort zone. If they were new to a bicycle, he didn't invite them to the hill climb. But he would invite them to whatever was appropriate as their next step. My friend Ben writes about how this played out in his life:

> [Scott] presided over our wedding. He taught me to make omelets. He gently pushed me into teaching Sunday school classes when I didn't feel quite ready (and I wasn't quite ready). It was those classes, not my graduate education or

chemistry teaching assignments, that actually taught me how to teach. That's what I do every day now. At his prompting I taught the Psalms, a post-September 11 course with Kevin, and a History of Church and State course. I would not have done them without his prompting, or even known how to teach without his example. I wouldn't even be able to read the books I'm reading now without what he gave me[107].

That's what this is about. We listen for the voice of God as He challenges us to take the next step, to ascend to the next level. When we go there, we won't remain comfortable for very long before we hear God's voice inviting us up higher still. As we respond, new challenges, new beauty, new adventures await us. And all the while, almost unbeknown to us, we're becoming more and more like Jesus.

Chapter 18

Celebration

Isn't it bewildering…that everything is so beautiful, despite all the horrors that exist? Lately I've noticed something grand and mysterious peering into my sheer joy in all that is lovely—the sense of a Creator whom innocent creation worships with its beauty. Only man can be hateful or ugly, because he possesses a free will to cut himself off from the chorus of praise. It often seems that he will succeed in drowning out this chorus with his cannon thunder, curses, and blasphemy. But it has become clear to me this spring that he cannot. And so I must try to throw myself on the side of the victor.

Sophie Scholl

Some of the best meals have come on the heels of the heaviest breathing. After the summit, there's always a feast. The same is true after running or going for a long bike ride. The meal at the end of the task is a celebration of effort and accomplishment. And it's more, or at least can be; it can be the articulation of gratitude to God for the ability to do whatever has just been done, whether climbing a mountain, laying a foundation for a church building in an impoverished part of Costa Rica, or running a three-day medical clinic in a village in the heart of Nepal. Rising to a challenge, moving out of our comfort zones, watching something unfold that is somehow beyond what we'd sought, what we thought we were capable of doing, or what we thought we deserved: These are the moments when celebration is a natural response.

The spirit of celebration also infuses those times in our lives when we see ourselves as the recipients of grace and mercy. On Christmas Eve, I watch my children, dressed for sleeping, as they watch *A Muppet Christmas Carol*. This is our family tradition on that night. In one song, Kermit lifts a glass and sings a prayer: "Bless us all!" I've never been able to listen to it and watch my children without feeling profoundly grateful for all I've been given to enjoy. I know my greed, lust, failure; I know much of it anyway. I know that I don't deserve what I have, that I've not earned it by my own wit and wisdom. I have this sense, as I look at my family and my life, that I'm the recipient of oceans of mercy. I am profoundly grateful that I can enjoy this moment, and my gratitude spills over into the next day's celebration of Christmas.

Even as I'm writing I know it sounds sappy, like I'm some wide-eyed romantic. *Yes. Here's the middle-class American white guy with a Master's degree, privileged beyond at least 90 percent of the world, and he's feeling pretty good about it. That's not so hard to understand.* Actually, it's a little trickier than that, because statistics indicate the relationship between happiness and material well-being is far less direct than we'd like to think. The American mind is largely convinced that our sense of contentment is proportional to our economic welfare. And so we think education, home ownership, central heating, clean water, cheap cable, Internet access, fine food and wine for Christmas day, and an unlimited selection of sweaters purchased at Goodwill will make us happy and turn Christmas Eve into a Currier and Ives moment.

Let's take the equation even a bit further. If I'm happy because of the stuff I have, more stuff will make me happier, right? Wrong. Bill McKibben points out that a heavy weight of evidence indicates that income increases produce a hefty increase in contentment and satisfaction in those places in the world marred by stark poverty. However (and this is the part that confounds the developed world), in already prosperous cultures, the capacity shrinks for increased wealth to contribute to a person's sense of well-being. In an extremely wealthy culture such as our own, more income actually serves to diminish the odds for happiness.

> What this means is: if you are a poor person in China, you have plenty of friends and family around all the time; perhaps there are five people living in your room. Adding a sixth doesn't make you much happier. But adding enough money

so all five of you can eat some meat from time to time pleases you greatly. By contrast, if you live in a suburban American home, buying another coffeemaker adds very little to your quantity of happiness—indeed trying to figure out where to store it, or wondering whether you picked the perfect model may decrease your total pleasure. But since you live two people to an acre, a new friend, a new connection, is a big deal indeed[108].

Perhaps is this why parties among people of means so often seem strained, as if everyone is trying a little too hard to have fun. We're overworked, isolated, lonely, and often bored. In our attempt to escape from these various ailments, we often resort to participation in events that are supposed to tell us that we're beautiful, well-connected, and important. Perhaps you remember the scene from *Forrest Gump* in which the character Jenny is contemplating suicide. She has good looks, intelligence, and easy access to sex and drugs. Hers is the life to which many seem to aspire, believing that these things will fill the void and quench the aching of their hearts. Sadly though, our possessions and attributes serve ultimately only to remind us that in spite of our health, prosperity, good looks, and access to therapies, drugs, education, and even money, we still have a gigantic emptiness in our souls. Jenny looks around and is tired of it all as she comes within a high heel of jumping off a balcony.

Compare that with a woman who gave lunch to a few of us in her hut in Nepal. She was a Tibetan refugee who had come to faith in Christ. We had a medical team in the refugee camp, offering services to those with ailments, so this woman hosted a few of us for lunch one afternoon. Here she was. She'd lost her homeland. She was alienated from her own people because she'd chosen the path of faith in Christ, which put her in direct conflict with the overwhelming culture of Tibetan Buddhism surrounding her. Her products were being boycotted by her own Tibetan people, creating extra economic hardship in an already stark environment. To say that she'd had a hard life and was barely getting by would be an understatement.

Yet she invited us to her home for lunch. When we arrived, she greeted us, her eyes twinkling like Santa Claus as she cut down some sausage links that were hanging from the ceiling, offering us her generosity out of her poverty. She had no refrigerator, and the flies were eating the sausage before we were, but she was giving freely, so we received it in the spirit in which it was given. We prayed and drank yak butter tea. We had conversations about how she came to follow Jesus and the economic challenges she faced. She was profoundly grateful for the person of Jesus and for the things He had done in her life, even though she was in a state of very real material need. We even sang a little. We bought some of her handmade bags; we bought *most* of them, actually, to take home and sell to people so that she'd have enough. It was one of the best celebrations I'd ever experienced.

In fact, through the years, I've seen again and again that celebration, joy, and gratitude have virtually no relationship to wealth or lack of it. Something else is going on. Finding that something else and nurturing it is what this chapter is all about.

The Third Way

For many thoughtful people, the very notion of celebration seems unwarranted in days such as these. Famines, terrorism, the loss of liberties, the increasing gap between the wealthy few and the impoverished masses, wars, genocide, threats to safety and security, environmental threats, and the tragedies of human trafficking are such present realities that anger or mourning or activism seem to be the only proper responses.

Of course, underneath this global angst, this front-page stuff, lurks an entirely different level of reality that also causes mourning or anger. It has to do with our personal losses and schisms, be they emotional, financial, vocational, or physical. Not everyone feels these pains and losses, but many who *do* feel them embrace their reality with such intensity that they develop an air of superiority over the supposedly naive ones who walk through the world living from concert to concert or movie to movie, or who catch a thrill as the newest mobile phone hits the market. "Blessed are those who mourn," they say disdainfully as they don their black, whether literally or metaphorically, and prepare to face another day in this bleak and fallen world.

And so it appears, at least at first glance, that two options are available to us as we attempt to relate to joyfulness and celebration in this broken world. We can either live honestly with our eyes wide open to the sufferings of this world and become dark, angry, and weighed down, or we can shut our eyes and pretend our world doesn't include the untidy realities of the Fall. Plastic surgery, positive thinking, and a ban on listening to the news, especially National Public Radio, ought to make you happy. Isn't that the conventional wisdom of the day?

Thankfully, a third way avoids the blind optimism of denial as well as the disabling pessimism of pseudo-solidarity with the suffering and brokenness of this world. Not contingent on health or wealth, this third way germinates in prisons and refugee camps, in hospitals, and among impoverished or persecuted peoples. But this third way is not *contingent* on suffering and deprivation; it is also found on Ivy League campuses and in wealthy cities. Sickness or health, wealth or poverty, education or "ignorance" seem not to determine whether a spirit of celebration permeates a person or community. Other factors are at work, and we must uncover those factors if we're to be the people of hope and celebration that we're called to be. What are those other factors?

Celebration and Seeing

Throughout the Bible, people have claimed to know God when their hearts were actually far from Him. These people were often characterized by complaint rather than gratitude. It's easy to see this attitude in the nation of Israel after their deliverance from slavery. One would think that parting an ocean and drowning the opposing army would be evidence enough that the God who was guiding them had their best interests in mind. But the chapters that follow this miraculous deliverance, whether in Exodus or Numbers, are a litany of whining. The water, the food, the leadership, the leadership's wife, the timing of events, the directions God gives them all are cause for complaint and gossip. The people seem unable to see God's provision, direction, and love for them, and as a result, they waste away their days in petty complaining and cynicism[109].

I'm struck by the paradox that I whine about people who whine. In our glorious and beautiful world, having received the many gifts we're given to enjoy, how can people of faith have a reputation for declaring the cup to be half-empty and draining quickly? Churchgoers complain about moral decline, about politics, about our church's music or pastoral leadership—or if not our church, perhaps the church down the road. This crowd seems to continually sense that the world is about to end. It's been that way as far back as I can remember. And it's one of the reasons that Christians have a reputation as people you'd like to have in your neighborhood but not have over for dinner. This does a great disservice to the calling of the church, as indicated by James Joyce's portrayal of his hero in *A Portrait of the Artist as a Young Man*. The hero makes his decision not to become a priest based in part on the reputation "men of the cloth" had for being sour and negative.

This was clearly the case among the religious elite of Jesus' day. They were upset because His disciples went to parties and spent time with the lower classes. In their assessment, Jesus missed the point and disqualified Himself for His claims of Messiahship precisely because He went to the wrong events and even allowed an "unclean woman" to crash a party and disrupt a delightful theology discussion. Once there, she offered her love to him by weeping at His feet, wiping the tears from His feet with her hair, and anointing Him with expensive perfume. It was scandalous.

But from Jesus' perspective, the woman "got it," and the religious elite didn't. She was the only one in the room who understood what real worship was[110]. Her gender, her profession, and her level of education were three strikes against her in a league where one strike is enough to get you out. But Jesus turned the tables completely and said that hers was the real celebration. Why? Because she saw. She saw her sin, saw her need for forgiveness, saw that Jesus had the authority to forgive and restore, saw that He had seen fit to do so in her case. His healing and transformative power captured her heart, and she was living a life of obedience and celebration in spite of her social standing.

We become worshippers as we accurately see ourselves, our world, and what God has done for us, as we become celebrants who are rejoicing and participating in the vast redeeming work that God is doing in the universe. Several things in particular will spark our joy if only we can see them.

Seeing the Finished Work of Christ

The last words that Jesus cried out from the cross were these: "It is finished." He was talking about much, much more than simply the completion of His physical life on earth, though the phrase would certainly include that. This completion also had to do with the triumph over all the forces in the universe intent on darkness, death, fear, hatred, disease, division, and oppression. His death opened the door for all that is life-giving, as evidenced by what happened immediately after His physical death.

> And Jesus cried out again with a loud voice, and yielded up His spirit. And behold, the veil of the temple was torn in two from top to bottom; and the earth shook and the rocks were split. The tombs were opened, and many bodies of the saints who had fallen asleep were raised; and coming out of the tombs after His resurrection they entered the holy city and appeared to many (Matthew 27:50-53).

This is the first overt hint that death has been defeated by the work of Jesus. This hint would go on to become a full-blown clue through the resurrection of Christ, and it would be developed into a foundational doctrine of the church through teachings of Paul and the testimony of the Revelation[111].

The triumph over death encompasses all other triumphs as well. History is headed toward the end of all evil, the wiping of every tear from every eye, the healing of every disease. Those who are the most hopeful among us are those who have been baptized into optimism, but not a mushy romantic optimism that denies the realities of suffering in this present world. Some of the religious systems of the world reduce suffering to the realm of illusion, seeking to do away with the distinctions between good and evil, portraying them as false categories.

Christianity does no such thing. From the very beginning, humanity chooses to follow an evil presence in the garden and thus sets history on a course of great suffering and loss. Yet the redemptive story is that the curse has been broken. If we're living in C.S. Lewis's Narnia, the snow has started to melt, signifying an end to the perpetual curse of a winter that had created such misery for millennia. Knowing that the melt has begun and spring is coming changes everything.

Of course, our calling is to embody and make real some small measure of this beauty and triumph that Christ is bringing. This is what it means to be artisans of hope. This is why we exhale. But exhaling is sometimes difficult, because our means for blessing others have been curtailed. We've become victims of something: cancer, infidelity, oppression, loss. What form does celebration take amid such suffering, amid situations that rob us of our own capacities to serve and bless? Celebration takes the form of hope.

It's why slaves have sung in the face of oppression, rape, and abuse. It's why terminal cancer patients have said to me when I've visited them in the hospital, "But enough about me. How are you doing? How can I pray for you?" It's why my dad wanted Handel's "Hallelujah Chorus" sung at his funeral, rather than some dirge about loss. It's why Dietrich Bonhoeffer had the reputation during his imprisonment as being that pastor who was able to spread an atmosphere of joy throughout the camp. It's why some POWs from the war in Vietnam talk about communion with a stale crumb of bread and seaweed soup as being the most profound and beautiful memory of captivity. All of these were living out of an assurance that history was headed in a certain, hopeful direction, and this belief became their basis for joy. It is ours as well.

Seeing Our Completion in Christ

"For in Him all the fullness of Deity dwells in bodily form, and in Him you have been made complete" (Colossians 2:9-10).

A theme runs through Jesus' ministry. He meets people who are carrying a weight of failure, shame, social marginalization, fear, or anger and calls them to become other than what they perceive themselves to be. Look at His word to the woman caught in adultery: "I do not condemn you, either." Only moments before, she was condemning herself. The religious establishment was condemning her too. But now, Jesus has confounded the religionists, and He tells her that He has forgiven her and that she should get on with the business of living out her life as the whole and righteous person that she is[112].

He meets the weak-willed Simon Barjona and changes his name to Peter, which means "The Rock." Jesus sees the wavering one as solid, steady, trustworthy[113]. He tells all of His followers that amid the darkness that comes from shame, greed, failure, lust, war, and so much more that is destructive, that they are the light of the world, and He exhorts them to let the light of hope shine without fear or apology[114]. Paul the apostle says that he no longer recognizes people "according to the flesh," which means he sees people the same way Christ sees people[115].

Of course, such seeing must include not only our assessment of others but also our capacity to believe what God says about our own selves: that we're loved, that we're forgiven, that we're adopted into God's great family, and most significantly, that there is no longer any condemnation for those who are in Christ Jesus[116]. If Jesus doesn't beat me up, manipulate me, and play mind games, perhaps I shouldn't do those things either.

This is right where the rub comes, isn't it? We all have old recordings playing inside our heads, portraying a reality entirely different from the one God sees and declares. These messages come from our childhood, significant teachers and friends, and numerous random yet profound experiences. Verbal or sexual abuse, disapproval, shame, mocking, marginalization, and religious systems that demanded performance in exchange for affirmation are just a few of the recordings that coat our thawing hearts with a fresh layer of ice. And nothing will kill our capacity to be people of hope and celebration quicker than the deep freeze that comes from listening to old messages. This is just one of the reasons why inhaling the Word of God on a regular basis is so vital to our well-being and our capacity to bless others[117].

Seeing the Riches We Can Share

The story of Ernest Gordon in the book *To End All Wars* documents the transformation that came over a community of prisoners working on the Burma-Siam railway at the hands of the Japanese. One man was unjustly accused, but he offered his life in order to spare others from suffering, and this became a fulcrum point in the camp. That single action set forces in motion that transformed the prisoners' culture from theft, greed, fear, and selfishness to mutuality, interdependency, generosity, and sacrifice. A university of sorts developed among the prisoners, with each sharing his talents and learning from the talents of others. Gordon would later write this:

> Death was still with us—no doubt about that. But we were slowly being freed from its destructive grip. We were seeing for ourselves the sharp contrast between the forces that made for life and those that made for death. Selfishness, hatred, envy, jealousy, greed, self-indulgence, laziness and pride were all anti-life. Love, heroism, self-sacrifice, sympathy, mercy, integrity and creative faith, on the other hand, were the essence of life, turning mere existence into living in its truest sense. These were the gifts of God to men[118].

These gifts came into being in the camp because of one man's generosity, giving the only thing he had left in the suffering and abuse of captivity: his life. As we have already seen, we're blessed by God in order to be a blessing to others, in order to spill the colors of hope onto the canvas of the world. This is why learning, contentment, and gratitude are such vital ingredients in our lives. Without them, we begin to feel impoverished, obsessing over what we don't have. Of course, we needn't go far to begin seeing what we *don't* have. The world of advertising offers ever-present fodder for discontentment about our health, hair, weight, eyesight, wrinkles, car, clothes, education, and income. If an area of our lives can be changed, advertising is there to make us discontent and motivated to drop some dollars in an attempt to change it. If that doesn't work, try playing a few of those old recordings.

A better way would be to look through a different lens, discovering what you *do* have! Take a cue from the psalmists. Theirs was no sense of syrupy optimism. They saw loss and suffering. They were willing to express their frustration with how God was running things. But as they stayed engaged, pouring out their hearts to God, they began to see His provision, mercy, and generosity as well. This capacity to see both—the suffering and the beauty, the loss and the provision—develops a seasoned, profoundly powerful capacity for blessing and celebration.

As our medical team was leaving a village in Nepal, our hostess came to me with a gift. It was a tall, bamboo-like stick, which I assumed she offered to me as a walking stick. I presumed she'd heard rumors of how weak we all were, how unaccustomed to mountains and walking in them, and she'd wanted to help. Apparently, she'd singled me out as the person most needing the help of a third leg, and so gave me the stick. I thanked her, and as we began to walk away, I realized that this stick was too tall to be of value. Breaking off the top, I turned back and smiled, waving as I tossed the extra piece of stick into the grass.

Immediately, she began running toward us, agitated, even irritated, waving her hands and imploring us to stop. Through translation she asked me why I was throwing the gift away. I told her the walking stick was too tall, and she immediately began laughing. "This is not a walking stick for you. This is sugarcane—food. And it's for you to share with everyone." It's one thing to receive gifts; it's another to know what they are and then to share them generously with others.

This will only come about when we begin to open our eyes and see what God has given us to share.

Seeing a Monism Rather Than a Dualism

For a number of reasons beyond the scope of this book, Christianity is often suspicious of the physical pleasures of this world. This is unfortunate, because these very pleasures are gifts given to us by our Creator, who designed the world as a place of pleasure, though pain has been introduced and pleasures perverted as results of the fall. Still, God's intention is that His kindness would lead us to repentance by causing us to see God as the source of blessing, provision, pleasure, beauty, and gladness in our lives and so to respond as grateful worshippers[119].

Sadly, the church has sometimes hindered people from seeing God as the giver of these good gifts. The church's wholesale condemnation of how these gifts have been perverted has resulted in a perception that God is against good food, good drink, and good sex. I doubt that. Why would the wise man write, "Let your fountain be blessed, and rejoice in the wife of your youth. As a loving hind and a graceful doe, let her breasts satisfy you at all times; be exhilarated always with her love" (Proverbs 5:18-19)? Or this: "Go then, eat your bread in happiness and drink your wine with a cheerful heart; for God has already approved your works. Let your clothes be white all the time, and let not oil be lacking on your head. Enjoy life with the woman whom you love all the days of your fleeting life which He has given to you under the sun; for this is your reward in life" (Ecclesiastes 9:7-9)? Or this: "The Lord of hosts will prepare a lavish banquet for all peoples on this mountain; a banquet of aged wine, choice pieces with marrow, and refined, aged wine" (Isaiah 25:6)?

Prudish? Hardly. I could be in Bible study or in bed with my spouse; I could be eating an omelet or listening to Bach or Hamilton or my church choir. I could be watching a good movie with friends. The contexts for celebration are as vast as creation itself. Where grace breaks through in our lives, the Scripture is fulfilled: "God saw all that He had made, and behold, it was *very* good[120]."

A few years ago my two eldest children and I drove halfway across the state to an outdoor concert in an amphitheater overlooking the Columbia River. As the sun dipped over the mountains, the music began. Dave Matthews was singing a song about a woman who was lonely and bored, whose significant other never listened to her, who felt stuck in her dead-end life. The lyrics went on to tell of her calls, her prayers for help, and how, ultimately she learned that she needed to work hard to live out her dreams.

The song never mentioned Jesus. It didn't provide a final solution to her problem. This was not a Christian concert and thus not a crowd that you'd necessarily find at your church potluck. Alcohol seemed to be flowing pretty freely all around us. And yet something in the lyrics of that song and the way in which it clearly resonated with so many people around us reminded me that we can find truth and beauty in many places beyond the walls of cathedrals in this world if we'll but look carefully, prayerfully.

This song was neither a blind denial of suffering nor a disabling fixation on it. Rather, this song and many others throughout the night seemed to share a message: In this broken world, we must commit to finding, making, and celebrating beauty, genuine intimacy, and hope. Particularly as I looked around at the crowd during the singing of this one song, people's hearts appeared to be dripping with desire for those very things. The experience was poignant, powerful. All the right questions were being asked, formulated in some of the best music I've ever heard.

So what was I attending with my young adult children? A secular rock concert, to be avoided lest the mind be poisoned? Perhaps. I would be arrogant to judge anyone who had decided not to be there. Each of us must, by our own histories, upbringings, and consciences, decide what to consume and what to avoid in this world[121]. But when Paul was sharing the good news of Christ with some Greeks in his day, he began his articulation of the good news, not with Bible passages from the Old Testament but with that which was familiar to his audience: Greek deities and secular poetry. And where do you suppose that Paul, a Jew converted to Christianity, learned about such things? I suspect that he went to the cultural equivalent of concerts, so that he could articulate the longings of the heart in the language of the day[122]. Celebrations, be they weddings, concerts, or parties, reveal a great deal about cultures in which we're called to live. We'd do well to show up once in a while.

Celebration As Fruit

The life of Wladyslaw Szpilman is recollected in *The Pianist,* his autobiographical chronicle of living through the German persecution of Polish Jews during World War II[123]. In the film version, there is a powerful moment when, after the war, Szpilman is back in the studio of radio Warsaw, playing a live piano concert. A violinist friend of his, also a Holocaust survivor, enters the studio, and their eyes meet. What unfolds next is one of my favorite nonverbal scenes in all film. Through facial expressions alone, they communicate all they've suffered, all they've lost, all they've survived. They are celebrating, but theirs is a celebration that has been born out of the realities of living and serving in this fallen world.

These are the real celebrations, the kind of celebrations that will become each of ours as we begin to breathe more fully. Regardless of our financial, educational, or physical lot in life, we simply cannot escape the effects of living in this fallen world. "All these died in faith," the author to the Hebrews says, "without receiving the promises[124]." And yet, these same ones lived their lives as doxologies of hope.

A world as dark and oppressive as ours has little need for sanitized celebrations carried out in prosperous bubbles, hermetically sealed off from the realities of suffering. On the other hand, no one needs the debilitating nihilism that is shouted from the "realists" of the world, inflaming rage but doing nothing to facilitate redemption, hope, or beauty. Rather, we need a spirit of celebration borne as fruit from the tree of brokenness and beauty that is this world of ours.

Such fruit will come where people are seeing the world with the eyes of Christ. Such seeing will come where people are inhaling—where they are taking the time to open their eyes and ears, absorbing all that God is offering us. But inhaling is not enough, for taken in large doses it leads to a self-absorbed preoccupation with one's own little life. We simply must be exhaling too: Serving others and living generously, opening our homes and seeking to embody the justice and mercy of God's reign. When these elements are thrown together and stirred consistently, real celebration is born. This is, it seems, the only way.

Endnotes

1 Jeremiah 6:16

2 In the iTunes app under podcasts, see "Richard Dahlstrom" and look for all the "Soil Care for the Soul" podcasts.

3 Sayers, Mark. *Disappearing Church: from Cultural Relevance to Gospel Resilience*. Moody Publishers, 2016.

This work catalogs the ongoing decline of the church.

4 You can read about the skepticism towards creation care articulated in some churches here: http://nyti.ms/2sfqK27

5 Stanley Hauerwas and William H. Willimon. *Resident Aliens: Life in the Christian Colony*. Abingdon Press, 1989.

6 For more reading on this subject, consider Brian McLaren, *More Ready than You Realize*. Grand Rapids: Zondervan, 2002.

7 There are plenty of places in the Bible where this happens, but few churches help people express these emotions in worship. For some reason, the gathered church has found room for celebration and rejoicing but has censured mourning. A quick reading of Psalms, or of Job's complaint, or Jeremiah's, or Moses', is enough to give us permission to struggle and doubt. In fact, the struggle and doubt that are parts of any normal relationship are vital parts of our relationship with God. Honest dialogue and wrestling lead to greater intimacy with our Creator.

8 Romans 12:1-3 indicates the the parchment of our lives will, indeed, be written upon by forces outside ourselves. The only question is who the author will be, and the answer to that question, we're told, is in our hands. We'll either live passively, and the the forces of culture will author our script, orient ourselves to God's reference point and God will become the author.

9 Cited in Dennis Hoover, "Love Thy Neighbor," *Faith and International Affairs*, vol. 4, no.2, p.1

10 Dietrich Bonhoeffer, *Life Together*. San Francisco: Harper, 1978.

11 Henri Nouwen, *The Way of the Heart*. San Francisco: Harper, 1991.

12 When Jesus was tempted by Satan (see Matthew 4:1-8), He responded by quoting from the Scriptures. He obviously knew them well, as indicated in this and many other passages.

13 Mark 2:7,16,18,24.

14 Though this appears to be what Paul did in Acts 16:31, Paul is actually inviting this jailer to a moment of justification, which will

257

begin a lifelong journey of salvation. We change from glory to glory as God peels away layers, invites us to further repentance, challenges our assumptions, and shapes us to become blessings to the world (see 2 Corinthians 3:18).

15 Compare Matthew 5:3,6 with Luke 6:20-21,25.

16 Brian McLaren, *A Generous Orthodoxy.* Grand Rapids: Zondervan, 2004, p. 160.

17 See 1 Corinthians 13:12. The context is a reminder that this whole project God has undertaken in offering us His Word and His Son has been done in order that we might learn to love God, our enemies, each other, the whole world. When that happens, some of our interpretive problems will be less vexing.

18 Leviticus 15:19

19 Leviticus 19:19

20 James 1:22-25

21 "Behold, I am making all things new" (Revelation 21:5)

22 Hebrews 3 and 4

23 Compare Acts 15:20 with 1 Corinthians 8:4-6.

24 2 Corinthians 3:18

25 1 Corinthians 9:24

26 See www.stepbystepjourney.com

27 John 10

28 The lessons learned through my years of ministry at Bethany Community Church can be found in my newest book, *The Map is Not the Journey.*

29 Genesis 12

30 Exodus 3

31 Genesis 50:20

32 Judges 6:11-16

33 Esther 4:14

34 Luke 2:10-12

35 1 Corinthians 10:1-11 articulates the story of nearly two million people who stopped short of the journey's destination. We're told that the story is given to us as an example in order that the fate that befell them might not fall to us.

36 Hebrews 11:32-38

37 Wayne Muller. *Sabbath Finding Rest, Renewal, and Delight in Our Busy Lives.* Bantam Books, 2000.

38 This exchange has been well documented in Major Ian Thomas' books, the latest of which is *The Indwelling Life of Christ: All of Him in All of Me.* Colorado Springs: Multnomah Books, 2006. Major Thomas writes, "So long as Christians are busy doing for God what is best in their own eyes, they will never enter into His

rest and the true inheritance that is theirs to enjoy now. They will only be sweating it out, and end up weary, discouraged, depressed. They will likely become deeply cynical. They will finally want to quit, and quit they must. They quit depending on self-effort, and instead recognize the Truth: 'I cannot—God never said I could; but God can, and always said He would!'" (p. 31).

[39] Sleep replaced tossing and turning through the night. I became confident that God was in control, that He was active in the work that was unfolding. I realized good fruit would come from the work that He was doing because His life is by its very nature fruitful. This confidence led to a capacity to be more fully present in the midst of all moments, both easy and difficult. The struggles, doubts, and old habits didn't disappear, but this new vision of living out from His sufficiency has made for palpable fruit and rest in every area of life—physical, emotional, and spiritual.

[40] Matthew 15:3-6

[41] Henri Nouwen. *Clowning in Rome: Reflections on Solitude, Celibacy, Prayer and Contemplation*. Darton, Longman and Todd, 2001.

[42] This is what we saw in the chapter on generosity.

[43] Timothy Ware, ed. The Art of Prayer, *An Orthodox Anthology.* London: Faber & Faber, 1966, p. 110.

[44] John 15:5

[45] John 14:13

[46] 2 Corinthians 12:7-10 is one of many examples

[47] Ephesians 5:22-33

[48] Matthew 22:36-38

[49] Matthew 22:39-40

[50] James 4:2

[51] Luke 18:1-8

[52] 2 Samuel 12:22-23

[53] Resources to help you practice this kind of prayer can be found on my Web site, www.stepbystepjourney.com.

[54] Maggie Jackson. *Distracted: The Erosion of Attention and the Coming Dark Age.* Prometheus Books, New York, 2008.

[55] John 7:37,38

[56] The metaphor comes from I Corinthians 10:4, where we're told that those in the wilderness who drank from the rock which delivered water were drinking from the rock that was Christ.

[57] Philip F. Reinders, *Seeking God's Face.* Co-published by Faith Alive Christian Resources and Baker Books, Grand Rapids, MI, 2010.

[58] John 8:32

[59] David C. Needham. *Birthright: Christian Do You Know Who You Are?* Multnomah Books, Portland, Oregon, 1979.

[60] A list of identity truths can be found here: http://bit.ly/identityinChrist

[61] https://www.christiantoday.com/article/a-growing-church-why-we-should-focus-on-the-bigger-picture/49362.htm

[62] For more on this, see Jayson Georges. *The 3D Gospel: Ministry in Guilt, Shame, and Fear Cultures.* Time Press, 2014.

[63] I Corinthians 4:19,20

[64] Exodus 14:18

[65] I Kings 18:37

[66] Ephesians 1:20

[67] This is the reason you shouldn't fast if you have certain physical issues, including blood sugar issues and diabetes. Please check with your doctor before beginning a practice of fasting from food.

[68] Colossians 1:23

[69] Adam Smith, *The Wealth of Nations.* New York: Knopf, 1991. This is a reprint of Smith's 1776 original work, *An Inquiry into the Nature and Causes of the Wealth of Nations.*

[70] Bill McKibben, *Deep Economy.* New York: Times Books, 2007, p. 35.

[71] We're told in Genesis 2:15 that our calling is to sustain. God develops this calling in His commands to Israel to allow the land to rest and to proclaim a Jubilee every 50 years that would function as an arrest to the disappearance of the middle class. You can learn about these things in Richard Austin's book, *Reclaiming America.*

[72] Revelation 21:5

[73] Matthew 6:25-34

[74] Such communities are seen through the work of Agros International and World Vision

[75] Quoted in Wendy Wilson Greer, ed., *The Only Necessary Thing.* New York: Crossroads, 1999.

[76] Genesis 12:1

[77] Mark 1:32-34

[78] I John 2:16

[79] John 13:8

[80] Jeremiah 2:13

[81] Quoted in Greer, *The Only Necessary Thing.*

[82] Golf was a hobby that I tried for a few months because I thought all pastors needed to golf just as all pastors needed to

pray and read the Bible. How liberating to discover that golfing was an optional spiritual discipline. I quickly discarded it.

[83] Psalm 24:1

[84] Matthew 10:8

[85] Matthew 10:42

[86] Francis A Schaeffer, *The Church at the End of the Twentieth Century*, 1970, pp.100-101. Used by permission of Crossway Books, a publishing ministry of Good News Publishers, Wheaton, IL 60187. www.crossway.com.

[87] Ephesians 2:14

[88] Chuang Tzu, *The Way of Chuang Tzu*, New York: New Directions, 1965, p. 154.

[89] Proverbs 10:19; James 1:19; 3:2

[90] Romans 12:1-3

[91] Matthew 18:20

[92] Psalm 73

[93] John 10:10

[94] Matthew 11:28

[95] Deuteronomy 6:6-9;12

[96] Colossians 3:16

[97] http://bit.ly/northumbriarule

[98] I John 3:9

[99] I Timothy 4:8

[100] http://bit.ly/soilcrisis

[101] Romans 12:2

[102] As it turns out, these textual experts were the primary movers in Jesus' execution. A stunning verse in Acts reveals that these teachers of law fulfilled the very texts they studied. They knew their beloved Messiah would be killed, yet they became His murderers: "For those who live in Jerusalem, and their rulers, recognizing neither Him nor the utterances of the prophets which are read every Sabbath, fulfilled these by condemning Him" (Acts 13:27).

[103] Willi Graf, friend of Sophie Scholl. See www.jlrweb.com/whiterose/willi.html.

[104] James 3:2

[105] Matthew 25:14-30

[106] Colossians 2:16-23 warns us that developing a list of rules might appear to be a form of wisdom but that these rules are of no value in truly liberating us. If the rule of life is only a list of rules, we're missing the point.

[107] Taken from Ben McFarland's blog, *Arrow Through the Sun*, posted September 14, 2007. Used by permission.

[108] Bill McKibbon, *Deep Economy: The Wealth of Communities and the Durable Future*. New York: Holt and Company, 2007, pp. 108-9

[109] Exodus 15–19; Numbers 11–17

[110] Luke 7:36-50

[111] See 1 Corinthians 15; 1 Thessalonians 4:13-18; Revelation 1:17-18; 22:1-5

[112] John 8:1-11

[113] Matthew 16:13-19

[114] Matthew 5:14-16

[115] 2 Corinthians 5:16-17

[116] Romans 8:1

[117] For further reading on this subject, you might consider Bob George, *Classic Christianity.* Eugene, OR: Harvest House, 2000.

[118] Ernest Gordon, *To End All Wars*. Grand Rapids, MI: Zondervan, 1963, p. 105.

[119] Romans 2:4

[120] Genesis 1:31

[121] This principle is articulated in Romans 14:2-3. Paul is clear that it would be wrong for those who are living out their convictions to judge one another in matters of conscience. Go or don't go, but don't make a big issue over it. Lately, the celebration of liberty in Christ seems to have become the flag people are flying higher than Christ Himself. The Christian life is, after all, not about drinking beer and smoking cigars but about faith, love, hope, service, beauty, justice, and so much more that matters a great deal. We mustn't allow ourselves to lose our focus.

[122] Read Acts 17 to more fully understand Paul's heart and his brilliant capacity to move toward people, beginning right where they live. This, after all, is exactly what Jesus does with us.

[123] Władysław Szpilman, *The Pianist.* London: Picador Publishing, 2002.

[124] Hebrews 11:13

Made in the USA
San Bernardino, CA
06 August 2018